CHOCOLATE–SOUR CHERRY
BREAD

PRETZELS

RAISIN BRIOCHE

ITALIAN RING BREAD
AND *FICELLE*

RYE-CURRANT BREAD

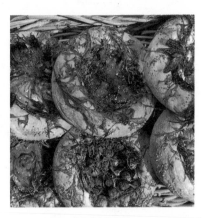

FOCACCIA

OLIVE BREAD

SESAME-SEMOLINA
SANDWICH ROLLS

NORMANDY RYE

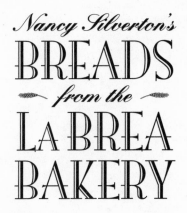

Nancy Silverton's
BREADS
from the
LA BREA
BAKERY

NANCY SILVERTON
IN COLLABORATION WITH LAURIE OCHOA
FOREWORD BY RUTH REICHL

VILLARD NEW YORK

Nancy Silverton's
BREADS
from the
La Brea
BAKERY

Recipes for the Connoisseur

Library of Congress Cataloging-in-Publication data is available.

ISBN: 679-40907-6

Manufactured in the United States of America on acid-free paper

2 4 6 8 9 7 5 3

First Edition

BOOK DESIGN BY BARBARA MARKS
PHOTOGRAPHS BY STEVEN ROTHFELD

To STEVE SULLIVAN, of Acme Bread Company, whose wonderful bread proved to me once long ago that even though we might not have the right water, the right flour, or the years of tradition in the United States, it's still possible to turn out a superior product. His bread continues to be a benchmark of excellence at La Brea Bakery.

AND TO IZZY COHEN, for being there in the beginning, when I was just learning how to make sourdough breads and there were as few books as there were experts to turn to. Izzy, when I'm seventy years old and retired, I want to be just like you.

FOREWORD BY RUTH REICHL

The first time I met her, Nancy Silverton was standing in the kitchen at Spago while her two-week-old daughter lay in a basket on the pastry table, cooing. Nancy was shaking her head at a disappointed-looking farmer. Pointing to a half-eaten berry, she said, "They're not ripe enough. The flavor's not very good." Turning away, she announced to the kitchen, "No berry tarts tonight."

I didn't know it then, but I had just gotten a perfect snapshot of Nancy. Every kitchen she has worked in has had children underfoot, because she has always known how to integrate her family into her work. At the same time, she has never compromised on quality.

In a city where desserts were traditionally made by men, hers was radical behavior. In the early eighties, young chefs in Los Angeles created a food revolution. They served simple, seasonal dinners. Then the cake came out and it was some sweet, fancy concoction that looked better than it tasted. Nancy changed that, holding herself to the same standards as any good nondessert chef. She insisted on using local ingredients and cooking with the seasons. She tasted her fruit before she bought it, and if nothing pleased her she simply did without. Her desserts were often more savory than sweet: I once watched her hold up a chocolate cake and tell the waiters, "This will not be loved by children."

No matter where she cooked, Nancy's standards never changed. She once showed up at my house for Thanksgiving dinner carrying an apple pie and an ice cream maker. "Ice cream tastes so much better when it's fresh," she said blithely, setting the contraption on the only available surface, the floor, and measuring out vast quantities of cream. I tripped over her as I was carrying the turkey into the dining room, but she never even looked up.

Given her dedication to quality, I was not surprised that Nancy decided she had to bake the bread when she and her husband, Mark Peel, opened their restaurant, Campanile. And it was pretty predictable that once she took on the bread project, she would become obsessed.

But I think even Nancy was surprised by the depth of her obsession; it went on for years. (In fact, it's *still* going on.) Long after everyone acknowledged that Nancy made the best bread in Los Angeles, she was still wrestling with it. We were thrilled to have such good bread; Nancy thought it could be better. She now had two young children and a restaurant to run, but most nights you could find her in the bakery at 3 or 4 or 5 A.M., dusted with flour and delving into the mystery of wild yeast.

"What's wrong with it?" we'd ask, and she would mutter something about the size of the holes or the thickness of the crust. She'd get a knife and slice open a loaf and show you why the rise had been too fast, or too slow, or too something.

Just about the time Nancy seemed sufficiently satisfied to begin living a normal life, the bakery outgrew its original quarters; La Brea Bakery bread had become too popular. So Nancy moved the operation to a larger space, bought new, state-of-the-art ovens, and started all over again.

While most people thought the new bread was the same as the old, Nancy thought it was a disaster. "This bread is terrible," she wailed. "I have to learn how to bake all over again in the new ovens." Anybody else would have been in despair, but Nancy seemed secretly pleased to be back in the bakery poking at loaves and peering at flour.

All great cooks, of course, are obsessed; it is what separates great cooks from good ones. They cook for themselves, to some inner compulsion, and they are never satisfied. Great cooks also share another quality: generosity. You will never meet a great cook who is stingy. On the other hand, you are unlikely to meet another cook as generous as Nancy.

Nancy is profligate with her bread, handing it out as if it grew on trees. She is even more generous with her knowledge, which she seems willing to share with anybody who asks. This amazes many people: "She told me everything," said one man who went on to open his own enormously successful bakery on the East Coast. "I never did quite figure out why."

I think the reason is that Nancy thinks everybody deserves good bread.

And that she knows that each loaf of bread is only as good as the person who bakes it.

In the end, it really doesn't matter what her reasons are, for they are the guarantee that you can trust this book. Nancy has written it with all the passion and care she has dedicated to her craft. And, as always, she has held nothing back.

ACKNOWLEDGMENTS

When I look at the pages of this book, it's hard for me not to think of the many talented, hardworking people who've assisted me along the way. My thanks go to all the following:

To my editor, Peter Gethers, and his assistant, Amy Scheibe, who displayed the patience of true bakers while waiting for me to finish the manuscript.

To my loyal agents, Eric and Maureen Lasher, who probably never believed that I'd finish this book but kept pushing me nonetheless.

To my meticulous copy editor, Susan M. S. Brown, and my production editor, Benjamin Dreyer, who made sure that my repeated instructions always matched.

To Steven Rothfeld, who always showed a genuine feeling for bread. I can't wait to see his photographs.

To Barbara Marks, who promised me that this book would be as pleasurable to look at as the bread would be to make.

To my tireless assistant, Teri Neville (pronounced *Nah-Ville*), and the day she decided to quit hostessing and come upstairs and give me a hand.

To the bakery production manager, George Erasmus, who has pulled countless all-nighters in order to keep our sourdough starters fed and our bread from being burnt, and who took our little bakery far beyond my wildest dreams.

To Hugo Robles, our first employee at the bakery, who does a first-rate job in backing up and supporting George.

To Manfred Krankl, Phil Shaw, Brad Springer, Yolande Van Heerden, Amy Erasmus, and all the hardworking bakers who keep things running smoothly at the bakery.

To the investors of La Brea Bakery and Campanile, whose money allowed us to open our initial bakery.

To German Alarcon, who fixes our broken-down equipment.

To Paul Schrade and Jack Stumpf, my two former students, who read my manuscript, gave me pointers, then went home and baked such great bread that I knew others could do it too.

To Kerry Caloyannidis, who came in every day dressed in bathers and helped me get the bakery off the ground.

To Kathy Bergin, who allowed me to test recipes in her professional oven before the bakery was built.

To Michel Suas, who designed our wholesale bakery, sold us most of our equipment, and generously allows me to use him as a twenty-four-hour sounding board for bread-making questions, and to Steve Bloom, who sold us the rest of our equipment.

To Steve Lowe and John London from Capitol Milling, who answered my endless list of questions about flour.

To my fellow bakers on the East Coast, Pammy Sue Fitzpatrick, Paula Oland, and Mary Kay Halston, who were always there for me in the wee hours when I had no one to talk to.

To my best friend, Margy Rochlin, whose occasional bouts of insomnia provided me with someone fun to talk to during the night shift.

To Tom McMahon of the Bread Baker's Guild, who combed pages for inconsistencies and reassured me that many of my instinctive observations about bread were scientifically well founded.

To Jason Asch, of the conveniently located Diamond Foam and Fabric, who sells us *couche* at a moment's notice.

To Jonathan Gold for unselfishly donating his editing and writing skills. (Same goes for you, Margy.)

To Charles Perry, who always knew the answers to my questions about words and their meaning.

To Professor Jurgen-Michael Brümmer, I can't thank you enough for helping me to understand the sourdough bread–making process.

And, most important:

To Edon Waycott, who tested and retested all the breads in this book to ensure that fancy equipment and years of expertise are not prerequisites for good bread.

To Laurie Ochoa—this book is as much hers as it is mine. She listened to me babble endlessly, then somehow managed to reconfigure my words into a book that I hope will inspire thousands of pounds of dough and an equal number of sourdough bread loaves.

To my husband, Mark Peel, and my children, Vanessa, Ben, and Oliver. I love you all.

CONTENTS

4 BREADS MADE WITH WHITE STARTER 61

ILLUSTRATIONS

The

BAKING

LIFE

A Loaf of Integrity

I don't like ugly bread. The most important thing in bread is flavor, what you might call the inner beauty of the loaf. Yet we're all attracted to good looks, in bread as well as in people. And while you can't judge the worth of a person by his or her physical attributes, in bread making looks tell. The more beautiful the loaf, the better it tastes.

Of course, standards of beauty, in bread as in art or music or love, are subjective. We've all been fed images of fresh-baked bread, usually a fragrant mom-made pan loaf, pale gold and soft and squishy, hot from the oven and ready to be slathered with butter. This is what bread companies hope we think of when we buy their supermarket loaves, but this isn't what we get. Their loaves are pale, soft, and squishy all right, but you'll need that butter if you want any flavor at all.

My ideal loaf is neither squishy nor pale. It is a sourdough loaf that *earns* its character and its beauty. Natural leavening, slow by nature, gives this more rustic loaf the time it needs to develop texture and flavor. And while no two naturally leavened loaves are exactly alike, this bread has a standard of its own. Rustic bread is not ugly bread.

A beautiful sourdough loaf, burnished brown on the outside, has a solid but not impenetrable crust, subtly blistered with tiny fermentation bubbles that say, this is a loaf of integrity, a loaf made with care and with time.

If I had to choose a Crayola-box crayon to describe its color, it would be burnt sienna. There is a natural sheen to the skin of the bread—neither highly polished nor dull as unglazed ceramic—almost like the inner glow that signals health in humans.

There is a solidness to a good loaf, yet, when you take it in your hands, it feels slightly lighter than its appearance would lead you to imagine.

The shape is neither lopsided nor disfigured by the bulges, fissures, and cracks that lesser loaves develop when they are given either too little or too much time to rise. Its edges are rounded, never sharp, and the loaf looks complete, allowed to develop to its full, inherent form. Bakers call this elusive characteristic *oven spring* because it is in the oven that a loaf finishes its rise. Approximately a third of a loaf's volume is realized during baking.

Pull apart this perfect loaf and you'll find that the texture is elastic but not rubbery. This comes, in part, from its long, slow rise. Tearing into the interior or crumb, what the French call the *mie,* you'll see that the bread is porous, almost spongelike: not a sponge stamped into uniformity by some automated machine (the texture of commercial, brand-name breads) but a natural sponge, in which an irregular cell structure has been preserved. This look mirrors the appearance of the sourdough starter itself in its earlier stages. Examine the interior surface of a properly shaped loaf and you will find neither empty holes nor gaping air pockets; the interior of each bubble is laced with a network of thin strands. These are strands of *gluten,* the substance that holds a loaf together, the structure of a piece of bread. Formed when flour and water are combined, gluten is what allows a loaf of bread to rise before it is baked and, finally, to expand in the oven. It is the key to oven spring.

All this is really just a prelude to that first bite, the moment of truth after the days spent growing and feeding a starter, the hours spent mixing a dough, shaping a loaf, baby-sitting the rise and the bake.

The crackle of the crust is the first thing you notice, not just from the bubbly outer skin but from the thin, caramelized layer of crunch that surrounds the *mie.* This is where you find most of the flavor—the slight sweetness from the crust and the developed tang of fermentation—concentrated in one wonderful bite. There should be a natural, almost cavelike coolness to the interior of the bread, which I like to think comes from the aging of the dough. You taste the time and sweat it took to make this loaf. You taste perfection.

ON BECOMING A BAKER

The best way to learn to bake bread is to watch a baker, to ask questions of a baker, and, finally, to bake with a baker. I didn't have that luxury. It's true that when I first thought of opening my own bakery I knew how to bake a fairly good loaf of bread, but it wasn't the bread I dreamed of making. For the longest time, I assumed that great, crusty loaves of bread—bread with flavor and substance, made only with natural leavening—could be made only in Europe. America lacked the right flour, the right water, the years of tradition.

I turned to cookbooks for guidance, but they weren't much help. Most of them made it seem as if loaves made without the crutch of commercial yeast were beyond the skills of a talented home cook. A few books I scanned mentioned the existence of naturally leavened sourdough loaves, but the authors always seemed to chicken out when it came time to describe how such a bread might be made. They'd give either an adapted recipe that included commercial yeast or a recipe so vague and confusing that it seemed best just to close the book and bake a cake.

In France, when I studied pastry making, I learned how to temper chocolate, how to make a reliable tart crust, how to glaze a petit four. But even there, the bread I learned to bake was made with commercial yeast. In my off-hours, I'd go to local *boulangeries* and eat wonderful baguettes and hard-crusted country loaves, many certainly made on a *levain* (the French method of natural leavening). I never did figure out if I missed out on the class in which *levains* were discussed or if the instructor gave directions for the process and I simply didn't understand. French is a language I never managed to master.

When I came home to Los Angeles, bread was still a mystery to me. I baked bread for Wolfgang Puck and Barbara Lazaroff at Spago, both before and after my studies in France, but I wasn't obsessed by the process. Bread making was a tiny part of my job as pastry chef, and the bread I made was good enough.

At the time, few restaurants in Los Angeles cared much about the bread they served. Pale rolls with Styrofoam-like interiors, heated to hide their lack of flavor, passed for bread at even the most famous places. When my husband, Mark Peel, and I were planning to open our restaurant, Campanile, I decided I wanted to serve great bread, and the only way I knew how was to bake it myself.

In the process of building what would eventually become La Brea Bakery, I talked to oven manufacturers, flour millers, bakery consultants, to any expert I could find. I read crumbling nineteenth-century cookbooks and jargon-filled papers on the scientific properties of sourdough baking. All the while I felt no more confident in my ability to bake a great loaf than in the days when I relied on fast-rising bread recipes and every loaf turned out exactly the same as supermarket bread, only warm.

Few of the people I talked to in the bakery industry had dealt with anyone like me before. Most were polite but wondered why in the world I'd *want* to bake without commercial yeast. Why did I want to use different flour? Why didn't I like the expensive proof box contraption that took up most of the space in my bakery? After all, it was designed to help dough rise as quickly as possible. Why wouldn't I want to use the most *efficient* bread-making methods available?

Finally, I came to the conclusion that should have been obvious from the beginning: In order to become a baker, I'd have to stop looking for answers and just bake some bread, not four times a year as a special occasion, not even once a month. To learn to bake the bread I wanted to eat—bread like the kind I'd eaten in France and at the breakthrough Acme Bread Company in Berkeley, California—I'd have to raise my own sourdough starter and start baking every day.

This is the most frustrating and ultimately satisfying thing I discovered: Bread is alive.

Sourdough bread in all its states, as a starter, as a dough, as a shaped loaf about to go in the oven, is a product not only of its ingredients, but of its surroundings. The sourdough loaf you might bake in St. Louis with the same ingredients, equipment, and recipe as I use in Los Angeles will not be exactly the same as mine. It will have its own characteristics and idiosyncrasies.

Sourdough is temperamental, and it reacts to its environment in ways you'd expect of a human. If the air is too cold, the sourdough's "metabolism" slows down in an attempt to conserve warmth; too hot or humid, and the metabolism speeds up. A starter needs to be fed a steady diet of flour and water to stay alive. If it's given too much, it binges, then gets lazy; not enough and it literally starves to death.

What's more, bread can even seem to have emotional reactions to the way you treat it. Strange as it sounds, baking can be like marriage: There's a lot of give and take. If you try to be too controlling, the bread rebels. If you ignore your bread and think it's going to be there when you decide to come back around, think again.

And if you're not careful, the bread can take over your life. When I started baking every day, the relationship was completely out of balance. The bread essentially ruled me. If I wanted the dough to be ready to put in the oven after four hours of rising, it wouldn't be ready for six. Or worse, it would be ready too soon. The bread seemed to need attention as much as it needed flour, even more attention than my husband or kids.

Eventually I discovered little tricks to help push the bread in the direction I wanted it to go. I raised the water temperature for some breads; I lowered it for others. I found that some breads worked better as one-pound loaves, others as two-pound loaves. I let some doughs rise only at room temperature; others went straight into a cooler to ferment as slowly as possible. Many got a combination of both environments. I left some doughs in bulk form longer than others before they were shaped. When I learned (the hard way) that rye doughs cannot ferment as long as white doughs, I tried using what bakers call a sponge, a predough of sorts made of starter, flour, and water, which gave the rye doughs more time to rise and develop flavor.

Toward the end of the first year, I felt as if I were working *with* the bread rather than against it. Finally, there was a more or less equal partnership. "OK," I'd tell myself when I got to the bakery in the morning, "it's not as warm today as it was yesterday, so I need to leave the dough out a little longer. And it's probably going to be cold outside for the rest of the week, so I'm going to have to adjust my schedule a bit."

It was a huge revelation. If I were only slightly more tolerant, more observant—more flexible—the bread would work with me, no matter what the conditions or the climate.

As with anything else worth learning you get better with practice. Whether playing the harpsichord or painting a portrait, you eventually learn to rely on your own instincts. There is plenty of room for experimentation in bread making. Often unorthodox methods produce better results; often they become your new standards.

If you have a baby and you feel her forehead, you know right away whether she has a fever. You're connected enough to know what her normal temperature should be, whether she naturally feels warm or cool. It's the same with bread. Is the dough stickier than usual, the air moister, the starter too sour?

It takes time. It takes patience. But the rewards are great. Every loaf you bake is slightly different, but most of all, it is uniquely your own. Nothing you can buy at a store will give you as much satisfaction.

WAITING FOR SOURDOUGH

There are those who will tell you that great bread takes very little time to make. They will praise the efficiency of bread machines and the wonders of fast-rising yeast. I am not one of those people. Great bread, in my opinion, does take time. Great bread is not, however, difficult to make.

Many of the breads I make at La Brea Bakery are different from the breads most people make at home. But this is not because my breads are tricky or complicated. They are sourdough breads, leavened naturally with sourdough starter—a simple combination of flour and water left out where it can "catch" the wild yeasts that occur naturally on the flour, in the air, and on your hands.

Sourdough is not, as some people think, a San Francisco invention. It's a way of baking bread that goes back thousands of years before the discovery of commercial baker's yeast. Visit one of the dwindling numbers of great bakeries in France, and alongside the lovely yeasted cakes and crackly baguettes you'll still find wonderful rustic sourdough loaves made with only natural leavening, water, flour, and salt.

Great bread like those European loaves is the result of slow risings. The strains of yeast in a sourdough starter are slower acting, more sluggish than those found in commercial baker's yeast. But what they lack in speed they make up for in the flavor, texture, and good looks they give to a loaf of bread. With a sourdough starter, you can produce bread with a complexity that no fast-rising bread could ever achieve.

OK, you might ask, if sourdough is so wonderful, why can't more people use it to make bread?

For one thing, I think people have been scared off. Few things are as intimidating as bread making. The techniques—mixing, kneading, shaping, baking—are not hard to master. But the simplest step, waiting—for the bread to rise, for the bread to rest, for the bread to bake—is for many a difficult hurdle. The phenomenon of rising bread, and the mysteries of yeast and how it works make people nervous. They think they can't control the bread the way they can a pot roast. This is why most home bakers rely on commercial baker's yeast, which seems to them more predictable than a smelly substance that grows spontaneously and doesn't come in a refrigerated package.

What I hope to do with this book is make the process less mysterious. Every so often, one of my customers at La Brea Bakery pulls me aside and asks me to reveal the secret of my bread. The request is always made with a skeptical tone, as if I wouldn't, couldn't really share such privileged information. When I start to describe how we make the bread, and even offer a recipe or a little starter, the conversation turns conspiratorial, as if I have just delivered a spy code or something. But sourdough shouldn't be kept a secret.

You don't need any special cooking talent or science training to bake sourdough bread; patience is the only requirement. Even after spending years working with sourdough and after reading tons of scientific material on the subject, I don't pretend to understand the whole process. I learned by doing. You should do the same. Read this book as a guide, but know that to understand sourdough you've got to make the breads. Start with the Country White Bread, which I explain in Chapter 3, "A Lesson in Bread Making." To me, it's the perfect model of pure sourdough bread, with no added ingredients to get in the way of the essential flavors of sourdough and wheat. After you make it once, remake it, then remake it again. Keep practicing. You'll find a bread that is worth the wait.

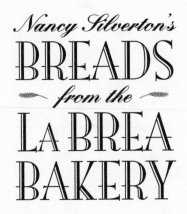

Nancy Silverton's

BREADS

from the

LA BREA
BAKERY

THE ELEMENTS

of

BREAD

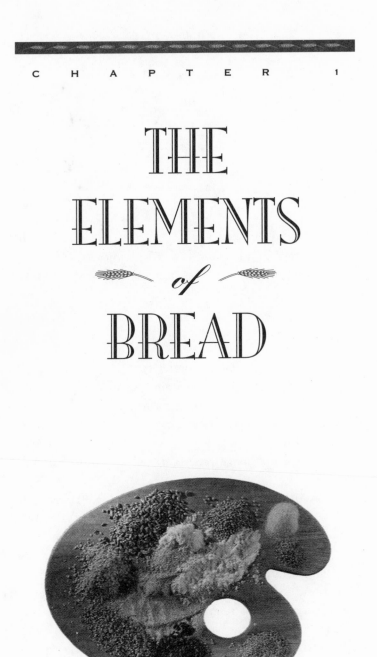

A LOAF OF BREAD NEED CONTAIN only two ingredients: flour and water. Together, in reaction to their environment—and sometimes with supporting elements—the two create a universe of possibilities.

FLOUR

With its mysterious ability to interact with water, heat, and unseen living organisms, flour is both the medium and the mechanism of bread's natural leavening. Wild yeasts and bacteria, which make sourdough rise, live not only in the air but in the flour itself. Combined with water and left at the proper temperature to ferment, flour "catches" or activates the wild microorganisms, beginning the sourdough process. Later, flour is the food that sustains the process.

Of course, not all flours are alike. Flour may be made out of any grain, and even among wheat flours there are numerous variations beyond white and whole wheat.

Wheat itself is categorized as hard or soft and winter or spring depending on its growing characteristics and its optimum growing season. Soft wheat, for instance, is widely grown in Europe, where the soil, worn down by centuries of farming, is unable to support the robust hard-wheat varieties common in the United States. (Hard wheat is best for baking bread; soft wheat is best for pastries. This is why most European bread flour is blended with hard wheat imported from North America.) Spring wheat tends to be grown in harsh climates such as those in Montana and the Dakotas; winter wheat is grown all over the Midwest.

Farming and processing methods, climate conditions, and luck also influence the subtle and not so subtle variations in flour. Even if a miller processed flour from wheat grown by the same farmer year after year, and neither varied his methods, a different product would emerge with each season—almost like the year-to-year variations of wine. Most millers buy their wheat from several sources, then blend the processed wheat like a flour cocktail to get a more consistent product. The choices are vast. I've never met two professional bakers who use the same flour.

The two main components of flour are starch and protein. The starch is food for the yeast—it converts into various sugars during fermentation and proofing. Gluten, the musclelike strands that give bread the structure it needs to rise, is formed when the protein contained in the wheat kernel is mixed with water.

Serious bread makers try to get flour with a relatively high protein content. A good hard-wheat white flour contains 12 to 12.5 percent protein, which converts to 40 to 42 percent gluten when mixed with water. Compare this with all-purpose flour, which is 10.5 to 11 percent protein and converts to 35 to 37 percent gluten when wet.

But two flours with the same amount of protein might produce completely different *sorts* of gluten. The quality of gluten is more important than the quantity. Consider two 180-pound men, one a couch potato, the other an athlete; it's not hard to imagine that the weight lifter will be much stronger than the remote-control jockey. It's the same with flour. In some varieties the gluten might be superstrong, making the dough tough, rubbery, and hard to mix. Flour with weak gluten makes wet and sticky dough. For the most part, the stronger the gluten, the longer the dough needs to be mixed, the more water it will absorb, and the longer it can ferment.

As you become more experienced at baking sourdough bread, you may want to experiment with different flours. Unfortunately, unless you are a professional baker it's unlikely that you'll be able to fine-tune your flour requests in terms of gluten quality. Still, there's a lot of flour out there to try, some made from organically grown wheat, some that is stone ground. Pester your local miller as I did (even cities as large as New York and Los Angeles have a miller or two), or seek out mail-order sources (see Appendix, "Sources"). Health food stores stock organic flour.

Some people buy their flour from tiny boutique mills, insisting that only fresh-milled flour should be used for home baking. Some grind their own flour, which may make the very best bread of all. Century-old baking manuals teach that flour must be aged at the mill at least a month to be effective in baking. You've got to decide for yourself.

If you're just starting out, though, there are more important things to worry about. To tell the truth, I've never had the time to grind my own flour. And while conventional wisdom dictates that organic flour is necessary to grow a natural leavening, I've done fine growing a sourdough starter with nonorganic flour. Keep things simple. As long as you don't use pastry flour, which is too soft for bread, you should do fine.

WHITE FLOUR

You can certainly make an acceptable loaf of bread using supermarket-bought all-purpose flour. But for bread making, you'll get better results from an unbleached hard-wheat white flour known as baker's flour. I like unbleached flour because it gives the finished loaf a naturally creamy color. The white flour I use at the moment is blended from hard winter wheat and dark hard northern spring wheat, and has a protein content of 12.5 percent.

When you look at a sack of white flour, you may notice the word *enriched*. During the milling process, some of the nutrients contained in the whole kernel are removed. The enriching process restores these nutrients but in a synthetic form.

UNBLEACHED HIGH-GLUTEN FLOUR

High-gluten flour has from 13.5 to 14 percent protein (45 to 47 percent gluten when wet). This flour should be used only under certain conditions for certain breads in this book, such as Normandy Rye, Multigrain, and Bagels. Tough and rubbery gluten is good for very heavy breads that contain such inert ingredients as rye flour, grains, and cracked wheat, which have no gluten strength of their own. These "deadweight" ingredients dilute the gluten of a lower-strength flour too much to allow the necessary lift. (Only a high-gluten flour will stand up to such deadweight.)

Unfortunately, you probably won't find high-gluten flour at the local supermarket, although you can order it by mail (see Appendix, "Sources"). All the breads in this book (except Bagels) that call for high-gluten flour will come out fairly well with unbleached hard-wheat bread flour, but the resulting loaves won't have as much volume as they should. You can also strengthen bread flour by adding vital wheat gluten, which is almost pure protein; it's sold at health food stores. You need to add only a bit of this gluten, 2 to 3 percent of the measured amount of flour, to strengthen it. For whole-wheat or rye breads, add 1½ teaspoons per cup of flour; for white breads, add 1 teaspoon per cup of flour. You can also add wheat gluten to coax all-purpose flour into working more like a bread flour. Gluten absorbs water, and you must add an equivalent amount of extra water to your dough.

WHOLE-WHEAT FLOUR

To a lot of people, whole-wheat bread is sacred—and white bread is the devil. But I have to admit that I use whole-wheat flour mainly for its good looks and flavor, not its vitamins. You may have grown up thinking that whole-wheat bread is more nutritious than white bread, but that's not really true. Whole-wheat flour *does* contain more nutrients than white flour, but our bodies can't absorb most of them because whole-wheat flour works its way through our systems too fast. Most of the vitamins in white flour, on the other hand, do get absorbed, so the battle between white and whole wheat turns out to be a draw.

When wheat is milled to make white flour, the bran—or outer coat of the wheat berry—is removed. Most often the germ, or seed, of the berry is removed too—it's at the bottom or widest tip of the kernel. The bulk of what remains and becomes white flour is called the endosperm. In whole-wheat flour, however, all the bran and all the germ are always preserved and milled. You can get whole-wheat flour milled in varying degrees of coarseness. The most common whole-wheat flour is medium ground. I prefer very coarsely ground whole-wheat flour (milled from hard wheat), which leaves visible flecks of bran in the bread. Finely ground whole-wheat flour produces a loaf with more volume but without the hearty texture of breads made with coarser flour.

Some bakers prefer stone-ground whole-wheat flour because the oil from the germ becomes evenly distributed throughout the flour when wheat is ground between stones. Because this process does not heat up the flour, it tends not to harm the delicate balance of the wheat berry, resulting in a loaf that may have a better flavor. Still, whether the flour is ground by stone or by the more commonly used high-speed rollers, the finished loaf will look the same—it's the granulation that makes the difference.

Whole-wheat flour needs to be used fairly quickly after you buy it; the extra oils generated by the germ tend to make whole-wheat flour go rancid after a couple of months. For longer storage, keep whole-wheat flour refrigerated.

Breads made with a substantial amount of whole-wheat flour will never have the volume of those made with white flour. The bran contributes weight to the loaf, but helps neither with the fermenting nor the rising of the bread. It also slashes the strands of gluten, inhibiting the bread's growth. If you use 100 percent whole-wheat flour, you'll have dense, heavy bread, the sort most people associate with bad health food. But there are ways to prevent this loaf-as-rock texture. The most common is to blend in white flour. You might, for instance, add 30 percent white flour to a whole-wheat dough and still get a dark, flavorful, and well-risen loaf. If you're not satisfied, experiment with the proportion of white to whole-wheat flour. Keep in mind, the coarser the whole-wheat flour, the more white flour must be used.

RYE FLOUR

Rye flour contains more starch and has a poorer gluten quality than wheat flour, which means rye flour doughs can't be left out to proof as long as wheat flour doughs. Baking a dough made mostly with rye flour is a lot like baking a hunk of oatmeal. This is why most rye breads actually contain a combination of rye flour and white flour. The problem is that people tend to add too much white flour and end up with loaves that have few of the flavor characteristics that make rye bread so wonderful. Be suspicious of a fluffy, lightweight rye loaf. Chances are very little rye flour was used.

On the other hand, a few tablespoons of dark rye flour can give white bread a nice peasanty quality—it makes the crust darker, gives the flavor a little more tang, colors the interior a dusty off-white, and adds to the keeping quality of the loaf.

I usually think mixing dough by hand is better than mixing by machine, but I make an exception for rye breads. Rye doughs are wet, sticky, and difficult to work with. Mix the dough by hand and you might be tempted to add more flour than is really needed because it just won't feel right. Even when you use an electric mixer, you have to be careful. The gluten quality is so poor that doughs made from rye flour are much more susceptible to being overmixed. When a rye dough is overmixed, the dough becomes very slack, and will not keep its shape as it rises.

Rye flour comes in three grades: white (or light), medium, and dark. The variations have to do with how much bran is removed from the flour during milling. White rye flour is the most common, though years ago only dark rye, the sort that went into rustic Old World breads, was sold. But as white bread became more popular, dark breads were more and more thought of as food for the poor. Millers began processing rye flours to make white bread the same way they were processing wheat flours. When you go into a Jewish bakery today, the rye bread you buy will likely be pale tan, rather than hearty and dark.

I happen to prefer darker rye bread. But when I began making the bread I call Normandy Rye, it took a long time to persuade the people at the mill that I really did want dark rye flour. "But nobody buys that!" I was told. *I* bought it, and with such low demand I got a good price too. Don't expect to get the volume or airiness of a white bread when you bake with dark rye flour. Not only does its poor gluten quality work against you, but the residual bran slashes what few strands of gluten do exist and adds extra weight to the loaf.

You can't go against public expectations without a fight, so for my Jewish-style rye bread, I use white rye flour. Even so, I use a starter made with dark rye flour, which makes the bread *slightly* heartier and darker—I consider this my subtle revenge against the status quo. In the Pumpernickel, Rye-Currant, and most other breads that use rye flour, I call for dark rye flour. If you have trouble finding the dark grade, look for medium, and keep in mind that white rye flour *will* work. Your bread just won't look the same as mine.

White rye flour is ideal for one other purpose: I use it to dust the lining of my proofing baskets and cloths and the work surfaces where I shape and knead, no matter what kind of bread I'm baking. Because rye flour absorbs less moisture than wheat flour, it isn't incorporated into the dough—it adheres better to the surface. If you can't find white rye flour for dusting, rice flour works well too.

DURUM AND SEMOLINA FLOURS

Durum is the hardest of all wheat varieties. It has lots of protein and therefore little starch. If you baked bread made with pure durum flour, you'd get a tough loaf, almost impossible to bite into. This chewy quality makes durum flour and semolina (a coarser grind of durum wheat) perfect for making pasta. Despite their drawbacks, I find them useful in some breads when I want to add texture and bulk. You just have to be careful to balance them out with other kinds of flour. I also use semolina to dust sticky doughs like that of the Rustic Bread, which prevents the doughs from sticking to the baker's peel or parchment paper. I prefer to dust with semolina rather than the more widely used cornmeal or polenta because semolina is coarse but not so coarse that it distracts from the inherent texture of the bread.

WATER

The moment flour is combined with water, fermentation begins. Many bakers insist on mixing bread dough with only bottled or purified water. This makes sense: You always want to use the best ingredients you can find, especially when the ingredients are as exposed as they are in a loaf of bread. Even so, I'm not sure bottled water is worth the extra money. I think that water good enough to drink is good enough for baking. If the tap water in your area isn't over-chlorinated and tastes fine, use it for your bread.

NATURAL LEAVENING

Most of us are familiar, at least in concept, with commercial baker's yeast. Packaged dry in small envelopes or moist in cake form, it's the most common leavening in bread. But there are other ways to make bread rise. To me, the most exciting leaven is the yeasts from a sourdough starter that has been nurtured from just flour and water. (I also add grapes to help kick-start the fermentation.) Not only do you get better-tasting bread with a natural starter, but you actually participate in the "growing" of your food, like a gardener or a farmer—yeast, after all, is a plant, a fungus like mushrooms.

There are many ways to raise a starter. The most basic method is simply to stir together flour and water and let the mixture sit out, covered, at room temperature for a few days. During that time, the paste, which starts out looking like some sort of papier-mâché concoction, becomes a bubbly, active mass that looks as if it's breathing with life. In fact, it *is* alive, transformed by and host to some of the microorganisms that exist on the flour and in the air: the wild strains of yeast that act as the rising agent, and lactic and acetic producing bacteria, which give the bread its slightly sweet, slightly sour tang.

How does a vile-looking, smelly goop make something so beautiful and delicious as a loaf of bread? Explaining this process is as difficult as explaining the essence of life.

Science can explain some of the mechanics. Elizabeth David, in her book *English Bread and Yeast Cookery*, quotes the 1921 edition of *The Technology of Bread Making* in her discussion of the process: "Leaven fermentation is due to the presence in the leaven of certain species of yeast, which grow and multiply in that medium. These induce alcoholic fermentation of the sugar of the flour." Still, even food chemists are hard-pressed to define what exactly draws the so-called wild yeasts from the air to a simple mixture of flour and water.

Throughout history, bakers have tried all sorts of methods to promote the growth of wild yeasts and beneficial bacteria in a batch of flour and water: starter. Many, like me, add a few grapes to the initial flour-water mix.

After all, if the microorganisms on the skins of grapes promote fermentation in the making of wine, why not in sourdough bread?

Some bakers ignite fermentation with potatoes or just the cooking water from potatoes. Still others use sweetened peaches. I've even seen instructions for making a starter with bananas.

On the rare occasion a cookbook addresses the subject of sourdough starters, it instructs readers to use commercial or baker's yeast in the initial batch. But commercial yeast is so much stronger than wild yeast that I have to wonder: What's the point of going to the trouble of raising and maintaining a starter over days, weeks, and years, if you're going to include a strain of yeast guaranteed to bully out the wonderful, naturally occurring organisms in the air?

Commercial yeast is efficient and fast acting. With it, you can produce almost foolproof bread. But the bread you get will have neither the depth of flavor nor the texture—the character—of true sourdough. Wild yeasts are unpredictable and take a long time to develop, but with them you'll never get a bland loaf of bread. In the production of baker's yeast, almost all lactic acid bacteria are eliminated before the yeast is packaged for sale. While the yeast causes the dough to rise, it does so without the help of flavoring agents from the acidic bacteria. To me, it's the difference between baking a cake from scratch and baking one from a mix: Both of them are still cakes, but the taste is miles apart.

Most of us have heard the myths about the extreme fragility of a sourdough starter—some bakers keep their starter under lock and key—but starters are pretty hearty after they've developed a few weeks. Once a friend spilled some Coca-Cola into a tub of starter and the bread wasn't affected at all. After a disgruntled employee at another bakery poured all the shop's carefully nurtured starter into the alley, another friend managed to regrow it from a single tablespoon of the stuff.

The only thing I worry about contaminating my starters is commercial yeast—even a little will quickly take over the natural starter batch. Suddenly, you'll have doughs that rise too quickly, and bread that tastes less wonderful than it should. But even a dab of Fleischmann's doesn't have to be too much of a problem: Commercial yeast strains don't survive long in the highly acidic environment of a sourdough starter. With regular feedings, even a starter infected with commercial yeast should eventually become healthy again.

Most of the starters I keep are almost liquid in form, basically slurries. Think of a milk shake or pancake batter and you'll get an idea of what a starter looks like. The consistency is similar to that of the leavening the

French call *poolish* and the Italians call *biga*, though a *poolish* and a *biga* are slurries made with commercial yeast the day before baking and are not strictly natural leavenings.

Another way to form and keep natural leavening is to shape a small ball of unyeasted dough—simply flour and water—and leave it to ferment for a few days in a flour-filled sack. The ball of dough, called the *chef*, or seed, is built up with "feedings" of flour and water and is eventually used to make the initial batch of bread dough. After the dough is mixed, you form the new *chef* by holding back a small piece of the dough to use in the next baking session. This is the method the French call *levain* sourdough.

I prefer liquid sourdough starters because they're easier to maintain, and, once developed, they're ready to use more quickly. Feed a working starter three times a day by adding just flour and water, then stir and it's ready to use in 12 hours. To maintain a *levain*, you have to age the *chef* for a minimum of 24 hours first and then give it its three feedings.

That doesn't mean there isn't work involved in keeping a liquid sourdough starter. You can't just whip up a batch and ignore it. I've found that with starters, there is a fountain of youth: regular feedings of flour, water, love, and attention. Like a human, an uncared-for starter will weaken and show signs of age. A fresh starter is always better than an improperly cared for older starter. But if you find yourself swamped with everyday life and unable to bake for a few weeks, you can keep a starter dormant in the refrigerator up to a few months, then bring it back to full strength with only a few days of regular feedings. There should be little change in its effectiveness.

Another thing to remember: You only have to go through the two-week process of growing the starter culture once in your life. A strong starter becomes what some bakers call a *mother* and can be used to "conceive" other kinds of starters, such as ones made with whole-wheat and rye flour. As long as you maintain it properly, a starter will last as long as you do.

BAKER'S YEAST

Sometimes, when people hear that I bake most of my bread with natural leavening instead of baker's or commercial yeast, they assume I'm a bread snob—as if I feel that anyone who doesn't take the time to make his or her own starter isn't somehow a real baker. They become very defensive and even snippy, saying things like "Well, she's just trying to show off or something."

But I'm not a purist. It's true that I think the best bread I make is baked only with natural leavening, but even within my style of baking there is a place for commercial yeast, sometimes by itself and sometimes in conjunction with a sourdough starter. I don't think bread making was necessarily ruined with the discovery of baker's yeast. After all, the greatest French baguettes—the kind I don't make because in Los Angeles it's impractical to sell a bread that must be eaten within a few hours—depend on baker's yeast for their lightness. A bread made with natural starter won't necessarily come out better than one made with commercial yeast. The most important thing in bread making is knowing how to control the fermentation process.

The manufacture of compressed baker's yeast didn't come about until the mid–nineteenth century, but bakers had been using a form of brewer's yeast from the making of beer and ale for years before that. Some speculate that the ancient Egyptians, who were known for their wine making, included some of the leftover fermenting liquid in their breads to help them rise.

I use baker's yeast for a few of my sourdough breads when I need to get a lighter texture. Often, I'll add a bit when a bread is loaded down with lots of ingredients. The Fruit-Nut Bread and the Multigrain Bread, for instance, would both be too heavy and dense without a little boost from commercial yeast.

When using commercial yeast in conjunction with sourdough starter, be careful to add only a tiny amount of baker's yeast; otherwise it will overpower all the subtle flavor characteristics of bread made from a sourdough starter.

Most bakers feel that both compressed cake yeast and active dry yeast are fine, but I've had better success using fresh cake yeast for sourdough baking. Dry yeast works well in sweet doughs or pastries that contain lots of sugar. According to Harold McGee, in his book *On Food and Cooking: The Science and Lore of the Kitchen*, "Compressed and dry yeast . . . are different genetic strains of the same species and have significantly different traits." Dry yeast, for instance, must be mixed with hot water to be activated and works better in doughs that are proofed in warm temperatures. Sourdough bread making requires cool water and cool proofing temperatures.

Both fresh yeast and dry are perishable (always check the labels for expiration dates), and both can be frozen for longer storage.

The only thing I don't recommend is fast-rising yeast, which works too quickly for the rising times required for most of the breads in this book. When you make a bread that relies solely on commercial yeast for its leavening (this is called the *straight-dough method*), be conservative with the amount—too much yeast will make the bread rise too quickly, give it an off flavor, and cause the bread to become stale or dry up more quickly.

Note: Dry yeast is more concentrated than wet yeast because it contains no moisture. When converting a recipe from dry to fresh yeast, remember to weigh twice as much fresh yeast as you would dry yeast and do the same when you measure by tablespoons.

SALT

In bread, as in all cooking, salt brings out flavor. But it does a lot more than that. It slows down fermentation, allowing a dough to benefit from a long proofing time so that it can develop flavor and texture. (This is why it's often added to a dough late in the mixing process—after fermentation has had a chance to begin.) Without salt, an overnight dough, one that produces a well-risen loaf with a good, irregular interior hole structure, would be impossible. The dough would be ready to go in the oven long before baking time.

Salt also stabilizes and toughens the gluten, strengthening the dough for shaping. And it preserves the natural off-white color of the flour by protecting against overoxidation during the mixing process. If you start with unbleached white flour, the color of the bread you end up with will be almost identical. Bakers in Tuscany are among the few who prefer bread without salt. Slice into a loaf of Tuscan bread and you'll often find that the interior is bright white.

You'll also notice that the texture of the saltless Tuscan loaf is drier than that of a loaf made with salt. Salt, as most weight watchers know, helps cells retain moisture. In bread making this is good—loaves made with salt go stale less quickly.

I use fine-ground sea salt at the bakery, but kosher salt and ordinary table salt work well too. Coarse sea salt is delicious for cooking, but in baking it doesn't blend well into the dough. You will, however, need coarse salt to make the Pretzels in this book—it's part of the crunch that makes the pretzel worth eating.

Note that if you use kosher salt, you need to add a little more than these recipes call for because the slightly larger flakes take up more room in a measuring spoon.

WHEAT GERM

You can get white flour with the germ still attached, especially if you buy organic flour. However, the oils in this portion of the kernel make flour go rancid rather quickly. At the bakery, I use white flour with the germ removed—we order so much flour in bulk that I need to be sure none goes bad. But I then add wheat germ (which I keep refrigerated) to certain white doughs to replace the nutrition that has been taken away. Feel free to add wheat germ to all your doughs. I add about 1 tablespoon of germ per 4 ounces (or about 1 cup) of flour.

BRAN

There's already bran in whole-wheat flour, but because I usually blend in a little white flour, I add extra bran to my whole-wheat breads to make them coarser and more rustic.

RYE CHOPS

Rye chops are simply the coarse grinding of rye berries. I use them mainly for texture in breads such as the Pumpernickel, Fruit-Nut, and Rye-Currant breads and the English Muffins. I find rye chops work better than whole rye berries because they blend into the dough, rather than working as a separate crunch. If you can't find rye chops, buy rye flakes or pumpernickel meal, available at health food stores.

MALT

Nondiastatic barley malt syrup is available at health food stores. It's a mild sweetener that adds malt sugars and flavor and gives a loaf of bread good crust color. I use it mainly in highly acidic doughs, especially those made with rye flour. It provides a little extra sugar for the yeast, which is always looking for something to feed on. In fact, sugar has many of the same chemical properties as malt. For darker breads in which sugar would be inappropriate, I use malt to help spark a warmer crust color and add an extra dimension of flavor. A lot of bakers use malt in all their white doughs—for a time, I did too, but I started to think of it as too much of a crutch. I'd rather get good crust color and flavor by letting a dough's long, natural fermentation take its course. One warning if you're planning to experiment: Too much malt will make the dough too slack and cause the yeast to become too active and the dough to ferment too quickly.

Hint: Malt is very sticky. If you lightly oil your measuring spoon, the malt will slide right off.

MILK

I add milk to some breads for flavor, as well as to soften the crumb, or interior. It also enhances crust color and adds to the keeping quality. You can use milk in its liquid or its powdered form. If you're going to add powdered milk in a recipe that calls for liquid milk, make sure you follow the directions on the package to determine the milk-to-water ratio.

HERBS

Some herbs are wonderful in bread—rosemary is a perfect match with olive oil bread; dill is just right with potato bread. But I don't like to overdo it, and I don't think every herb works in bread. Basil, for instance, belongs fresh on top of bread, not in it.

Even though the process of baking bread dries the herbs that go into a dough, I always prefer to use fresh herbs. Unless you dry your own herbs, you don't know if a bottle has been sitting on the shelf for three months or three years.

TOOLS

for

GETTING
STARTED

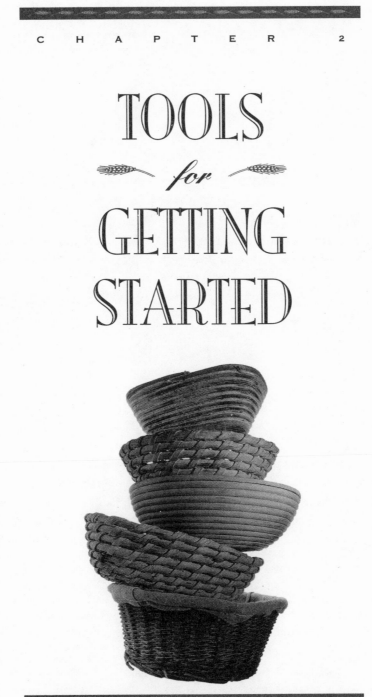

YOUR HANDS AND A HOT OVEN are the only essential pieces of equipment to bake a loaf of bread. Of course, even centuries ago bakers might have had a favorite stone mixing bowl or an improvised method of checking dough temperatures. Once, in desperation, I used an upside-down metal serving tray as a baker's peel and it worked just fine. But there are certain tools that you may want to invest in, simply to make the baking process go as smoothly as possible. And if you're just starting out as a baker, you can use all the help you can get.

THERMOMETERS

It's important to be able to accurately gauge the temperature of both your ingredients and your environment. A long-stemmed, digital, instant-read cooking thermometer works well for measuring dough and ingredient temperatures—just plunge it in. You may want to have a separate room thermometer as well. Finally, you should have an oven thermometer, because most ovens are quirky and run either hot or cold. Good-quality thermometers are available in kitchen shops or through mail order (see Appendix, "Sources").

SCALE

It's possible to bake sourdough bread using only measuring cups to measure your basic ingredients, but I wouldn't recommend it. A pound of starter, for instance, might measure 2 cups one hour and 1¾ cups the next, depending on its fermentation activity: The more active the starter, the more it froths . . . and the more of a measuring cup it fills. Think of how quickly beaten egg whites deflate after you've stopped whipping them.

Flour and other dry ingredients are also best weighed on a scale—in a measuring cup, they can shift and settle, making it difficult to get an accurate reading. In this book, 4 ounces of flour is about 1 cup. As you experiment with brands of flour, you'll find that they differ not only in the kinds of breads they make but in volume as well.

Still, in the recipes in this book, I provide measurements for both a scale and a measuring cup. Lack of exactly the right equipment should never stop you from making bread.

MEASURING CUPS AND SPOONS

You'll need measuring cups and spoons, especially if you don't have a scale. Even if you do, they are useful for measuring small amounts of ingredients. A tablespoon of salt may not be heavy enough to register on most ordinary kitchen scales. Remember, liquids need to be measured in a wet-measure cup, one that can be topped off. For dry ingredients use a *dry measure:* Scoop a heaping amount into the cup or spoon, then level it off with a knife. To be sure you're using the amounts of flour listed in the recipes of this book, don't sift the flour before measuring.

MIXING BOWLS

A mixing bowl should hold at least 5 quarts if you're going to use it to mix dough. You should know, however, that it's possible to mix dough right on a counter. Even so, you'll need bowls to hold the dough in bulk as it ferments. For this purpose, use a wood, ceramic, glass, or plastic bowl—metal bowls are fine for the mixing, but because the metal readily conducts heat, it could interfere with the rising of the dough.

MIXER

Most of the doughs in this book can be mixed by hand—in fact, I think they come out better that way. Even so, I know that most people are more comfortable using an electric mixer. If you use a mixer, be sure it's a freestanding heavy-duty machine, such as a KitchenAid. You'll need one with an attachable dough hook, adjustable speed, and a mixing bowl that holds at least 5 quarts. For wetter, stickier doughs (the few exceptions when a mixer actually is better than hand kneading), you may need a paddle attachment—use it just during the first few moments of mixing to form a dough from the wet ingredients, then switch to a dough hook.

Note that if you're using a KitchenAid, the expression "mix to combine" in the recipes refers to speed 1, "slow" mixing is speed 2, "medium" is speed 3, and "high" is speed 4.

PROOFING BASKETS

Technically, you can let dough rise—or "proof"—free form, with no basket, bowl, or special equipment. But to help the loaf keep its shape, it's best to put your dough in a cloth-lined *banneton* or unlined willow proofing basket. Without it, dough spreads too far and has trouble rising properly in the oven. A basket is better than a bowl because it protects the dough while allowing it to breathe. Also, once the basket linings have seasoned, you get a more interesting-looking crust—the bread takes on the pattern of the cloth lining (or the unlined willow) and picks up the flour used to dust the basket, which then bakes onto the loaf. Season lined baskets the first few times you use them by rubbing flour into the cloth. (There's a photo of proofing baskets on page 17.)

At the bakery we use baskets made especially for proofing. Most of them are woven from wood and lined with unbleached linen. You can order these by mail (see Appendix, "Sources"), but it's simple to improvise. You can, for instance, buy some heavy linen or canvas at a fabric store and sew it into—or simply drape it over—the basket. You can also use a dish towel, but be sure to choose a smooth-textured cotton or linen one—with an ordinary terry cloth towel, loose threads may stick to the dough and leave tiny indentations, which you don't want. The basket should be high enough to allow the dough to double in volume (when properly proofed, some doughs will rise just above the lip of the basket); its width should be just slightly greater than that of the shaped bread.

If you get really serious, you may want to try using different types of baskets for different breads. For Walnut Bread, I like to use circular willow baskets without any lining—because the spiral pattern allows less air to circulate than an open-weave basket and also leaves a beautiful marking on the bread. For whole-wheat breads and most rye breads I use an unlined open-weave willow basket because it allows more air to circulate. And the bread proofs more evenly.

PLASTIC WRAP

It's always useful to have a roll of plastic wrap around when you bake sourdough bread. It protects your starter if you don't have a lid for its container. And dough that is set out to ferment or proof may be covered at different stages with plastic wrap and with a proofing cloth (see following section).

COUCHE/PROOFING CLOTHS

Some breads—baguettes, *bâtards*, and rolls, for instance—never see a basket. They are proofed instead in what the French call a *couche*, or diaper (which is simply a large piece of heavy linen or canvas) that has been dusted with flour, then rippled around the shaped dough to help hold the shape of the loaves and protect the bottom and sides from drying out. Another proofing cloth is then placed on top of the dough. As with your favorite cast-iron skillet, you don't wash proofing cloths (or the linen that lines a proofing basket)—which is just as well, since loose flour can really clog up a washing machine. Instead, after each use set the cloth out to dry, then scrape or shake off the excess flour. If you forget to let the cloth dry completely before you put it away, it will become moldy. After you've used your *couche* and proofing cloths awhile, they will become saturated with the natural yeast from your starter, making them effective tools in helping your bread proof properly. (This happens with proofing baskets too.) Season proofing cloths the same way you season the lining of proofing baskets—by rubbing them heavily with flour the first few times you use them. Once they have been seasoned, a lighter dusting will be sufficient.

It's a good idea to have several sizes of proofing cloths: a few just large enough to drape over your proofing baskets, a couple large enough to cover a 26-by-36-inch board or baking sheet, and some long enough to be rippled.

You can order *couche* by mail (see Appendix, "Sources") or purchase the linen at a fabric store.

PLASTIC TRASH CAN LINERS

Odd as it sounds, a trash can liner can be extremely useful in bread making—and not just for cleaning up. Like plastic wrap and proofing cloth, liners (especially clear ones that allow you to watch the process) are used to protect some doughs when they're left either at room temperature or in the refrigerator to proof. Their size makes them ideal for larger amounts of dough—baking sheets of rolls or baguettes, for instance.

SHOWER CAPS

When my friend Paul Schrade travels, he stays only in hotels where there are shower caps to steal. He insists they make perfect covers for proofing baskets and bowls. The best thing about them is that they can be used over and over.

REFRIGERATOR

Sourdough bread made with natural leavening needs a lot more time than yeasted breads to develop. To get the most flavor, texture, and crust color in a loaf, bakers slow down the fermentation process by putting the dough in a cooler called a retarder. One way to do this at home is to place shaped dough for either several hours or overnight in the refrigerator, where the cooler temperature slows but doesn't stop the activity going on in the dough.

OVEN

Professional bakers have one big advantage over home bakers—their ovens. Bread specialists use steam-injected stone-lined ovens whose extremely high temperatures help develop crispness and color in the crust and promote oven spring. Some devoted small-scale bakers have wood-burning brick ovens, which give their loaves not only great crust but a woody aroma as well. But this doesn't mean a home baker should invest thousands of dollars in a professional-quality range; nor should you start searching empty lots for bricks. It just isn't necessary. There are tricks you can use—spraying the oven's interior to create a steamy atmosphere, lining the oven with baking stones or tiles—to manipulate your oven to simulate a professional bread oven. You may not get the same results as a professional, but you can get wonderful bread.

One thing you should check out before you start baking bread is the size of your oven. The recipes for most of the breads in this book instruct you to bake two loaves at the same time. But you can only do this if your oven is large enough to accommodate not only both loaves but enough space between them so that they don't fuse during baking. If your oven is too small, simply bake one at a time. This will take a little adjusting in rising times (see Chapter 3, "A Lesson in Bread Making"). Another option is to make one large loaf instead of two smaller loaves. If you do this, you will have to refigure your baking times. A 4-pound loaf, for example, should bake about twice as long as a 2-pound loaf, and at a slightly lower temperature.

BAKING STONES OR TILES

A baking stone provides insulated heat, which helps the bread cook more evenly than it would on a metal surface. A stone also absorbs moisture from the dough as it bakes, which gives the loaf a crisper bottom and chewier crust. Ideally, you should have an unglazed ceramic tile cut to fit the bottom of your oven. Buy one at a store listed under "Tile" in the Yellow Pages. You can also use a pizza or baking stone from a gourmet cooking store or mail-order catalog (see Appendix, "Sources"), but try to get one large enough to accommodate at least two loaves. In a pinch, you can even use fire bricks placed in a sheet pan. At home, I leave the baking stone on the bottom of my oven so it's always in place when I want to make bread. When you first use a baking stone or tile, *season* it in the oven at a low temperature for several hours or overnight so it won't crack when you turn the heat up high to bake.

BAKING SHEETS

While the majority of the breads in this book are baked directly on a baking stone, it's easier to bake some doughs on a baking sheet—especially if the dough is too sticky or the shape is too small or fragile (for instance, *Fougasse*, Rolls, Hamburger Buns). At the bakery, we use full sheet pans; you'll do fine with a half-sheet pan (13 by 18 inches), which is the size most stores carry. And if you ever see perforated sheet pans for sale, buy a couple. They're exactly right for bread baking—the tiny holes across the bottoms of the pans help the hot air of the oven reach the bottoms of the loaves, and you get a crisper crust. Your sheet pans must be made of a heavy-duty metal—otherwise the hot oven will warp them.

PARCHMENT PAPER

When I bake bread on a baking sheet, I line the sheet first with parchment paper, which prevents certain doughs from sticking to the baking sheets. Parchment paper can usually be reused a couple of times. It is available in gourmet cooking stores or supermarkets. An alternative is the Magic Baking Sheet (see Appendix, "Sources"). This is a paper-thin Teflon-coated insert that fits inside your baking sheet and will last for years. It is especially useful when baking pretzels, which have a tendency to stick even to parchment paper. The Magic Baking Sheet is interchangeable with parchment paper in all this book's recipes.

BAGUETTE PANS

Baguettes (or *bâtards*) are best baked directly on a baking stone or tiles, although they come out fine baked on baking sheets. In home ovens, they turn out even better when they're baked in a specially designed baguette pan. Baguette pans come in different widths. Perforated and curved to hold the shape of a baguette or *bâtard*, these pans make it much easier to handle the dough, which proofs overnight right in the pan. Most versions are French-made and are available by mail order (see Appendix, "Sources"). If you don't have proofing baskets, most of the doughs in this book can be shaped instead to fit a wide baguette pan. The dough can be proofed in the pan and turned out onto a baker's peel just as if it had proofed in a proofing basket.

LOAF PANS

Even bakers of rustic, boule-shaped loaves crave sliceable sandwich bread once in a while. And for that you'll need loaf pans. If you've already got a couple of loaf pans in your kitchen, don't go out and buy special ones to fit the sizes called for in the recipes. Just adjust the number and weight of the loaves you make. If a recipe calls for 10-cup loaf pans for two loaves and you've only got 5-cup pans, simply make four loaves instead of two and adjust your proofing and cooking times. Determine the capacity of your pans by filling them with water and measuring the contents.

PULLMAN PANS

A pullman pan is a lidded loaf pan that prevents the bread from rising over the rim during baking. With it you get a true rectangular loaf. I use this sort of pan when I bake the *Pain de Mie,* but if you don't have one, simply use a regular loaf pan. The pullman pan can also be used without its lid to make more traditional sandwich loaves.

SPRAY BOTTLE OR PLANT MISTER

In the first minutes of baking, you want to provide a moist, hot environment for your bread. Most professional bakers do this with steam-injected ovens. Home bakers can create steam by spritzing hot water on the sides of the oven and on the baking stone just before the bread is put in the oven. Spray again two or three more times during the first 5 minutes of baking. Use hot water because spraying with cold water will lower the oven temperature too drastically.

A spray bottle is also useful when you are shaping dough. Often it's hard to get enough friction to round a piece of dough into a boule shape. You can create more friction on the work surface by misting the air just above the counter, allowing the mist to fall onto the counter.

There is one other critical use of a spray bottle: If you notice your dough crusting over as it proofs, you must get rid of the crust as quickly as possible because it prevents the dough from rising. Lightly spray the surface with water to dissolve the crust.

You may also want to try gently spraying the surface of smaller breads such as rolls and baguettes as you remove them from the oven to prevent the crust from becoming too hard when it cools.

RAZOR BLADE

Bakers slash the tops of loaves just before placing them in the oven; this is less to make them look pretty than to allow the bread to achieve the oven spring it needs to develop to its full potential. The best tool for the job is a double-edged razor fitted with a metal stick—called a *lame* in French—which functions both as a handle and as a device to curve the blade slightly so it can enter the dough at an angle of about 45 degrees. (*Lames* are available by mail; see Appendix, "Sources.") A single-edged razor (safer to work with) or a sharp knife will also do, though it's harder to cut at an angle with these, and you don't want to cut straight down into the dough. Of course, as with most things in life, there is an exception to this rule: For denser breads, such as the Pumpkin Bread, the Normandy Rye, the Fruit-Nut Bread, and the Multigrain Bread, you *do* want to cut straight down into the dough, and a single-edged razor is best for this use.

SCISSORS

If you're baking dinner rolls, instead of slashing them you can snip the tops with scissors and create peaks that toast nicely in the oven, giving a little extra crunch. I use scissors with 4-inch blades.

DOUGH CUTTER

You can certainly make do without one, but a dough cutter, often called a baker's bench knife, is one of the most versatile tools you can have on hand. You can cut large bulks of dough with its broad rectangular blade (usually made of stainless steel, but also of plastic or wood), and you can use it to lift and stretch doughs—especially soft doughs, such as the Rustic Bread dough. When you're done baking, use your dough cutter to scrape off the excess flour that clings to your work surface and proofing cloths.

RUBBER SPATULA

If you use a mixer, you'll make good use of a rubber spatula, especially a flexible one without a handle. With it, you can scrape the dough out of a proofing bowl or away from the sides of a mixing bowl and prevent the dough from clumping too much on the dough hook.

FINE-MESH STRAINER

Use a fine-mesh strainer to sift flour over your proofing baskets and *couche* to ensure a light, even dusting.

BAKER'S PEEL

A critical moment in the baking process occurs when you transfer the dough from its proofing place to the oven. If you're not careful, you can deflate the dough, preventing it from acquiring its proper shape. A peel helps make the transfer easier. If you're using a regular home oven, a simple short-handled peel will do. Baker's peels are available by mail order or in specialty shops (see Appendix, "Sources").

WOOD WORK SURFACE

I like to knead and shape dough on a sturdy, porous wood surface. I can get more friction on a wood table or board than on, say, marble, Formica, or stainless steel, and that makes it easier to work with the dough.

WOOD BOARD

Sometimes, instead of proofing in baskets, bread is set out on a cloth-covered board that can be moved into a refrigerator during the retarding process. If your kitchen has a cutting board built into the counter, pull it out and use it. Remember, the board has to fit in your refrigerator. If you don't have a suitable board around the house, go to a lumber mill and have a piece of plywood cut to fit. Don't buy anything fancy—this is one piece of equipment you shouldn't spend a lot of money on. If you've already mixed a batch of dough and are just now reading this, don't panic—improvise. You can, for instance, use a cloth-covered baking sheet.

COOLING RACK

When your bread is hot out of the oven, you need to set the loaves on a rack that will allow air to circulate all around them—even under the bottom crust. If you set the loaves out on a counter, the bottoms will steam as they cool, destroying the fine, crisp crust you've just spent hours creating.

SERRATED KNIFE

Use a serrated knife to slice the finished bread. It will cut through the crust without tearing the interior.

YOUR HANDS

The most important tools of all are your hands. Don't hesitate to do as much as possible with them instead of a mixer, a spoon, or any other tool that distances you from the dough. The more you are in direct contact with your dough, the better you will get to know its idiosyncrasies and the better baker you will become.

A LESSON

in

BREAD
MAKING

IF YOU MAKE ONLY ONE BREAD in this entire book, make the one in this chapter. In it, you'll find all the elements that make sourdough baking worthwhile—crisp crust, subtly tart crumb, and a beautiful, irregular interior. There's nothing to interfere with the basic flavors of sourdough bread: wheat and time. This is the one bread I felt I had to perfect before I could open for business as a baker.

You should know that this isn't what most people would consider a beginner's bread—there's no commercial yeast to push the sourdough starter into action, so you've got to make sure the starter you grow is strong enough to do the work on its own. Then again, there's no blandly efficient commercial yeast to get in the way of that characteristic sourdough flavor and texture. And if you've never baked bread before, this is the loaf you need to know how to make. Start here and you won't have to unlearn any bad bread-making habits.

It's a good idea to take notes—especially as you make this bread the first few times. Jot down how it looks, feels, and smells through each part of the process. The environment you're in and the ingredients you use will ultimately determine the character of your bread. For instance, the more you bake bread, the more *desirable* wild yeasts you let loose in your kitchen, and the better your bread will be. It's almost like seasoning a cast-iron pan, only you're seasoning the whole room.

Once you get the basics down, follow your own instincts, not my instructions. And don't despair if your first few loaves don't look the same as the examples pictured in this book. I went through a lot of flour and time before I got the loaf I wanted. And I always learned from my mistakes. Besides, in bread making, mistakes are edible.

THE STARTER — 14 DAYS

The starter is, of course, the essential element of sourdough bread making. And it does take fourteen days to raise this starter from scratch—nine to grow the culture and five to build the starter to the strength you need to bake a loaf of bread.

What's in a starter culture? Nothing more is necessary than flour and water, which attract wild yeasts and beneficial bacteria. (I also add grapes, an abundant source of these wonderful flora.)

But don't be put off: You only have to grow a starter once. After that, as long as you feed and maintain it, your starter will be ready to use over and over again, any time you feel like baking, for the rest of your natural life.

*T*HE FERMENTATION PROCESS:
(LEFT TO RIGHT) DAY 1, DAYS 2 TO 3, DAY 4, DAYS 10 TO 14 AND ON . . . (BACK)

The yeasts cause the bread to rise; this is a complex chemical reaction that plays a vital role in the flavor development, structure, and keeping qualities of the bread. The lactic-acid-producing bacteria contribute to the tart flavor in the dough. Both are essential to a great sourdough loaf.

You could actually bake with your starter after just a few days, but if you invest the full two weeks it takes to build a truly strong starter, you will have leavening that not only makes your bread rise but gives it great flavor as well. And once again, remember that you only have to grow a starter once. After that, it's nothing but loaves in the afternoon.

DAY 1: GROWING THE CULTURE (FERMENTATION BEGINS)

HAVE READY:
Cheesecloth
Scale
One 1-gallon plastic, ceramic, or glass container
Rubber spatula, optional
Plastic wrap, optional
Long-stemmed, instant-read cooking thermometer
Room thermometer

1 pound red or black grapes (pesticide free)
2 pounds (about 4 cups) lukewarm water, 78 degrees F
1 pound 3 ounces (about 3¾ cups) unbleached white bread flour

The first thing you need to do is clean everything that will come in contact with the ingredients of the starter culture—scale bin, culture container, and especially your hands—to prevent the starter from being contaminated with unwanted bacteria. Once you've got an active starter, you don't have to be as meticulous. A healthy starter is hard to kill off. But in the early stages of development, a starter is a fragile living thing.

Ideally, you will use unsprayed, organically grown grapes; if you leave the grapes unwashed, the culture can take advantage of beneficial wild yeasts that cling to the grape skin's waxy coating. If you can't find organically grown grapes, wash the grapes you buy.

Lay the grapes on a double layer of cheesecloth. Tie together the opposite corners of the cheesecloth to form a bag around them. Set them aside.

Use the instant-read thermometer to check the water temperature. Use the scale to measure the water and flour, and place them in a 1-gallon container. Stir together, using your hands or a rubber spatula. The mixture does not have to be completely smooth. Hold the bagged grapes over the container and lightly mash them with your hands, squeezing the juice into the flour mixture. Swish the grapes through the mixture a few times, then push them to the bottom. Cover the container tightly with its lid or a piece of plastic wrap secured tautly around the rim with either a rubber band or a second piece of plastic—this traps the fermentation gases that will form over the next few days. Leave the culture at room temperature, ideally at 70 to 75 degrees F. Move the culture to a cool place, a basement, for instance, if your kitchen is hotter than room temperature; if it's below room temperature, move the culture to a warm place, possibly near, but not too close to, a heater or oven. You could even wrap the container in blankets—after all, gold-mining bakers used to sleep with their starters when they camped outdoors.

DAYS 2 AND 3: FERMENTATION CONTINUES

The second and third days are when the culture evolves from something that looks like a kid's papier-mâché mix into an alive and growing thing. On the second day, you will notice a few tiny bubbles in the mixture, and the bag of grapes may have begun to inflate. On the third day, depending on how active the culture is, it either takes on the appearance of a milk shake, full of frothing bubbles, or resembles a less exciting pancake batter, with only a few more bubbles than on the day before. Remove the plastic and smell the mixture. You should notice a fruity or yeasty aroma, and the bag of grapes may have become fully inflated. Replace the plastic as before.

DAY 4: REFRESHING THE CULTURE

HAVE READY:
Scale
Rubber spatula, optional
½ pound (about 1 cup) lukewarm water, 78 degrees F
4 ounces (about 1 cup) unbleached white bread flour

By the fourth day, the mixture may begin to turn a brownish purple, and it may seethe with large bubbles. If the culture was especially active on its third day, the activity may subside on the fourth. A distinct, unpleasant, alcohol-like smell should be present, and the culture will taste sharp and acidic. The bag of grapes may be deflated by now.

To refresh this culture through its growing period, you need to feed it. Without food, the acidic bacteria will overwhelm the wild yeasts. What you want is a balance between the yeast and bacteria. The yeasts in the culture—and the starter it will soon become—get their nourishment from the sugars that naturally occur in flour. Water helps give the mixture the proper consistency. Uncover the culture, add water and flour, and mix everything with your hands or a rubber spatula. Reach into the mixture for the grape bag and swish it through. Return the bag to the mixture. Cover the culture securely, as before.

It's technically possible to make bread at this point. The culture has already developed the activity it needs to make a loaf rise. But the bread you'd get wouldn't taste or look as good as it could.

DAYS 5 THROUGH 9: FERMENTATION CONTINUES

There's not much you have to do to the culture at this point, though you should check on it once a day to see how it's changing. The mixture normally separates, forming a yellowish liquid top layer. Mold may appear. If it does, remove it and add a cup of flour and a cup of water. If it's removed fairly promptly, mold won't hurt the culture, but it may be a sign that the yeasts and bacteria are out of balance. If everything goes well, the unpleasant smell of a young culture will eventually be replaced by the yeasty aroma you might have noticed on Days 2 and 3.

DAY 10: REGULAR FEEDING BEGINS

HAVE READY:
One 6-quart, covered but not airtight plastic, ceramic, or glass container

Begin early today, because this is the day the culture becomes a starter—and the day you put it on a permanent feeding schedule.

Uncover the culture and remove the bag of grapes, squeezing any remaining liquid into the culture. Discard the grapes. Stir the contents of the container well. Pour off and discard all but about 1 pound 2 ounces (about 2 cups) of the culture. You make more than you need because I find it easier to launch fermentation with larger amounts of flour and water. (If you can't stand to throw out so much of the culture you spent ten days raising, you're not alone. Many people give theirs away to friends, or freeze or refrigerate it to use if something happens to their working starter.)

Transfer the working culture to a clean, sealable but not airtight, container. (The carbon dioxide created from the yeast can cause the top of an airtight container to pop off.) The culture is now ready to be fed. Time and regular feeding are what distinguish a starter from a culture. Starter is still essentially a mixture of growing yeast and bacteria, but now it needs regular nourishment, and you can bake with it once you build it up to strength. Feeding instructions follow.

DAYS 10 THROUGH 14: BUILDING THE STARTER

What you'll be doing for the next five days is feeding the starter three times a day to get it into shape for baking. After this five days—and for the rest of your baking life—you will continue the feeding schedule, not to build up the starter's strength but to maintain it. The yeast in the starter *lives* off the sugar from the starch in the flour. After the yeast has eaten all the starch, it will starve. So the starter needs to be regularly replenished.

During this time, it's critical that you watch over your starter as a parent watches over a newborn. Don't miss a feeding! Other recipes may require starters to be fed only once a day, but think how *you* feel at the end of the day if you don't eat until dinner. If you absolutely can't be around to feed the starter as often as it needs to be fed, you can adjust the feedings and make a fine loaf of bread (see "Making Your Own Bread Schedule," page 58), but I've found that bread turns out a *lot* better when the starter has been fed three times each day. The main thing is to pick a schedule and then try to stick to it. On the days you are not going to make bread, you may choose to reduce the feedings. If you know in advance that you are going to bake, try to put your starter back on a three-times-a-day feeding schedule a couple of days before you do.

You determine how much to include in the first feeding by approximately matching the amount of the starter base with equal amounts of flour and water. If you begin, for instance, with 1 pound 2 ounces (about 2 cups) of starter, add ½ pound (about 1 cup) of water and 5½ ounces (about 1¼ cups) of flour (since the starter feeds on the flour, you add just a bit more than what you'd need to double the amount). Now the contents measure 1 pound 13½ ounces (a little more than 4 cups). For the next feeding double this amount: Add 1 pound (about 2 cups) of water and 11 ounces (about 2½ cups) of flour. For the third feeding double the previous amount by giving it 2 pounds (about 4 cups) of water and about 1 pound 6 ounces (about 5 cups) of flour. At the end of the day, you will have a little more than 7 pounds (or about 12½ cups) of starter.

First Feeding:
½ pound (about 1 cup) lukewarm water, 78 degrees F
5½ ounces (about 1¼ cups) unbleached white bread flour
1 pound 2 ounces (about 2 cups) starter

Stir the water and flour into the starter base and cover the container. The mixture does not have to be completely smooth. You may not notice much activity in the beginning; this is normal. You've got a new culture, and this is only its first feeding.

Second Feeding: 4 to 6 hours later
Starter
1 pound (about 2 cups) lukewarm water, 78 degrees F
11 ounces (about 2½ cups) unbleached white bread flour

Uncover the starter, stir the water and flour into the mixture, and cover the container.

Third Feeding: 4 to 6 hours later
Starter
2 pounds (about 4 cups) lukewarm water, 78 degrees F
1 pound 6 ounces (about 5 cups) unbleached white bread flour

Uncover the starter and stir in the water and flour. Cover the container and let it ferment 8 to 12 hours, definitely not more than 15 hours. The starter reaches its optimum strength 8 to 12 hours after it's been fed. Remember this when planning your baking schedule.

The next day, no more than 15 hours after the third feeding, repeat the feedings. You will continue this feeding schedule for the next four days, until you get through Day 14. But each day, before you begin, pour off all but 1 pound 2 ounces (about 2 cups) of starter. (If you kept doubling the amount of starter during each feeding, you'd eventually have enough starter to fill a swimming pool.)

DAY 15: MAINTAINING THE STARTER

Today you are ready to bake. Know that the first loaf made with the new starter won't be as good as the fifth—just as you need to get used to handling dough, your starter needs to adjust to its surroundings.

How can you be sure the starter is ready to go? Stick your clean hands right in the starter. Listen to the bubbles crackle. Even when you're not touching the starter, bubbles pop and slowly form, bulging and pulsing. The starter is really alive. You can crush the bubbles between your fingers, as if you were popping bubble wrap. You should also be able to smell a slightly nutty aroma and taste a pleasant, yeasty flavor. These are signs of a healthy starter—and of delicious bread to come.

To begin, measure out the amount of starter called for in the recipe you choose. Then set aside 1 pound 2 ounces (about 2 cups) of starter from what remains, as you've been doing for the past four days. (Most recipes in this book call for no more than 1 pound 2 ounces of starter, or about 2 cups, at once.)

Now that the starter is strong, you may want to maintain a smaller amount. Try setting aside 9 ounces or about 1 cup of starter. *Match* the starter with flour and water each time instead of doubling it. This method wastes the least amount of flour. If you ever need more starter, return to the original formula and grow as much as you like.

No matter what method you use, keep the starter on a regular feeding schedule. Otherwise, you'll throw off what you might call the starter's metabolism. Take care of your starter, and it will be ready to work whenever you are.

If you can't bake on the day your starter is ready, continue feeding it three times a day until you *can* bake. If for some reason you find that you won't be able to make bread for a week or two, put the starter in the refrigerator, where it will remain dormant. The day before you bake, reactivate it. If

---

When White Sourdough Starter Is Too Sour

Many people assume that because I like strongly flavored sourdough bread, I must *really* love sour bread. The sourer the bread, the better, right? Wrong. Overly sour bread has a flavor that zaps the back of your tongue when you eat it, a flavor that dominates all components of the bread, especially the subtle taste acquired from the age of the loaf. Rye bread is the only exception: The flavor of the rye and a good sour flavor are a well-balanced marriage.

I've had more than a few people proudly tell me that they've left their starter for several weeks without feeding so that it could acquire extra sourness (each time you feed a starter, you not only nourish it but tame the funkier aspects of the fermenting liquid). But when I taste these starters, they have an awful flavor.

What's more, an overly sour starter is weak in leavening power. It produces undesirable acidity, which in turn produces an undesirable flavor, almost a sign of illness. It's as if the starter is so weak from lack of flour refreshment that it has the strength neither to make the dough rise to its full potential nor to fight off the bad flavors. This is why a sour-tasting starter doesn't always make a good sour-tasting bread.

As long as you give a starter regular feedings, you shouldn't have to worry about it becoming too sour or too weak. Think of a bell curve graph; a starter is at its optimum strength and flavor 8 to 12 hours after it's fed, and drops off considerably in quality beyond that range.

Harold McGee, in his book *On Food and Cooking,* points out that starters that have been well maintained for decades are resistant to contamination, possibly because of some sort of penicillin-like antibiotic action.

---

the starter has been dormant up to one week, let it come to room temperature for 2 hours, then give it a full day of feeding. The next day it will be ready to use. If the starter has been dormant more than one week (and up to several months), put it on a regular feeding schedule for *three* days before using.

If you feed a dormant starter for several days and there's no activity, it's likely your starter is no longer alive. If the starter seems sluggish, put it in a warmer place and increase the water temperature during feedings. If the starter seems too active and tastes too sour, put it in a cooler place and feed it with water that is slightly colder than the usual 78 degrees F.

Another way to preserve a starter is to dry it. Pour out 1 or more cups of starter in a thin layer on a parchment-lined baking sheet and let the starter dry at room temperature about 3 days. Once dry, peel the flaky sheets of starter from the paper and store it in a tightly sealed plastic bag. To revive the starter, dissolve the dried pieces in water (78 degrees F), stirring as the starter softens. Once dissolved, feed the starter with flour and water as before. It will take about 5 days for the starter to regain its strength.

Storing Bread

Bread is best stored at room temperature, either cut-side down on the counter or in a paper bag. Never store bread in plastic bags—you'll make the crust spongy and it will become moldy more quickly. And if you've baked too much, remember: Yesterday's bread makes tomorrow's toasts (see pages 248–49) or croutons (see pages 250–51).

If you find that you've made more bread than you can eat within two or three days, wrap it in a plastic bag and freeze it. Note that smaller breads, baguettes and rolls, freeze less well than boules and sandwich loaves. Thaw frozen loaves by removing them from their freezer wrapping and allowing them to stand at room temperature for a few hours—microwaving will spoil the texture. Once a loaf is thawed, you may want to heat it for 3 to 5 minutes in a hot oven to crisp up the crust. Ordinarily, I don't like oven-warmed bread, but loaves that have been frozen seem to benefit from the crisping process. Never store bread in your refrigerator. Science tells us that the staling process takes place faster at the cooler temperature ranges of a refrigerator.

THE BASIC LOAF: COUNTRY WHITE

MAKES TWO APPROXIMATELY 1-POUND-10-OUNCE BOULES.

Congratulations: You've raised your starter and are ready to bake. Don't be put off by the two-day process this loaf involves. It's not two full days of work. Remember, to get a great loaf of sourdough bread, you don't need technique, you just need a little patience. The dough does most of the work. You simply activate the processes.

TWO-DAY BREAD—FIRST DAY

HAVE READY:

Scale
Room thermometer
Long-stemmed, instant-read cooking thermometer
Mixing bowl, at least 5 quarts
Proofing cloth
Mixer with attachable dough hook, optional
Rubber spatula, optional
Ceramic, glass, or plastic bowl
Plastic wrap
Fine-mesh strainer
2 cloth-lined proofing baskets
Spray bottle, filled with water

12 ounces (about 1⅓ cups) White Starter
2 pounds plus 2 ounces (about 7 cups) unbleached white bread flour, plus extra for dusting
1 pound plus 2 ounces (about 2¼ cups) cool water, 70 degrees F
½ cup raw wheat germ
4½ teaspoons sea salt
Vegetable oil

PLANNING

Don't do a thing until you read the recipe carefully and calculate the times involved. It wouldn't hurt to look at the section called "Making Your Own Bread Schedule" (see page 58).

INITIAL MIXING

Check on your starter. It should be bubbling and healthy. Now weigh it carefully. When you're making just a few loaves of bread, it is especially important to have exactly the right amount of starter.

Proper Temperature: A Baker's Secret Weapon

Home-baked bread *is* different from bakery bread, but it doesn't have to be dramatically different. One crucial element in the process should be exactly the same in your kitchen as it is in my bakery: temperature. If you want to match the characteristics of the bread I bake, be sure your dough is the same temperature as mine after mixing.

The friction generated during mixing and kneading heats the dough. You control this heat by controlling the temperature of the water you use for mixing. Test your tap water with a long-stemmed cooking thermometer. If the temperature is too low, add some hot water; if it's too high, fill a container with water, add ice to chill it, then measure.

In each of my recipes you'll see that a suggested water temperature is listed, based on the assumption that you'll be working in an environment that is room temperature, about 73 degrees F. First, read ahead in the recipe you're using and check the temperature the dough should be at the end of mixing. Next, take readings of the room temperature and the temperature of your flour. Most of the time, the flour and room temperatures are identical. For every degree above 73 degrees F, reduce your water temperature one degree. For every degree below 73 degrees F, increase your water temperature one degree.

It's important that you end up with approximately the same dough temperature as indicated in the recipe, as this will dictate how quickly your bread rises.

You need to do one more thing before you start mixing: Get a reading of the room temperature and the temperature of your flour. These measures will help you determine how hot or cold the water should be. (The water temperature recommended here assumes that the room you're working in is room temperature, 70 to 75 degrees F. You should always double-check this before starting.) Check the box on page 41 to help you figure out the proper water temperature. Once you've got your ingredients measured, you're ready to mix.

Your goal is to blend all the ingredients into a homogenous mass, a stretched, resilient object ready to benefit from the effects of fermentation. This blending, whether performed by hand or by machine, transforms the proteins in the flour into gluten (gluten strands hold the carbon dioxide that allows the dough to grow) and converts the starches into sugars. Mixing helps the yeast to begin feeding on the sugars and to start forming the carbon dioxide and alcohol that is a result of the fermentation process.

TECHNIQUE: BY HAND

Heap the flour in a large mixing bowl, at least 5 quarts, or on a sturdy work surface, and form a well in the middle of the mound. Place the White Starter, water, and wheat germ inside the well. (The bowl method makes less of a mess, though I prefer to mix everything on a wood work surface.) Using your fingertips, draw in just enough flour to form a slightly sticky, pliable dough.

Pause a moment to evaluate the dough. If it's too wet, add more flour; if it is too dry, this is the time to add more water. Water added too close to the end of mixing won't blend in properly. At this point, the dough is capable of absorbing more moisture than it can ultimately hold; if you add too much water, the moisture will seep out as the dough rises.

If you're not sure whether the dough is too wet or too dry, always err on the side of too wet. It's the softness of the dough that contributes to the open interior hole structure of the final loaf.

KNEADING

Once a sticky, pliable dough forms, it's time to knead. This action, the second phase of mixing, develops the gluten formed during the initial mixing of the dough. What you want to do here is make the dough as elastic as possible without stretching it so much that it breaks down like an overbeaten egg white and becomes limp. When you knead by hand, you don't have to worry about overmixing; most home mixers aren't strong enough to do much damage—but

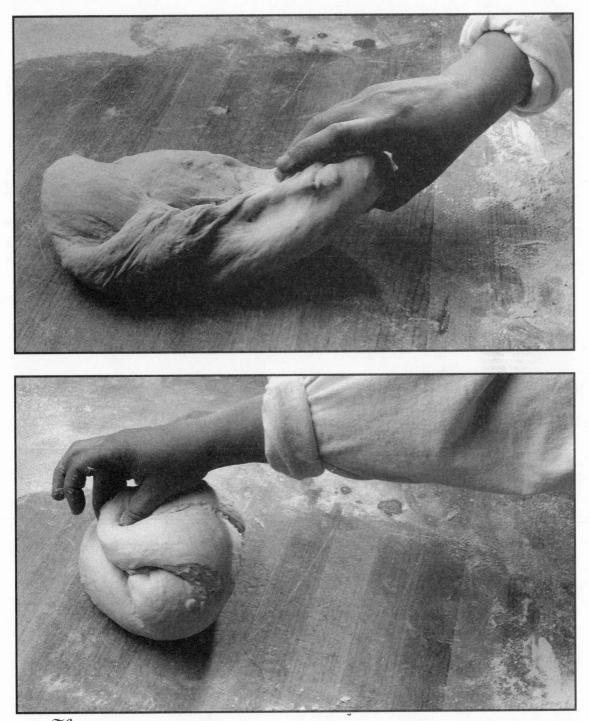

*K*NEADING BY HAND:

"WHEN YOU KNEAD BY HAND, YOU DON'T HAVE TO WORRY ABOUT OVERMIXING."

beware of food processors. You want a satin smooth, elastic texture. If the dough is still too sticky, add a bit more flour and keep kneading.

Though an electric mixer mimics the motion of kneading fairly well, I prefer to knead by hand. You've got to use all your upper-body strength if you're going to do it right. Kneading bread dough is less the pretty, two-handed massage motion that you may have learned when you first made bread than an aggressive, one-handed slam dunk that can be mastered with just a little practice. (When you're baking, it's nice to have one clean hand with which to answer the telephone, burp the baby, or pat the dog.)

Here's what you do: Remove the dough from the bowl, if you're using one, and place it on a sturdy work surface. With one continuous motion, grab the end of the dough closest to you, fold it toward the other end, gather one end in your fist, lift and flip the dough in midair, then whack it down hard on the work surface. Immediately grab the dough again and repeat the motion over and over for about 5 to 7 minutes. As you work, the dough will become less sticky, more elastic, and more difficult to manipulate. Slowly, it will start to take on the rough shape of a rounded loaf, or boule.

AUTOLYSE: A MOMENT OF REST

Stop kneading, cover the dough with a proofing cloth, and let it rest for 20 minutes. As it sits, the flour continues to absorb water. The dough is also regaining its composure, so to speak, after enduring the stress you've just inflicted on it during mixing and kneading. This respite makes the dough easier to handle, easier to shape, and it allows you to make a slightly better dough. In France, bakers call this period of rest *autolyse*. (Many bakers don't add their sourdough starter until *after* the *autolyse*. I've found that it works pretty much the same either way.) *Autolyse* was developed as a baker's trick of sorts to cut down on mixing times—the more you handle a dough, the more you mix out flavor and color. By letting the dough rest, you're helping your bread develop a more porous interior and a better crumb color.

I don't call for an *autolyse* with all my breads. The benefits are more noticeable with wheat breads and those breads with highly porous interiors.

SALT AND THE FINAL MIX

After 20 minutes, sprinkle the salt on the dough. The addition of salt slows the fermentation and toughens the gluten—you'll notice the dough becomes much stiffer as soon as the salt is added. Begin to knead again, using the same motion as before, until the dough reaches a temperature of 78 degrees F, looks satiny, and feels smooth and elastic, about 5 minutes. You should be able to stretch a tiny piece of the dough paper-thin without breaking it. (This trick only works with white doughs.) At this point, most people like to describe dough as feeling a little like a baby's bottom.

TECHNIQUE: MACHINE

If you decide to use an electric mixer, be sure you have a mixing bowl large enough to hold all the ingredients: at least 5 quarts. We always use a mixer at the bakery, but that's because we bake hundreds of loaves a day. When you're making just a few loaves, it's almost always best to mix by hand, and it's really not that much more work. (There are a few exceptions, including the Rustic Bread, the Fruit-Nut Bread, and other rye breads, doughs that are especially wet, chockful of ingredients, or hard to work with.)

Still, you may want to save your strength and mix by machine. If so, use a dough hook attachment and measure the water, White Starter, flour, and wheat germ into the mixing bowl. Mix on low speed for 5 minutes. The dough should be sticky and pliable. Watch the dough carefully in the first few minutes to see if it needs more water. If it does, dribble it in slowly and keep mixing. (Many bakers like to hold back a cup of flour and add it as needed to get the proper consistency.)

After 5 minutes, turn off the mixer, cover the dough with a proofing cloth, and let the dough rest for 20 minutes. Add the salt and mix the dough at medium speed until it reaches a temperature of 78 degrees F, looks satiny, and feels smooth and elastic—about 5 more minutes—scraping the dough down the sides of the bowl as necessary with a rubber spatula. (You may need to adjust the mixing time to get the desired temperature: mix a little less if it reaches 78 degrees F before 5 minutes, mix a little more if you haven't reached 78 degrees F after 5 minutes.) The dough should cohere enough to clean the sides of the bowl by the end of the mixing time.

Remove the dough from the mixing bowl and place it on a lightly floured work surface. Knead the dough using the motion described earlier for another minute or so. This gives you at least some physical contact with the dough, and the assurance that it is mixed enough. It should look shiny and feel smooth and resilient.

FERMENTING: THE FIRST RISE

Fermentation, the slow stretching and development of the gluten in the dough, has actually already begun. It starts as soon as the flour and water are combined during mixing, and doesn't end until the gluten "sets" in the oven during baking. Of course, most of the work of fermentation occurs during the two to three rest periods for the dough. At least, this is when the effects of fermentation are most visible—most doughs double in volume.

What's happening? Picture each microsopic yeast organism as a little Ms. Pac-Man gobbling up the starch in the flour. One of the by-products of all this activity is alcohol. The coexisting bacteria from the starter consume some of this alcohol and produce lactic and acetic acids and other elements that flavor the bread. And as the yeast and bacteria do these marvelous things, they also release carbon dioxide gas, which causes the dough to inflate and rise as if it contained a million tiny gluten-walled balloons. When bakers talk about the process going too far (the balloons burst) or not far enough (the balloons fail fully to inflate), they use the terms *overproofed* and *underproofed.*

To help distinguish the stages of the rise, bakers traditionally give each segment of the proofing process a different name. Before the dough is shaped, it is *fermenting.* After the dough is shaped and set out at room temperature, it is *proofing.* When the dough is placed in a refrigerator or other cold environment to slow the proofing, the term *retarding* is used. (Retarding will be considered part of proofing in the recipes that follow this chapter.)

To get the dough ready for its first rise, or fermenting, place it in a clean bowl that has been lightly coated with vegetable oil. (Don't use metal bowls; they conduct heat too rapidly.) You don't need to put the dough in a proofing basket until the second rise. Cover the bowl tightly with plastic wrap. Let the dough ferment at room temperature (70 to 75 degrees F), away from drafts, until it doubles in volume, 3½ to 4 hours.

To make sure that the dough ferments at the correct temperature, bakers have special pieces of equipment called *proof boxes* to maintain a warm temperature and high humidity, and *retarders* to maintain a cooler temperature. If the temperature in your home is significantly hotter or colder than standard room temperature, you may have to create an artificial environment for the dough. Place it near a heater (but away from direct heat) or a warm stove if the air is too cold; if it's an especially hot day, let the dough rise in a cool basement. Avoid putting your dough in an air-conditioned room—air conditioning tends to dry out dough, and if the dough dries out, it may form a crust and have trouble rising.

If you're afraid the room you're working in is too dry or too cold, you can create your own proof box. Place the bowl on a baking sheet and slide the sheet into a clean plastic trash can liner. Gather the opening, inflate the bag by blowing in it, then close the bag and secure it tightly. (I've experimented with plastic trash can liners for proofing from the time I started baking, but I got the idea for inflating the bag from Paul Bertolli's bread chapter in *Chez Panisse Cooking*, which contains some of the best writing I've read on sourdough baking.)

Note that the dough is not simply increasing in volume as it rises; it is also developing characteristics that make white sourdough bread special: the sour tang, the chewy crust, the elasticity of the crumb, the open-holed interior and the creamy color.

Whenever you ferment or proof dough, you have to watch it carefully. My recommended time for this first rise is 3½ to 4 hours. But the surroundings in which you work could speed or slow this process. A better way to gauge whether the dough is ready is to look at it and touch it. Lay a hand over the loaf. When it is properly fermented, this dough should feel cool and slightly flabby on the surface, but the center core should still feel firm, and you should get a sense of the activity of fermentation. (It's difficult to describe this activity, but when you're working with a living thing—this sourdough is alive—there is a palpable internal energy: remember, this is not cookie dough.) Finally, when you press on the dough with your fingertip, a slight indentation should linger—the dough shouldn't spring right back, as it does immediately after mixing. Look for the same characteristics later, when the dough has proofed.

If your dough underferments at the early stages it will lack flavor, strength, and maturity, which cannot be compensated for later in the process. If the dough is overfermented, it will be too weak to hold its shape as it proofs, too weak to grow to its optimum size when baked.

Use these guidelines to check the dough at each rising stage—especially when looking for signs of overproofing or underproofing—and make note of how long your bread requires to reach the proper texture. You may have to adjust your baking schedule.

MISE EN TOURNE: PRESHAPING

Shaping, obviously, turns the dough from a mass of flour and water into something with form, something tangible. But bread is shaped not just to make it easy to handle once it's out of the oven; the form a loaf takes also helps determine how high the bread will rise, how porous the interior will be, and how well the crust (and the cuts slashed on top of it) will develop. Shaping is a sort of road map for dough—it tells it where it's going and how to get there.

This bread is formed into a rounded loaf, or a boule, a shape that has been used by bakers for hundreds of years. Before it's formed into a boule, however, you need to preshape the dough, or introduce the shape to come.

Turn the dough out onto a lightly floured work surface and cut it into two equal pieces (each half should weigh about 1 pound 14 ounces) with a dough cutter. Slap each piece gently against the work surface a few times to deflate the dough. Knocking the dough to deflate it puts the yeast into contact with fresh starch granules and closes up any air pockets.

Tuck all the edges under to form a sort of rounded mass. Don't bother to make the dough look like a loaf at this point—you simply want to suggest the shape to come. French bakers call this action *mise en tourne*, which means half turn or primary turn.

Cover the two pieces of dough with a piece of cloth. Let the dough rest for about 15 minutes. As with the *autolyse* during mixing, this rest period relaxes the dough, helps develop flavor and texture, and makes it easier to shape.

SHAPING

Using a strainer, sift a thin, even layer of flour along the sides and bottom of each cloth-lined proofing basket. (If you don't have proofing baskets, you may proof the bread directly on a proofing cloth similarly dusted.)

Wrap your hands around the side of one piece of dough and with a rolling motion rock it into a ball—the motion is similar to making a slow turn on a steering wheel. Use the work surface to create friction as you shift the dough. If you feel that the friction is insufficient, mist the work surface by spritzing water from a spray bottle into the air just above the surface. Bring the dough toward you as you work. One common mistake at this stage is overshaping—apply even pressure all around and don't worry about getting the ball super-compact. The skin shouldn't be stretched so tight that it starts to rip. You have just made a boule, a taut ball with a smooth skin that stretches over the surface of the dough.

Put the shaped boule smooth side down into a basket. Pinch the seam closed with your fingers. Shape the second boule and put it in the second basket. Cover each basket with a piece of plastic wrap to prevent the dough from drying out.

*S*HAPING A BOULE

PROOFING: INTERMEDIATE RISE

Place the baskets at room temperature (70 to 75 degrees F) away from drafts and let the dough proof just until it starts rising up the sides of the baskets and increases in volume by one fourth. This will take approximately 1 hour.

Remove the plastic and sprinkle the surface of the dough with flour. Cover the baskets with plastic wrap and secure tightly—I usually take a second piece of plastic wrap and tie it around the rim of the basket.

PROOFING: RETARDING

Now, after having invested most of your energy into encouraging fermentation, you want to slow it down; you want the dough to age. Retarding is the step that allows the dough to maintain the long, slow rise required to develop flavor and texture. Without this step, the dough would proof too quickly and would have to be baked much sooner, with far less delicious results.

The activity of fermentation generates heat; retarding is done by cooling the dough. Many bakeries have a special piece of equipment actually called a retarder; it provides an ideal environment—and temperature, 50 degrees F—for the dough. At this temperature, yeast activity is slowed down, while the lactic acid–producing bacteria that flavor the bread remain active.

At home, you can just put the proofed dough in your refrigerator. The dough is covered with plastic wrap to prevent it from drying out and to help accelerate the retarding process—you're trying to simulate the environment of a professional retarder. Your refrigerator, however, is much colder than a retarder and will put the yeasts and acid-forming bacteria into a near-dormant state. Later, you'll have to wake them up.

Leave the boules in the refrigerator for 8 to 12, but no more than 24 hours; you have plenty of flexibility. If there were commercial yeast in this dough, you couldn't let it sit this long—it would rise too quickly and the yeasts would polish off all the nutrients in the flour. Start checking the dough after 12 hours, using the guidelines described in "Fermenting: The First Rise."

SECOND DAY

HAVE READY:
Proofing cloth
Room thermometer
Long-stemmed, instant-read cooking thermometer
Baking stone or tiles
Baker's peel
Single-edged razor blade
Spray bottle, filled with water
Cooling rack

Shaped dough
Unbleached white bread flour for dusting

PROOFING: THE FINAL RISE

Remove the baskets holding the boules from the refrigerator and take off the plastic wrap. The surface of the dough may seem a bit wet because of the condensation caused by the plastic wrap. It will dry as the dough sits out at room temperature. Now cover the boules with proofing cloth. Left on, the plastic wrap would keep in the refrigerator's cold and prevent the dough from coming up in temperature in a timely manner; the cloth keeps the dough from drying out.

Note: If your oven is too small to accommodate two boules placed well apart (at least three quarters of the width of one boule), you should bake one at a time. This means you should take only one loaf out of the refrigerator now. Remove the second boule 1 hour after removing the first so that it will be ready to bake just as the first loaf is taken from the oven.

Proof the boules at room temperature (70 to 75 degrees F) away from drafts. The dough should be ready to bake when it has doubled in size, no longer springs back when poked with your finger, and has come up to a temperature of 62 degrees F, about 3 hours.

It's especially important at this point to follow the guidelines for determining whether the dough is overproofed or underproofed, described in "Fermenting: The First Rise." This is the dough's last rise—and your last chance to get things right. When dough is underproofed, or too cold, the bread will develop too much oven spring and the finished loaf will have a ceramic-like finish rather than one well blistered with fermentation bubbles, also an unappealing pallor, bulges or blowouts on the sides or a lopsided appearance, and a tight, restricted look. If the dough feels too firm and if it springs back at the touch of a fingertip, it is underproofed.

If the dough is overproofed, it won't have enough oven spring. The bread may not come up properly through the cuts, and instead of gently rounding into a dome shape, the boule may emerge from the oven with sharp edges. The interior of the loaf will be uniform, without an irregular hole structure. The bread may taste overly sour, and the crumb and crust will have an off-yellow color. No matter how long you bake it, an underproofed or overproofed loaf will never have the rich, burnished color of an ideal sourdough boule. You can tell that the dough is overproofed if it starts to form tiny rips in the surface and if it seems to be flabby all over, with no firm center or indication of life.

PREPARING THE OVEN

As the dough proofs at room temperature, line the bottom rack of your oven with ceramic baking tiles or a pizza stone and set the oven temperature at 500 degrees F. (Actually, you can keep your baking tiles or stone in your oven on a permanent basis.) Do this at least 1 hour before baking so the stone or tiles are well heated. Many home bakers also remove the lightbulbs in their ovens to prevent them from bursting when the ovens are spritzed with water.

DOCKING: CUTTING THE LOAF

The cuts you make on top of a piece of dough are not merely decorative but functional. Like shaping, cuts, called *docking, slashing,* or *scoring* by bakers, work as a guide for the dough so that the loaf can reach its proper shape and height. The cuts also allow moisture in the dough to escape. Bakers use several kinds of cuts—Xs, Cs, straight slashes, tic-tac-toe patterns, or indentations with their fingers—to help distinguish one type of loaf from another.

*C*UTTING A BOULE

It should be noted that softer doughs (ones made with, say, olive oil) don't rise as much during baking, so cuts in those breads are less functional.

If, as you read through the recipes, you find the instructions for cutting a certain dough too complex, know that with most breads a single slash down the middle or a simple *X* will work just fine.

In this loaf, expect the cuts to work for you. At the end of baking, they should have blossomed like a flower, exposing part of the loaf's smooth interior. The edges of each cut should be thin and sharp. Then the bread will have what bakers refer to as a beautiful *shag*.

When the boules are properly proofed, lightly dust them with flour. Carefully run a hand around one loaf to loosen it from the sides of the basket and gently invert it onto a flour-dusted baker's peel, smooth side down. Be careful—if you're too rough, you could deflate the dough and ruin the final shape.

Notice that much of the flour used to line the proofing basket remains on the top of the dough. Don't remove it, unless you need to remove *gently* any *hunks* of flour that managed to pass through your strainer. The flour will brown in the oven and give the loaf a nice, rustic look.

Anchor the dough by placing a hand around the side of the boule. With a single-edged razor blade held at a 45-degree angle to the surface of the boule, slash the top of the dough, beginning about 1 inch from the top edge of the boule, curving down to the bottom edge. Be sure to keep your anchored hand well clear of the blade. (Don't cut too deep or the lip of the cut will be too thick after it's baked.) You just want to create a thin flap, as horizontal as possible and only about ½ inch deep. When you're done, the cut should look like a backward *C*. Don't cut the second boule until after you load the first in the oven.

One thing to know if you think your dough isn't properly proofed: Adjustments in docking can improve the odds of getting a better-shaped loaf. If the dough is overproofed, for instance, cuts that are more shallow than usual help prevent the loaf from deflating during baking. Conversely, if the dough is underproofed, a deeper-than-usual cut can keep the loaf in check, preventing it from overexpanding to the point where the insides blow out in places. Proper docking complements the proof.

BAKING

When shaped dough is placed in an oven, it is surrounded by both top heat—the hot air on the top and sides of the loaf—and bottom heat, from the baking stone or tiles underneath. This heat causes the yeast, in the last gasp of its life, to lift the dough one more time: the process called *oven spring.* For oven spring to work properly, the oven must be moist and hot. If the oven is not moist enough, the bread will crust over too quickly, preventing it from growing to its full potential; also, the final crust will turn out too tough. Professional bakers use steam-injected ovens—they give the bread what is called *bloom,* which is the beautiful shine gained from the addition of steam and the full, rounded shape of the loaf. At home, use a spray bottle of water to create steam.

A minute before you place the bread in the oven, spritz water heavily onto the preheated baking stone or tiles and around the sides of the oven. Then quickly close the door.

Now there will be two forces ready to work simultaneously on the dough: heat, whose drying effect creates a skin on the dough, and steam, which moistens the dough. The bottom heat puts a skin on the bottom of the loaf virtually on contact, like that of an egg dropped onto a hot frying pan. The top heat creates a skin more slowly, but the moisture is needed to slow the process even further. Even when the oven conditions are perfect, the skin will tear or explode as it expands if you forget to dock the loaf before loading.

Open the oven door, slide the boule from the peel directly onto the baking stone or tiles, and close the door.

Quickly cut and load the second boule in the same manner as the first, being sure to spritz the oven with water again before putting the bread in.

Make sure the loaves are spaced well apart; if they're too close either to each other or to the sides of the oven, there won't be enough air circulation for them to brown properly and they'll attract each other like magnets during baking, spreading horizontally instead of vertically and even growing together as they expand. The safe distance for slow-dancing junior-high kids is said to be a ruler's length; for sourdough bread, place boules at a distance of at least three quarters of the width of an unbaked loaf. Don't forget, this goes for rolls and baguettes too.

Turn the oven temperature down to 450 degrees F.

During the next 5 minutes, spritz the oven with water two more times. There are two things to remember as you do this: Open the oven door as narrowly as possible (to prevent losing the steam and heat already in the oven), and don't spray directly on the boules (if you do, the flour dusted on top of the bread will mottle and discolor).

After the first 5 minutes, don't open the oven door for 20 minutes. You want to maintain the steam you've created. In a commercial oven, where many loaves of bread are baking, each loaf naturally gives off moisture, so the oven needs to be vented during the last 10 to 15 minutes of baking; this allows some steam to escape, ensuring that the loaves brown nicely and remain crisp. This is not necessary in a home oven.

After 25 minutes, check the bread and rotate the boules if necessary to ensure even baking. Continue baking another 20 minutes, for a total of 45 minutes. Remove the boules from the oven. (If you're baking another loaf, don't forget to turn the oven back up to 500 degrees F for preheating.) The loaves should have a burnished brown crust with lots of fermentation bubbles. The shape should be round and fully formed, with no bulges or rips. The cut should be curved open, with a crisp, thin edge. On top, where the baker's slash has left its mark, there should be a thin, sharp-edged ridge of crispness. Its terrain: somewhere between the rough outer crust and the smoother inner crust of the cut—the cut that helps guide the loaf to its proper shape.

One test to see if the bread is finished baking: Tap the bottom of the loaf solidly with your fingers and listen for an almost hollow thud. If the bread feels too dense to your tap, or if the crust color is too light, put the boule back in the oven for a few more minutes. If your bread has good crust color but is not fully baked, leave it in the oven 5 to 10 more minutes with the oven door open. If you don't trust your instincts, you may want to take the bread's internal temperature with a long-stemmed, instant-read cooking thermometer. I have found that most breads in this book will measure 210 degrees F when fully baked. (Denser loaves—walnut, fruit and nut, and multigrain—will measure less than 200 degrees F.)

If the bread is properly baked, place the boules on a cooling rack, rather than a counter, to prevent the bottom crust from steaming or softening.

Now comes the hardest step of all: Try to resist cutting into the loaf and eating it before it is cool. The sourdough flavor doesn't fully develop until the bread is cool; the open interior also looks better after you let it set. The bread is still "cooking" in a manner—it's giving off carbon dioxide, and if you eat it right away, you may end up with an upset stomach a few hours later.

Of course, when you're baking your first loaves of bread, it will be hard to listen to the crackle of the cooling loaves and not tear into them. It's a good thing this recipe makes 2 loaves.

BEFORE YOU EAT . . .

I f you want to become a great bread maker, think of every loaf you bake as a cooking lesson. You can teach yourself a lot just by taking a good look at what you've baked and noting how the process went. Anytime you encounter changes in weather or the temperament of your dough or starter, jot them down. Eventually, you'll find yourself changing my recipes slightly to fit your environment and your lifestyle. Ultimately, you should rely more on your own notes than on this book.

As you make adjustments in your own bread, remember that it's best to make one change at a time. It's the same as conducting a science experiment—change too many parts of the process at once and you'll never know what made the next loaf better or worse—and you won't be able to re-create your successes. Your checklist should look something like this:

DATE:

TYPE OF BREAD:

DAY NOTES:
(comments on weather, the type of day you're having, anything that could affect the baking process):

MIXING:
Starter characteristics (frothy or flat; strong smelling or weak, etc.):
Room temperature:
Water temperature:
Temperature of dough at end of mixing:
Dough characteristics:

FERMENTATION:
Start time of fermentation:
Room or refrigerator temperature during fermentation:
Dough temperature at end of fermentation:
End time of fermentation:
Dough characteristics:

SHAPING:

Time shaped:

Dough characteristics:

PROOFING:

Start time of proofing:

Room or refrigerator temperature during proofing:

Dough temperature at end of proofing:

End time of proofing:

Dough characteristics:

BAKING:

Oven temperature:

Baking time:

AFTER-BAKE:

Crust color:

Shape:

Volume (the loaf's heft in your hands):

Aroma:

Interior hole structure:

Taste:

COMMENTS:

(what you like or don't like about the bread; how you think you can make a better loaf next time):

MAKING YOUR OWN
BREAD SCHEDULE

One of the toughest parts of learning to make bread with a sourdough starter is trying to fit the demands of the bread in between the demands of everyday life.

Ideally, for instance, a starter should get three meals a day. But how do you give a starter three daily feedings if you leave for work at seven in the morning and don't get home until seven at night? There is the extreme solution of taking your starter to work with you—as long as you have a stable, well-ventilated place to put it (windowless office buildings are *not* good environments for living starters), and as long as your boss doesn't mind. I suppose you could get someone to check in on your starter and feed it in the middle of the day, as a baby-sitter would check on your children—after all, sourdough starters seem sometimes to require only slightly less care than a toddler or a recalcitrant Yorkie.

But most home bakers with jobs and busy lives will want a more practical solution, and the truth is, like many of us, a starter can survive on one meal a day. But you must give it the equivalent of three meals at once. (If you've got 9 ounces or about 1 cup of starter, that means you feed it 1 pound 3½ ounces or about 4 cups plus 5 tablespoons of flour and 1¾ pounds or 3½ cups of water at once.) And you should try to feed it at the same time each day. The important thing is to be consistent.

As you look at the recipes in this book, you'll notice that most of the breads take two days to make; a few take three days and some just one. But even these times can be slightly manipulated as well.

A two-day bread, for instance, may be done from start to finish in one day. A few two-day recipes can be stretched to three days. The Country White Bread, described as a two-day bread, can be made in as few as 17½ hours or as many as 34. Take your own schedule into consideration and then tailor a timetable to fit your needs—but make a timetable. I initially designed the recipes in this book to work for me and my schedule at the bakery. With a little planning, you can make the recipes fit your personal routine. Keep in mind that when you're away from the house or when you're sleeping, your dough works on.

To decide when to start baking, first figure out when you want to serve the bread. Say you're planning a 7:30 dinner on Saturday night. That means you should pull the bread from the oven by 6:30 P.M. at the latest, both to allow the loaves to cool and to have the freshest possible bread. A good time to start the bread would be when you got home from work, say Friday night at 5:00. Take a half hour to decompress and start baking at 5:30 that night.

Here are three plausible bread schedules for the Country White Bread. These aren't to be used as strict timetables but to give you an idea of the flexibility you have with these recipes.

Two-Day Bread:
Starting Friday Evening for Saturday Night Dinner

Ready to start: 5:30 P.M. Friday, using starter last fed Friday morning between 5:30 A.M. and 9:30 A.M.

Mixing: approximately 5:30 to 6:15 P.M.

Fermenting: 6:15 to 10:15 P.M. (assuming the full 4 hours, instead of 3½, will be needed)

Preshape and rest: 10:15 to 10:35 P.M.

Shape and intermediate rise: 10:35 to 11:45 P.M.

Into the refrigerator for retarding: 11:45 P.M. Friday

Out of the refrigerator for final rise: about 3:15 P.M. Saturday (assuming 15½ hours)

Into the oven to bake: about 5:45 P.M. (allows 30 minutes flexibility in case the dough doesn't come up to temperature as quickly as the recipe says it should)

Out of the oven to cool: about 6:30 P.M.

Ready to eat: 7:30 P.M.

One-Day Bread:
Starting Saturday Morning for Sunday Brunch
(and Saturday Late-night Snack)

Ready to start: 6:00 A.M. Saturday, using starter last fed Friday evening 6:00 P.M. to 10:00 P.M.

Mixing: approximately 6:00 to 6:45 A.M.

Fermenting: 6:45 to 10:45 A.M. (assuming the full 4 hours, instead of 3½, will be needed)

Preshape and rest: 10:45 to 11:05 A.M.

Shape and intermediate rise: 11:05 A.M. to 12:15 P.M.

Into the refrigerator for retarding: 12:15 P.M.

Out of the refrigerator for final rise: about 8:15 P.M. (assuming 8 hours)

Into the oven to bake: about 10:45 P.M. (allows 30 minutes flexibility in case the dough doesn't come up to temperature as quickly as the recipe says it should)

Out of the oven to cool: 11:30 P.M. (you can go to bed now)

Ready to eat: 12:30 A.M. (or next morning)

TWO-DAY BREAD:
STARTING SATURDAY MORNING FOR SUNDAY SUPPER

Ready to start: 9:00 A.M. Saturday, using starter last fed Friday evening 9:00 P.M. to 1:00 A.M.

Mixing: approximately 9:00 to 9:45 A.M.

Fermenting: 9:45 A.M. to 1:45 P.M. (assuming the full 4 hours, instead of 3½, will be needed)

Preshape and rest: 1:45 to 2:05 P.M.

Shape and intermediate rise: 2:05 to 3:15 P.M.

Into the refrigerator for retarding: 3:15 P.M. Saturday

Out of the refrigerator for final rise: 10:15 A.M. Sunday (assuming 19 hours)

Into the oven to bake: about 1:15 P.M. (allows 30 minutes flexibility in case the dough doesn't come up to temperature as quickly as the recipe says it should)

Out of the oven to cool: 2:00 P.M.

Ready to eat: 3:00 P.M.

BREADS MADE

with

WHITE STARTER

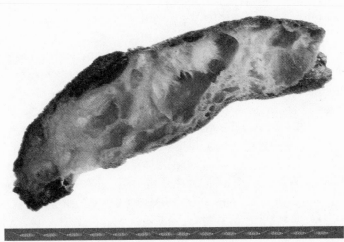

Baguette

The first great baguette I ever ate was in Paris. It was a rustic sourdough baguette, not one of the fluffy ones that most people associate with French bread. I never really liked the airy kind served in most Parisian cafés—mostly because good ones are so hard to find. The so-called classic baguette—which has actually been around only since about World War I—is always made with commercial yeast. And even in Paris, just a few Parisian bakeries still make perfect yeasted baguettes, skinny, wandlike breads that are so delicate they need to be eaten within two hours from the time they are taken out of the oven. Unfortunately, the majority of baguette bakers—both in France and in this country—jack up their doughs with conditioners and extra yeast and end up with bread that to me has the texture of Styrofoam, with neither the character nor the flavor of baguettes made with sourdough starter.

My rustic sourdough baguettes look different: They're a warm, caramelized brown instead of pale gold, their ends are pointy and irregular rather than rounded and smooth, and the crust is thicker than that of yeasted baguettes, so you do need a strong tooth to bite through it. Since most people know only baguettes made with commercial yeast, I've gotten more complaints at the bakery about this bread than about any other. People are especially bothered by the crust. But these baguettes are as rustic as the rest of my breads. Still, I sometimes think people would be happier if I called them something else.

Keep in mind, though, that there is a huge difference between a crusty baguette and a baguette with a crust that's too thick. What you want is a thin, caramelized crust, an almost candied layer that shatters when you bite into it. At the same time, the crust should be tender: When you take that first bite, the whole baguette should compress almost into flatness, then slowly rise back like a Naugahyde cushion and resume its shape.

Unfortunately, a crust like this is difficult to develop in a home oven, and, of all the breads in this book, the baguette is probably the hardest to make. The technique isn't difficult, but a baguette has a vast surface area in relation to the amount of its dough—it's almost all crust—and bakes best in commercial ovens, where the injectable steam keeps the interior soft and develops crispness and color in the crust. (Loaves and boules seem to have enough interior dough to help develop their own steam in the oven.) Still, you can get a nicely golden crust if you spritz enough water in the oven at the beginning of the bake, and open the oven door during baking no more than strictly necessary.

Be careful not to overbake baguettes—they can dry out in an instant. And home ovens are rarely as deep as commercial ovens, so the standard-size baguette, about 26 to 30 inches long, won't fit—measure the length of your oven and roll out your baguettes to that length. Think of them as your customized house baguettes. Traditionally, five to seven long slashes are made on the top of a baguette; you may have enough room for only three.

One last thing to remember: Baguettes, even rustic baguettes, are at their best about an hour after baking, though these will remain fresh for most of the day. The one advantage home baguette bakers have over commercial bakers is that they can eat their baguettes as soon as they're cooled. My own customers have to wait a few hours. If you do end up with day-old baguettes, don't worry—baguettes make great toast.

TWO-DAY BREAD—FIRST DAY

HAVE READY:
Plastic wrap
Dough cutter
Proofing cloth
Spray bottle, filled with water
French baguette pan or wood board or baking sheet covered with flour-dusted cloth
Plastic trash can liner

1 recipe Country White Bread (page 40)
Unbleached white bread flour for dusting

Mix, knead, and let dough ferment in bulk, covered with plastic wrap, for 3½ to 4 hours, as directed for Country White Bread.

Uncover the dough and turn it out onto a lightly floured surface. Cut the dough with a dough cutter into four 15-ounce pieces, each about the size of a softball. Slap each piece against the work surface a few times to deflate. Tuck under the edges of each piece, cover the dough with a cloth, and let it rest for 15 minutes.

Uncover the dough. Working with one piece at a time, flatten the dough into a 4 by 6-inch rectangle by placing one hand over the other, palms down, and patting the dough to an even thickness. (Begin in the center and work outward.) This gives you more control and ensures evenness—the top hand works as a guide.

Fold in the short ends to meet in the center, and press down firmly with the heel of your hand to seal the seam. With the short ends parallel to the edge of the work surface, fold the bottom edge of the dough to the center. Pat across the whole seam firmly with the heel of your hand. Fold the top edge of the dough over the seam, to about 1 inch from the bottom. Seal the seam in the same manner. Fold the dough once more so that the top and bottom edges meet. Seal the seam as before. Tuck in the ends at each side and press firmly to get a clean seal.

Turn the dough seam side up. Place one hand over the other, palms down, in the center of the dough and begin rolling the dough into a cylinder. As the dough starts to stretch, uncross your hands and continue rolling with light, even pressure, moving your hands slowly all the way to the ends of the baguette. (It may be necessary to repeat this motion, starting in the center, hand over hand, to get the proper baguette shape.) Use as little flour as possible to prevent sticking. If there is not enough friction between the dough and the work surface, spritz the work surface lightly with water from a spray bottle.

When the baguette is long enough to fit the size of your oven, lay your hands on top of each end. Taper the ends by alternately rolling each toward and away from you (think of the arm motions of a cross-country skier).

If you are using a baguette pan, lightly dust the pan with flour and invert the baguette, seam side down, onto the pan.

If you are using a cloth-covered board or baking sheet, place one baguette, seam side up, on the proofing surface. Pinch the cloth into a deep pleat alongside the baguette. (This will separate the baguettes, help them hold their shape, and prevent them from sticking together as they proof.)

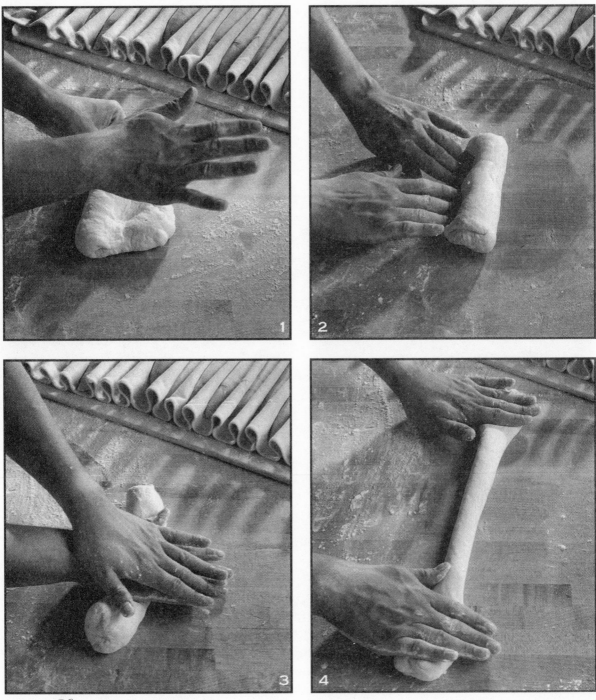

*S*HAPING A BAGUETTE

Shape the remaining three pieces of dough. As each baguette is formed, place it on the baguette pan or repeat the pleating process on the proofing cloth.

Dust the tops of the baguettes lightly with flour. Cover them with a cloth, slide the pan into a plastic trash can liner, and close the bag securely. Place the baguettes in the refrigerator, and let them proof for 12 to 20 hours.

SECOND DAY

HAVE READY:
Long-stemmed, instant-read cooking thermometer
Baker's peel, optional
Single-edged razor blade
Spray bottle, filled with water
Cooling rack

Shaped baguettes
Unbleached white bread flour

Take the shaped baguettes out of the refrigerator and remove the plastic bag. Keep the baguettes covered with the proofing cloth and set them out at room temperature to continue proofing until the dough reaches an internal temperature of 60 degrees F, about 2 hours.

Preheat the oven to 500 degrees F 1 hour before baking.

Remove the cloth when the dough is the proper temperature and lightly dust the baguettes with flour.

If the baguettes proofed on a board or baking sheet, place a lightly floured baker's peel on the work surface. Lift the ends of one baguette and flip it, seam side down, onto the peel.

Make sure the baguette is parallel to the edge of the work surface. Hold a single-edged razor blade at a 45-degree angle and, beginning about ½ inch from the end of the baguette, just to the left of center, make a straight cut about 5 inches long and ½ inch deep. The next cut should begin about ¼ inch below the center of the first cut and as close to the center of the baguette as possible. The last cut should end just to the right of the center, ½ inch from the end. The cuts should be not curved but straight and parallel to one another. All the cuts should be the same length. *Note*: If you hold the

*C*UTTING A BAGUETTE

razor at the correct angle, the flaps you've cut should be very thin. If you are using a baguette pan, simply make the cuts directly on the baguettes without removing them from the pan.

If you are using a baker's peel, open the oven door, spritz the oven heavily with water from a spray bottle, and quickly close the door. Open the oven door again, slide the baguettes from the peel onto the baking tiles, spritz the oven heavily with water, and quickly close the door.

Cut and load the remaining baguettes, spritzing the oven after each is loaded. Work quickly to ensure an even baking time and to get the best use out of the steam created by spritzing. Reduce the oven temperature to 450 degrees F. Refrain from opening the oven door for 15 minutes.

If you are using a baguette pan, spritz the oven first as just described. Load the baguette pan in the oven, spritz the oven heavily, and quickly close the door. Reduce the oven temperature to 450 degrees F. Spritz the oven three more times during the first 5 minutes. Refrain from opening the door for the next 15 minutes.

After 15 minutes, check the baguettes and rotate them if necessary to ensure even baking. Continue baking for 10 to 15 more minutes, for a total of 30 to 35 minutes.

Remove the baguettes to a cooling rack. They should have a golden-brown crust and a porous interior.

FICELLE

MAKES EIGHT APPROXIMATELY 6-OUNCE *FICELLES*.

Traditionally, *ficelles* are skinny baguettes—in French, *ficelle* means "string." But at the bakery, we make our *ficelles* only slightly thinner than our baguettes (which are thinner than French baguettes to begin with) but much shorter. They aren't authentic, but they are delicious. They're perfect when you don't have the appetite to eat a whole baguette, and they make ideal sandwich bread. Just don't overstuff them—they work best with only a flavor or two to complement the strong flavor of the crust.

To make *ficelles*, follow the instructions for making baguettes but with three differences. On the first day, instead of dividing the dough into four 15-ounce pieces, cut it into eight 8-ounce pieces. Each *ficelle* should measure 8 to 10 inches.

The second difference is in the cuts. Obviously, since the *ficelle* is a shorter bread, it has fewer cuts. There should only be two to three cuts in each *ficelle*, each about 3 inches long.

The last change is in the baking time, again because you are working with smaller loaves. If you don't have a special baguette pan, the *ficelles* can be baked directly on a baking stone or tiles. Do not open the oven during baking to rotate the *ficelles*—the total baking time is just 15 to 20 minutes.

CHAPEAU ROLLS

MAKES FIFTEEN ROLLS.

A lot of bakers have one basic dough that they use for all their breads, no matter what the shape. To change the flavor, they just add a few flavoring ingredients, such as herbs or cheese. This usually doesn't work for me. A few breads in this book do derive from a single base dough—the dough for the Rustic Bread, for instance, can be used in several recipes. But I've generally found that if you're going to change the shape of a bread, you're probably going to have to change the makeup of its dough as well. Even with something as simple as white bread rolls, I found I couldn't just use the dough for the Country White Bread.

The dough for these rolls has a little less starter than the Country White Bread; there's also a little whole-wheat flour added to the mix for color.

At the bakery, we make a few roll variations. My favorite are the *chapeau* rolls. *Chapeau* is French for "hat," and these rolls do wear a kind of hat, one essentially made of crust. My kids like these rolls too—sort of. They remove the "hats" and either set them aside or (occasionally) use them as Frisbees. They *will* eat the rolls underneath, but unfortunately they're missing out on the best part. The hat is crisp and brittle and wonderful.

The method for making these rolls is a little unusual. Part of the dough is used to make the "hats."

Rye flour (or rice flour) is essential to use for dusting the dough because you want to keep the "hat" of the roll distinct from the rest of the dough. If you use white flour for dusting, there's a chance that the flour will absorb moisture and the "hat" will melt into the roll underneath.

TWO-DAY BREAD—FIRST DAY

HAVE READY:
Mixing bowl
Mixer with attachable dough hook, optional
Proofing cloth
Rubber spatula, optional

Long-stemmed, instant-read cooking thermometer
Plastic wrap
Dough cutter
Rolling pin
One 2-inch round cookie cutter
Baking sheet or wood board, lined with proofing cloth and lightly dusted with rye or rice flour
Spray bottle, filled with water
Plastic trash can liner

1 pound 2 ounces (about 2¼ cups) cool water, 70 degrees F
11 ounces (about 1¼ cups) White Starter
2 pounds 2 ounces (about 7 cups) unbleached white bread flour
1½ ounces (about 4 tablespoons) whole-wheat flour
½ cup wheat germ
1 tablespoon barley malt syrup
4½ teaspoons sea salt
Rye or rice flour for dusting
Vegetable oil

Place water, White Starter, flours, wheat germ, and malt syrup in the bowl of a mixer fitted with a dough hook. Mix on low speed for 4 minutes. The dough should be sticky and pliable. (The dough may also be mixed by hand; see basic instructions on page 42.) Cover the dough with a proofing cloth and allow it to rest in the mixing bowl for 20 minutes.

Add salt and mix on medium speed, scraping the dough down the sides of the bowl as necessary with a rubber spatula, until the dough reaches an internal temperature of 78 degrees F, looks satiny, and feels smooth and elastic, about 5 minutes.

Remove the dough from the mixing bowl, place it on a lightly floured work surface, and knead it for a few minutes by hand.

Clean the mixing bowl and lightly coat it with vegetable oil. Return the dough to the oiled bowl, cover it tightly with plastic wrap, and let it ferment at room temperature until it doubles in volume, about 3½ to 4 hours.

Uncover the dough and turn it out onto a lightly floured work surface. Using a dough cutter, cut a 1-pound piece from the fermented bulk. Set aside and cover the remaining dough with a proofing cloth.

Shape the 1-pound piece of dough into a rough square or rectangle. Cover it with a proofing cloth and let the dough rest for 15 minutes.

Uncover the remaining bulk dough. Cut it into fifteen approximately 3-ounce pieces. Tuck under the edges of each piece, cover the dough with a cloth, and let it rest for 15 minutes.

Turn the 1-pound piece of dough out onto a work surface, lightly dusted with flour. Roll it out into a flat square or rectangle, about ⅛ inch thick, with a rolling pin. Lightly sprinkle the dough with rye flour and cover it with a proofing cloth. Allow the dough to relax for about 15 to 20 minutes to prevent it from shrinking when cut. Uncover the dough and cut fifteen circles out of it using a cookie cutter. These will become the "hats" of the rolls. Place each hat on a cloth-lined and lightly floured baking sheet or wood board, spaced about 2 inches apart. Sprinkle the tops of the circles with a thin, even layer of rye flour and set aside.

Uncover the fifteen reserved pieces of dough. Shape each piece (leaving the rest of the pieces covered) by cupping your hand lightly around the ball of dough and rounding it against the friction of the work surface. Begin slowly and increase speed as the ball becomes tighter and smoother. Use as little flour as possible on the work surface. If there is not enough friction between the dough and the work surface, spritz the work surface lightly with water. With a little practice, you'll be able to shape two rolls simultaneously, one in each hand.

As each roll is shaped, check to be sure it is smooth and taut and the surface of the dough is not torn, which would indicate overrounding. Place each roll, smooth side down, on top of a circle (the "hat") on the baking sheet or wood board.

Working with one roll at a time, dip your index finger into some flour, then press the finger through the center of the roll, all the way through the hat to the baking sheet or board. Remove your finger. Pick up the roll and turn it over. You want to see a pinch mark on the other side. This should ensure that the hat will adhere. If you don't see a pinch mark, turn the roll over and press your finger firmly through the dough again. Proof the rolls "hat" side down.

Dust the rolls lightly with flour and cover them with a proofing cloth. Slide the covered rolls on the baking sheet or board into a plastic trash can liner and close the bag securely. Place the rolls in the refrigerator for 8 to 12 hours.

SECOND DAY

HAVE READY:

Long-stemmed, instant-read cooking thermometer
Baking sheets, preferably perforated
Spray bottle, filled with water

Shaped rolls
Rye or rice flour for dusting

Take the shaped rolls out of the refrigerator and remove the plastic bag. Keep the rolls covered with the proofing cloth and set them out at room temperature until the dough reaches an internal temperature of 62 degrees F, about 1 to 1½ hours.

Preheat the oven to 500 degrees F 1 hour before baking. Be sure the oven racks are placed well apart to allow plenty of air circulation.

Uncover the rolls, lightly sprinkle them with rye flour, then place them, hat side up, on unlined baking sheets.

Open the oven door, spritz the oven heavily with water from a spray bottle, and quickly close the door. Open the oven door again, slide the baking sheets onto the baking tiles, and quickly close the door.

Reduce the oven temperature to 450 degrees F. Spritz the oven heavily three more times during the next 5 minutes. Refrain from opening the oven door for the next 15 minutes.

After 15 minutes, check the rolls and rotate them if necessary to ensure even baking. Continue baking for about 5 more minutes, for a total of 25 minutes. They should have a medium golden-brown crust. The *chapeau* will bake faster and should be darker than the roll.

OTHER ROLL SHAPES

MAKES TWENTY ROLLS.

With the basic *Chapeau* Roll dough, you can make several kinds of rolls. Follow the preceding recipe, but instead of dividing the dough into one I-pound piece and fifteen smaller pieces, cut it into twenty small pieces. Shape them into balls as directed in the *Chapeau* Roll recipe, and place them, smooth side down, on a cloth-lined and lightly floured baking sheet or wood board. Proof the rolls as directed in the preceding recipe, refrigerated in a plastic trash can liner. After the dough has been removed from the refrigerator and has reached an internal temperature of 62 degrees F, place the rolls smooth side up on unlined baking sheets.

Now you can cut the rolls in several ways. With a single-edged razor blade, you can cut either a curved arc slash or an *X* down the middle of each roll. Just be sure not to cut all the way to the edges of the roll. Or, with very sharp 4-inch scissors held vertically, make a I-inch-deep snip on the top of each roll. This will form a beak of sorts that will become extra crisp during baking.

CROWN

MAKES THREE CROWNS.

A crown looks like a fancy, difficult bread, but it's really just several dinner rolls joined at the sides to form a bread ring. It's an impressive party or buffet bread.

To make it, follow the directions for *Chapeau* Rolls, but instead of dividing the dough into one 1-pound piece and fifteen smaller pieces, cut it into twenty-one pieces. Shape them into balls as directed in the *Chapeau* Roll recipe. Instead of setting the rolls on cloth-lined baking sheets or wood boards to proof, use flour-dusted willow or unlined proofing baskets large enough to hold seven rolls. You'll need three round baskets. Place seven rolls, smooth side down, ½ inch apart, to form a circle in one basket. Repeat with the remaining rolls and baskets.

Cover the baskets with plastic wrap and place them in the refrigerator to proof for 8 to 12 hours.

Take the baskets out of the refrigerator, remove the plastic wrap, lightly sprinkle the dough with flour, and cover the baskets with a proofing cloth. Allow the rolls to proof at room temperature until the dough reaches an internal temperature of 62 degrees F, 1 to 1½ hours. By this time, the rolls should be proofed together so that their sides are just touching. The dough will continue to adhere as the rolls expand during baking.

Preheat the oven to 500 degrees F 1 hour before baking. Be sure the oven racks are placed well apart to allow plenty of air circulation.

Invert the rolls, one basket at a time, onto a lightly floured baker's peel. Adjust the rolls as necessary to restore circular shape. Snip the tops of each roll with scissors as directed for Other Roll Shapes. (See page 73.)

Follow the oven spritzing and baking directions for *Chapeau* Rolls. Note that each crown may have to be baked separately, depending on the size of your oven and baking sheets.

WALNUT BREAD

MAKES TWO APPROXIMATELY 2-POUND BOULES.

Walnut Bread is tricky to make, but it's worth the trouble. It's based on a classic French bread that is often served as part of the cheese course in fine restaurants. At Campanile, we toast our Walnut Bread for breakfast and serve it with rounds of goat cheese. It also makes terrific croutons for salad, and it's a good sandwich bread, especially if you're using rich-tasting ingredients such as avocado.

Three things make this bread difficult: walnuts, rye flour, and whole-wheat flour. It would have been simpler if I'd only added walnuts to a basic white dough, but the bread itself wouldn't have had good flavor. Besides, the whole wheat and the rye give the loaf a nutty brown color that contrasts beautifully with the walnuts.

This dough can't sit out proofing as long as other white sourdough breads because it will fall apart. This means you have to watch carefully as it proofs to make sure you put it in the oven as soon as it's ready. If you wait too long, you'll end up with an extremely sour flavor that camouflages the taste of the walnuts, and a chemical reaction from the walnuts that gives the crumb an unattractive purplish color. My solution was to make the bread using what's known as the sponge method, which allows it to benefit from overnight fermentation before a full dough is made—and before the walnuts are added.

THREE-DAY BREAD—FIRST DAY

HAVE READY:
Mixing bowl
Rubber spatula, optional
Plastic wrap

14 ounces (about 1¾ cups) cool water, 70 degrees F
6 ounces (about ⅔ cup) White Starter
2 tablespoons milk
1 tablespoon barley malt syrup

8 ounces (about 2 cups) whole-wheat flour, plus extra for dusting
3½ ounces (about 1¼ cups) dark rye flour
¼ teaspoon sea salt

Make a sponge by placing water, White Starter, milk, malt syrup, flours, and salt in a mixing bowl and stirring with your hands or a rubber spatula. Cover the bowl tightly with plastic wrap and leave it at room temperature just until bubbles begin to break on the surface, about 5 hours.

Check the sponge, resecure the plastic wrap, and place the bowl in the refrigerator for 8 to 12 hours.

SECOND DAY

HAVE READY:
Baking sheet
Mixing bowl
Mixer with attachable dough hook, optional
Proofing cloth
Rubber spatula, optional
Long-stemmed, instant-read cooking thermometer
Plastic wrap

14 ounces (about 4 cups) walnut halves
Sponge
6 ounces (about ¾ cup) cool water, 70 degrees F
1 teaspoon sugar
1 pound plus 6 ounces (about 4⅔ cups) unbleached white bread flour, plus extra for dusting
3¼ teaspoons sea salt
2 tablespoons walnut oil
Vegetable oil

Preheat the oven to 350 degrees F.

Spread walnuts in a single layer on a baking sheet and bake them until they are lightly toasted, 7 to 10 minutes. Set aside to cool.

Remove the sponge from the refrigerator and take off the plastic wrap. Place water, sponge, sugar, and flour in the bowl of a mixer fitted with a dough hook. Mix on low speed for 4 minutes. (The dough may also be mixed by hand; see basic instructions on page 42.) The mixture should appear thick and creamy and, unlike most doughs, will not clean the sides of the bowl. Cover the dough with a proofing cloth and allow it to rest in the mixing bowl for 20 minutes.

About Sponges

Sponge is a funny word for a baking method that helps the dough benefit from a long fermentation without mixing the whole dough hours ahead. It may get its name from its spongy texture. Basically, you make up a portion of the dough—flour, water, sourdough starter or commercial yeast, and sometimes salt (which helps keep the sponge from overfermenting)—and let it rise either several hours at room temperature or overnight in the refrigerator. The consistency can be either thin and watery or thick and porridgelike. Thin sponges ferment faster than thick ones. A thick sponge will rise like a piece of dough—ideally you want to use it just before it falls. The fermented sponge is mixed with flour and water and other ingredients to make the final, rejuvenated dough, which is again set out to rise. This way, the dough's total fermenting time is essentially doubled.

This method, also called a *pre-ferment,* is commonly used in yeasted breads, because it gives those doughs some of the benefits of a slow rise—the longer shelf life, better flavor, and better texture that are usually possible only with naturally leavened breads. As the sponge ferments, the yeast grows and multiplies and provides the time for lactic and acetic acids to grow. The sponge gives sourdough characteristics to the seed of the dough.

I use this method mainly with breads that I feel need a longer fermentation time. Doughs made with rye flour, for instance, cannot proof as long as white doughs because they do not have the same strength as doughs made with white flour. If you simply left a rye dough out to rise as long as you would a white dough, you'd end up with overproofed dough and a heavy loaf of bread. Use a sponge, however, and the final dough will benefit from the qualities of the sponge portion of the dough.

Note: Make sure the bowl you use is large enough for your sponge to triple in volume. The sponge grows as dough does and needs plenty of room.

Add salt and mix on medium speed for 5 minutes, scraping the dough down the sides of the bowl with a rubber spatula as necessary. Add the walnut oil and mix on low speed until the dough reaches an internal temperature of 65 degrees F, about 2 more minutes. Add the toasted walnuts and mix on low just until the walnuts are incorporated in the dough, 1 to 2 more minutes.

Remove the dough from the mixing bowl, place it on a well-floured work surface, and knead it for a few minutes by hand.

Clean the mixing bowl and lightly coat it with vegetable oil. Return the dough to the oiled bowl, cover it tightly with plastic wrap, and let it ferment in the refrigerator 8 to 12 hours.

THIRD DAY

HAVE READY:
Proofing cloths
Dough cutter
Two 2-pound-capacity unlined willow baskets or cloth-lined baskets
Long-stemmed, instant-read cooking thermometer
Baker's peel
Single-edged razor blade
Spray bottle, filled with water
Cooling rack

Dough
Unbleached white bread flour for dusting

Remove the dough from the refrigerator and take off the plastic wrap. The dough should have doubled in volume and feel soft but not sticky. If it hasn't doubled, leave the dough out at room temperature covered with a cloth until it has.

Turn the dough out onto a lightly floured work surface and cut it into two equal pieces with a dough cutter. Slap each piece against the work surface a few times to deflate. Tuck under the edges of each piece, cover them with a cloth, and let the dough rest for 15 minutes.

Uncover the dough and round each piece into a boule, according to the directions on page 48. Place the boules, smooth side down, into floured proofing baskets. Sprinkle the surface of the dough with flour, cover each basket with a cloth, and let the dough proof at room temperature until it grows by half its original volume and reaches an internal temperature of 60 to 62 degrees F, about 2½ hours.

Preheat the oven to 500 degrees F 1 hour before baking.

Remove the cloth and lightly dust the boules with flour. Carefully run your hand around one boule to loosen it and gently invert it onto a lightly floured baker's peel.

Holding a single-edged razor blade at a 45-degree angle, slash the top of the dough, making a backward *C* cut in the middle, about ½ inch deep, starting and ending 1 inch from the edges.

Open the oven door, spritz the oven heavily with water from a spray bottle, and quickly close the door. Open the oven door again, slide the boule onto the baking tiles, and quickly close the door. Cut, spritz, and load the second boule in the same manner.

Reduce the oven temperature to 450 degrees F. Spritz the oven two more times during the next 5 minutes. Refrain from opening the oven door for the next 20 minutes.

After 20 minutes, check the boules and rotate them if necessary to ensure even baking. Continue baking for 15 to 20 more minutes, for a total of 40 to 45 minutes.

Remove the boules to a cooling rack. The crust should be nut brown, with a nut-brown interior.

Rosemary–Olive Oil Bread

MAKES TWO APPROXIMATELY I-POUND-II-OUNCE BOULES.

With a bread that is essentially a white dough flavored with herbs, it's especially important that the bread have its own distinctive character. Too often, bakers think they can cover up the mediocrity of a loaf with strong-tasting herbs. This only succeeds in producing a bad loaf that tastes like rosemary.

In this Rosemary–Olive Oil Bread, you may not specifically taste the sourness of the sourdough, but you should get a multifaceted flavor in which the rosemary is a strong but not overpowering element. Olive oil goes into the dough—it's a classic match with rosemary—and it affects the texture of the loaf, coating the gluten strands and making a softer dough than usual. When it's baked, the interior will be slightly more uniform, less open than that of the Country White.

Just as your bread should be the best it can be, so should the herbs you use. I call for fresh rosemary in this dough. If it's impossible for you to use fresh, dried rosemary will work, but be sure it hasn't lost its flavor. There's no point in making this loaf if all you have on hand are three-year-old dried herbs.

Two-Day Bread–First Day

HAVE READY:
Mixing bowl
Mixer with attachable dough hook, optional
Proofing cloth
Rubber spatula, optional
Long-stemmed, instant-read cooking thermometer
Plastic wrap
Dough cutter
2 cloth-lined baskets, lightly dusted with flour

1 pound plus 2 ounces (about 2¼ cups) cool water, 70 degrees F
12½ ounces (about 1⅓ cups) White Starter

2 pounds plus 2 ounces (about 7 cups) unbleached white bread flour, plus extra for dusting
½ cup raw wheat germ
3½ teaspoons sea salt
1 tablespoon finely chopped fresh rosemary
4 tablespoons extra-virgin olive oil
Vegetable oil

Place water, White Starter, flour, and wheat germ in the bowl of a mixer fitted with a dough hook. Mix on low speed for 4 minutes. The dough should be sticky and pliable. (The dough may also be mixed by hand; see basic instructions on page 42.) Cover the dough with a proofing cloth and allow it to rest in the mixing bowl for 20 minutes.

Add salt and continue mixing on medium speed for 4 minutes, scraping the dough down the sides of the bowl as necessary with a rubber spatula.

Add rosemary and olive oil and mix on medium speed until the ingredients are incorporated and the dough reaches an internal temperature of 78 degrees F, about 5 more minutes.

Remove the dough from the mixing bowl. It should feel soft and resilient. Knead the dough for a few minutes by hand on a lightly floured work surface.

Clean the mixing bowl and lightly coat it with vegetable oil. Return the dough to the oiled bowl, cover it tightly with plastic wrap, and let it ferment at room temperature until it doubles in volume, 3 to 4 hours.

Uncover the dough and turn it out onto a lightly floured work surface. Using a dough cutter, cut the dough into two equal pieces. Slap each piece against the work surface a few times to deflate. Tuck under the edges of each piece, cover the dough with a cloth, and let it rest for 15 minutes.

Uncover the dough and round each piece into a boule, according to the directions on page 48. Place the boules, smooth side down, into floured proofing baskets. Cover each basket with a cloth and let the dough proof at room temperature until it begins to show signs of movement (it should rise just about 1 inch), 1½ to 2 hours.

Remove the cloth and sprinkle the surface of the dough with flour. Wrap each basket tightly in plastic wrap. Refrigerate for 8 to 12 hours.

SECOND DAY

HAVE READY:
Proofing cloth
Long-stemmed, instant-read cooking thermometer
Baker's peel
Single-edged razor blade
Spray bottle, filled with water
Cooling rack

Dough
Unbleached white bread flour for dusting

Remove the boules from the refrigerator, take off the plastic wrap, and cover each basket with a cloth. Let the dough continue proofing at room temperature until it reaches an internal temperature of 58 degrees F, about 2 to 2½ hours.

Preheat the oven to 500 degrees F 1 hour before baking.

Remove the cloth and lightly dust the boules with flour. Carefully run your hand around one boule to loosen it and gently invert it onto a lightly floured baker's peel.

With a single-edged razor blade held perpendicular to the boule, slash a tic-tac-toe pattern on top of the boule. Each cut should be ½ inch deep and 2½ inches long.

Open the oven door, spritz the oven heavily with water from a spray bottle, and quickly close the door. Open the oven door again, slide the boule onto the baking tiles, and quickly close the door. Cut, spritz, and load the second boule in the same manner.

Reduce the oven temperature to 450 degrees F. Spritz the oven two more times during the next 5 minutes. Refrain from opening the oven door for the next 20 minutes.

After 20 minutes, check the boules and rotate them if necessary to ensure even baking. Continue baking for 15 to 20 more minutes, for a total of 40 to 45 minutes.

Remove the boules to a cooling rack. The finished boules will have a rich brown color and look swollen, but will not have quite the oven spring of the Country White.

OLIVE BREAD

⟶ MAKES TWO APPROXIMATELY 1-POUND-14-OUNCE BOULES.

You'll find olive bread eaten in both Italy and France, and there are hundreds of variations. My favorites are the ones with lots of olives and plenty of character in the bread itself. That's why I use two types of olives—kalamata and oil cured. The soft-skinned oil-cured olives crumble into the dough during mixing, staining the bread and giving it a wonderful olive color and flavor; the kalamatas remain juicy and intact. Subtly scented with fresh thyme, this Olive Bread is for eating with meals, but it makes terrific sandwiches as well. And the natural oil from the olives keeps the bread moist longer than you'd expect.

TWO-DAY BREAD—FIRST DAY

HAVE READY:
Mixing bowl
Mixer with attachable dough hook, optional
Proofing cloth
Rubber spatula, optional
Long-stemmed, instant-read cooking thermometer
Plastic wrap
Dough cutter
2 cloth-lined proofing baskets, lightly dusted with flour

1 pound 2 ounces (about 2¼ cups) cool water, 70 degrees F
12½ ounces (about 1⅓ cups) White Starter
2 pounds plus 2 ounces (about 7 cups) unbleached white bread flour, plus extra for dusting
½ cup raw wheat germ
3 teaspoons sea salt
½ cup pitted whole kalamata olives
½ cup whole oil-cured olives, pitted
2 tablespoons fresh or 2 teaspoons dried thyme
Vegetable oil

Place water, White Starter, flour, and wheat germ in the bowl of a mixer fitted with a dough hook. Mix on low speed for 4 minutes. (The dough may also be mixed by hand; see basic instructions on page 42.) Cover the dough with a proofing cloth and allow it to rest in the mixing bowl for 20 minutes.

Add salt and mix on medium speed for 4 more minutes, scraping the dough down the sides of the bowl as necessary with a rubber spatula. The dough should feel soft and resilient.

Add olives and thyme and mix on low speed until the ingredients are uniformly combined and the dough reaches an internal temperature of 78 degrees F, about 4 more minutes.

Remove the dough from the mixing bowl, place it on a lightly floured work surface, and knead it for a few minutes by hand.

Clean the mixing bowl and lightly coat it with vegetable oil. Return the dough to the oiled bowl, cover it tightly with plastic wrap, and let it ferment at room temperature until it doubles in volume, about 4 hours.

Uncover the dough and turn it out onto a lightly floured work surface. Using a dough cutter, cut it into two equal pieces. Slap each piece against the work surface a few times to deflate. Tuck under the edges of each piece, cover the dough with a cloth, and let it rest for 15 minutes.

Uncover the dough and round each piece into a boule, according to the directions on page 48. Place the boules, smooth side down, into floured proofing baskets and sprinkle the surface of the dough with flour. Cover each basket with a cloth and let the dough proof at room temperature until it begins to show signs of movement (it should rise just about 1 inch), 1½ to 2 hours.

Remove the cloth and wrap each basket tightly in plastic wrap. Refrigerate for 8 to 12 hours.

SECOND DAY

HAVE READY:
Proofing cloth
Long-stemmed, instant-read thermometer
Baker's peel
Single-edged razor blade
Spray bottle, filled with water
Cooling rack

Dough
Unbleached white bread flour for dusting

Remove the boules from the refrigerator, take off the plastic wrap, and cover each basket with a cloth. Let the dough continue proofing at room temperature until it reaches an internal temperature of 58 degrees F, about 2 to 2½ hours.

Preheat the oven to 500 degrees F I hour before baking.

Remove the cloth and lightly dust the boules with flour. Carefully run your hand around one boule to loosen it and gently invert it onto a lightly floured baker's peel.

With a single-edged razor blade held at a 45-degree angle, slash the top of the dough, making a backward *C* cut in the middle, about ½ inch deep, starting and ending I inch from the edges.

Open the oven door, spritz the oven heavily with water from a spray bottle, and quickly close the door. Open the oven door again, slide the boule onto the baking tiles, and quickly close the door. Cut, spritz, and load the second boule in the same manner.

Reduce the oven temperature to 450 degrees F. Spritz the oven two more times during the next 5 minutes. Refrain from opening the oven door for the next 20 minutes.

After 20 minutes, check the boules and rotate them if necessary to ensure even baking. Continue baking for 15 to 20 more minutes, for a total of 40 to 45 minutes.

Remove the boules to a cooling rack. The crust should be a deep burnished brown and show small fermentation bubbles. The interior should have an open structure with well-distributed small and large holes, chunks of olive, and visible flecks of thyme.

POTATO-DILL BREAD

MAKES THREE APPROXIMATELY 1¼-POUND LOAVES.

Potatoes do two things in bread—they add moisture and they promote fermentation, which helps give the loaf a light texture. Another thing I've noticed is that the breads I've made using potatoes have the most beautiful crusts of all. There must be something in the converging potato and wheat sugars that produces a rich, almost reddish undertone. I bake the potatoes before they go into the dough. I tried boiling them, but too often I ended up with waterlogged potatoes, which in turn made the dough too wet.

You can make this recipe without the dill, but I find dill subtly enhances the flavor of the bread. And if you're in the mood for an old-fashioned tuna sandwich, there are few better breads to use than Potato-Dill.

Note: These loaves are smaller than many of the others in this book—and the loaves are football shaped, instead of round like a boule. This means the proofing baskets you may have used for the Country White and other basic breads will be too large for this dough. (Remember, if a dough is given too much space in which to proof, it will expand horizontally instead of vertically.) At the bakery, we use smaller, oval-shaped baskets for this bread, but unless you are a completely dedicated bread maker, you probably have only one size basket, for the basic 2-pound boules. One solution: Proof the bread on a pleated cloth, or *couche* (see page 21).

TWO-DAY BREAD—FIRST DAY

HAVE READY:
Ricer or strainer
Work bowl
Mixing bowl
Mixer with attachable dough hook, optional
Rubber spatula, optional
Proofing cloth
Plastic wrap
Instant-read thermometer

1 pound baking potatoes (about 2 or 3 potatoes)
14 ounces (about 1¾ cups) cold water, 55 degrees F
9 ounces (about 1 cup) White Starter
3 tablespoons milk powder
¾ cup raw wheat germ
1 pound 15 ounces (about 8¼ cups) unbleached white bread flour, plus extra for dusting
3 teaspoons sea salt
4 tablespoons finely chopped fresh dill
Vegetable oil

Preheat the oven to 400 degrees F. Bake the potatoes in the oven directly on a rack for 1 hour. Let them cool slightly. While they are still warm, peel the potatoes and force the pulp through a ricer or strainer. Measure out 10 ounces (about 1 cup) of pulp and place it in a work bowl. Put the pulp in the refrigerator until it is cold.

Place water, White Starter, milk powder, wheat germ, flour, and potato pulp in the bowl of a mixer fitted with a dough hook. Mix on low speed for 4 minutes, scraping the dough down the sides of the bowl as necessary with a rubber spatula. The dough should feel soft and sticky. (The dough may also be mixed by hand; see basic instructions on page 42.) Cover the dough with a proofing cloth and allow it to rest in the bowl about 20 minutes.

Add salt and mix on medium speed for 8 more minutes. Add dill and mix on low speed until the herbs are incorporated and the dough reaches an internal temperature of 72 to 74 degrees F, 2 to 3 minutes. The dough will feel slightly sticky but firm and elastic.

Remove the dough from the mixing bowl, place it on a lightly floured work surface, and knead it for a few minutes by hand.

Clean the mixing bowl and lightly coat it with vegetable oil. Return the dough to the oiled bowl, cover it tightly with plastic wrap, and let it ferment in the refrigerator 9 to 14 hours.

SECOND DAY

HAVE READY:
Proofing cloth
Dough cutter
3 oval-shaped proofing baskets or wood board

Plastic wrap
2 large cloths, lightly dusted with flour, optional
Plastic trash can liner
Baker's peel
Single-edged razor blade
Spray bottle, filled with water
Cooling rack

Dough
Unbleached white bread flour for dusting

Remove the dough from the refrigerator and take off the plastic wrap. The dough should feel softer and more relaxed and should have expanded by about half. If it hasn't grown enough, cover the dough with a cloth and set it out at room temperature until it does, 1 to 1 1/2 hours. Cut the dough with a dough cutter into three equal pieces. Slap each piece against the work surface a few times to deflate. Tuck under the edges of each piece, cover the dough with a cloth, and let it rest for 15 minutes.

Uncover the dough and round each piece into a boule, according to the directions on page 48. Then elongate each boule by placing one hand on top of the other, palms down, in the center of the dough and simultaneously rolling and molding the dough into a football shape, about 8 inches long. As the dough begins to stretch, gradually spread apart your hands and continue rolling with light, even pressure, moving your hands slowly all the way to the ends of the dough as it tapers.

If you are using proofing baskets, invert each oval, smooth side down, into a floured basket. Dust the surface of the dough with flour and cover each basket tightly with plastic wrap.

If you are proofing in a *couche,* cover a wood board with one large, flour-dusted cloth. Invert one oval, smooth side down, onto the cloth. Pinch the cloth into a deep pleat alongside the oval. (This will separate the ovals, help them hold their shape, and prevent them from sticking together as they proof.) Repeat with the other two ovals. Cover the loaves with the second flour-dusted cloth. Slide the board into a plastic trash can liner and close the bag securely.

Place the baskets or board in the refrigerator and let the dough proof for 10 to 14 hours.

Preheat the oven to 500 degrees F at least 1 hour before baking.

Remove the dough from the refrigerator. If the dough proofed in baskets, take off the plastic wrap and cover with a cloth. If the dough proofed in a *couche*, remove the trash can liner. Let the dough continue proofing at room temperature until it reaches an internal temperature of 60 to 62 degrees F, up to 1 hour. (*Note:* Test the dough's temperature as soon as it comes out of the refrigerator; sometimes it's ready right away.)

Remove the cloth and lightly dust the ovals with flour. Invert one to three loaves spaced well apart onto a lightly floured baker's peel.

Holding a single-edged razor blade at a 45-degree angle, slash the top of the dough, making a gently arching cut just to one side of the center of the dough. Begin the cut 1 inch away from one tip of the dough; end 1 inch away from the opposite tip.

Open the oven door, spritz the oven heavily with water from a spray bottle, then quickly close the door. Open the oven door again, slide the oval onto the baking tiles, and quickly close the door. If you are loading each loaf separately, cut, spritz, and load the second and third ovals in the same manner.

Reduce the oven temperature to 450 degrees F. Spritz the oven two more times during the next 5 minutes. Refrain from opening the oven door for the next 20 minutes.

After 20 minutes, check the ovals and rotate them if necessary to ensure even baking. Continue baking for 10 more minutes, for a total of 35 minutes.

Remove the loaves to a cooling rack. The crust should have a deep, rich brown color and show plenty of good fermentation bubbles. The interior should be soft and chewy, with a good distribution of small and large holes and a distinct aroma of dill.

ITALIAN RING BREAD

~ MAKES TWO APPROXIMATELY 2-POUND RINGS.

There's olive oil in this bread, but that's not what makes it Italian. The shape—big, round, and with a hole in the middle—is an Italian classic. The dough is similar to the one used for Rosemary–Olive Oil Bread, but this one is a softer dough with a more porous interior.

Marjoram subtly flavors my version of Italian Ring Bread, although you could try other herbs, or do as well without. You'll find this a useful dough—at the bakery we use it for a few other breads, including the Onion and Parmesan Cheese breads and the Olive-Onion Bread Sticks.

TWO-DAY BREAD—FIRST DAY

HAVE READY:
Mixing bowl
Rubber spatula, optional
Plastic wrap

9 ounces (about 1 cup plus 1 tablespoon) cool water, 70 degrees F
2 ounces (about ¼ cup) White Starter
8 ounces (about 2 cups) unbleached white bread flour, plus extra for dusting

Make a sponge by placing water, White Starter, and flour in a mixing bowl and stirring everything with your hands or a rubber spatula. Cover the bowl tightly with plastic wrap and let it ferment at room temperature for 8 to 12 hours.

If you're making this bread on a day when it's hotter than 80 degrees F, the sponge should be left at room temperature for half the fermenting time, then refrigerated for the remainder.

Second Day

HAVE READY:

Mixing bowl
Mixer with attachable dough hook, optional
Proofing cloth
Rubber spatula, optional
Long-stemmed, instant-read cooking thermometer
Plastic wrap
Dough cutter
2 cloth-lined proofing baskets, lightly dusted with flour
Baker's peel
One 4-inch round biscuit cutter
Spray bottle, filled with water
Cooling rack

1¼ pounds (about 2½ cups) cold water, 55 degrees F
1 cake (.6 ounce) or 2 teaspoons packed fresh yeast
Sponge
2½ pounds (about 8 cups) unbleached white bread flour, plus extra for dusting
4 teaspoons sea salt
4 tablespoons coarsely chopped fresh marjoram, optional
3 tablespoons extra-virgin olive oil
Vegetable oil

Place water and yeast in the bowl of a mixer. Uncover the sponge and add it to the yeast mixture, along with the flour. Attach the dough hook to the mixer and mix the dough on low speed for 4 minutes. The dough should feel soft and slightly sticky. (The dough may also be mixed by hand; see basic instructions on page 42.) Cover the dough with a proofing cloth and allow it to rest in the bowl about 20 minutes.

Add salt and continue mixing on medium speed for 4 minutes, scraping the dough down the sides of the bowl as necessary with a rubber spatula.

Add the marjoram and olive oil and mix on medium speed until the ingredients are incorporated and the dough reaches an internal temperature of 74 to 78 degrees F, about 5 more minutes.

Remove the dough from the mixing bowl. It should feel soft and resilient. Knead the dough for a few minutes by hand on a lightly floured work surface.

Clean the mixing bowl and lightly coat it with vegetable oil. Return the dough to the oiled bowl, cover it tightly with plastic wrap, and let it ferment at room temperature until it doubles in volume, about 3 hours.

Uncover the dough and turn it out onto a lightly floured work surface. Using a dough cutter, cut the dough into two equal pieces. Slap each piece against the work surface a few times to deflate. Tuck under the edges of each piece, cover the dough with a cloth, and let it rest for 15 minutes.

Uncover the dough and round each piece into a boule, according to the directions on page 48. Place the boules, smooth side down, into floured proofing baskets and sprinkle the surface of the dough with flour. Cover each basket tightly with plastic wrap and let the dough proof in the refrigerator for 8 to 12 hours.

Remove the baskets from the refrigerator, take off the plastic wrap, and cover each basket with a cloth. Let the dough continue proofing at room temperature until it reaches an internal temperature of 58 to 60 degrees F, $1\frac{1}{2}$ to 2 hours.

Preheat the oven to 500 degrees F 1 hour before baking.

Remove the cloth and lightly dust the boules with flour. Carefully run your hand around one boule to loosen it and gently invert it onto a lightly floured baker's peel. With your fingers, press a small indentation in the center of the boule the same size as the biscuit cutter. Cut a hole in the center of the dough with the biscuit cutter. Enlarge the hole by stretching it with your hands until it is triple its original size. (The excess dough cut from the hole may be baked as rolls.) Instead of cutting a hole with a cutter, some bakers use their elbow to puncture the hole and then rotate their arm to enlarge the opening.

Open the oven door, spritz the oven heavily with water from a spray bottle, and quickly close the door. Open the oven door again, slide the loaf onto the baking tiles, being careful not to distort its shape, then quickly close the door. Cut, spritz, and load the second loaf in the same manner.

Reduce the oven temperature to 450 degrees F. Spritz the oven two more times during the next 5 minutes. Refrain from opening the oven door for the next 20 minutes.

After 20 minutes, check the loaves and rotate them if necessary to ensure even baking. Continue baking for 15 more minutes, for a total of 40 minutes.

Remove the loaves to a cooling rack. The crust should have an even, golden color. The interior should be light and porous.

FOUGASSE

This is a flat bread that's almost all crust. The shape is so low and so thin that the dough needs extra olive oil to soften it. Without the oil, the bread would dry out faster than you'd want it to. *Fougasse*, like *focaccia*, comes from the Latin word *focus*, which meant "fireplace." The original meaning of *focaccia* or *fougasse* was a bread cooked on a hot hearthstone or in the ashes, rather than in an oven. In France, *fougasse* is often cut to suggest the tree of life, or a wheat stalk. I slice all the way through the dough in a treelike pattern to get one of those shapes that looks difficult but is really very simple to do. If you like, you can use this dough to cut any shape you want, even animals or fish.

Note: As you are shaping the dough, it is more important to be sure it's at least 1 inch thick when it's flattened than to get the exact length and width—the bread is thin and crisp enough as it is; any flatter and you'll need a hammer and chisel to slice the thing.

TWO-DAY BREAD—FIRST DAY

1 recipe Italian Ring Bread Sponge (first-day directions, page 90)

Make the sponge and let it ferment at room temperature for 8 to 12 hours, as directed for Italian Ring Bread.

SECOND DAY

HAVE READY:
Plastic wrap
Dough cutter
Proofing cloth
2 parchment-paper-lined baking sheets lightly dusted with flour
Baker's peel
Spray bottle, filled with water
Cooling rack

Sponge
1 recipe Italian Ring Bread Dough (second-day directions, see page 91), plus 3 extra tablespoons olive oil
Unbleached white bread flour for dusting

Mix the sponge and dough ingredients plus 3 extra tablespoons olive oil and let the dough ferment, covered with plastic wrap, until it doubles in volume, about 3 hours, as directed for Italian Ring Bread.

Preheat the oven to 500 degrees F 1 hour before baking. Be sure the oven racks are placed well apart to allow plenty of air circulation.

Uncover the dough and turn it onto a lightly floured surface. Stretch the dough into a rectangle about 24 by 18 inches and at least 1 inch thick. Cut the dough down the middle with a dough cutter into two 12 by 9-inch rectangles. Working with one piece of dough at a time (leaving the second one covered with a cloth), fold in the edges of the longest sides of the dough to meet in the middle.

Invert the dough, seam side down, onto a floured, parchment-lined baking sheet. Dimple the dough slightly with your fingertips to seal the seam underneath.

Cup your hands around the top end of the dough and shape it into a half oval using a pushing motion. With a similar motion, shape the bottom end of the dough, leaving the edges slightly squared off to resemble a tombstone. The dough should be 1 to 1½ inches thick. Uncover the second piece of dough and shape it in the same manner.

Cover the loaves with a cloth and let them proof at room temperature for about ½ hour.

Uncover the first piece of dough and, with a dough cutter, make two 4-inch vertical slits in the middle of the piece. The slits should be about 2 inches apart and about 2 inches from the edge.

Make three diagonal cuts on each side of each center vertical slit, each diagonal cut about 3 inches long, 1½ inches from the edge of the dough and from the vertical slits. The top cut on each side will end so that if it were continued, it would hit the bottom of the top slit, the second cut so that if it were continued it would end in the first third of the bottom slit, and the last so that if it were continued it would end ½ inch below the bottom slit.

Enlarge the cuts with your fingers so that the openings are 1 to 1½ inches wide. (If the openings aren't wide enough, they'll close up during baking.) Stretch the outside edges to return the dough to its original shape. Make three 1-inch cuts on the right edge of the *fougasse*, placed halfway below

*C*UTTING AND SHAPING THE *FOUGASSE* DOUGH:
CUT THE DOUGH (RIGHT), THEN ENLARGE THE SLITS (LEFT)

each diagonal cut. Repeat these cuts on the left side. Cut the second piece of dough in the same manner.

Lightly sprinkle each *fougasse* with flour, cover them with a cloth, and let the dough relax for about 45 minutes.

Open the oven door, spritz the oven heavily with water from a spray bottle, and quickly close the door. Open the oven door again, slide one baking sheet onto the oven tiles or rack, and quickly close the door. Open the door and spritz the oven with water. Spritz and load the second loaf in the same manner.

Reduce the oven temperature to 450 degrees F. Spritz the oven two more times during the next 5 minutes. Refrain from opening the oven door for the next 15 minutes.

After 15 minutes, check the loaves and rotate them if necessary to ensure even baking. The crust should be an even brown color from top to bottom.

ONION BREAD

➤ MAKES TWO LARGE ROUNDS.

Some people look at this Onion Bread and call it a deep-dish pizza. Others call it a focaccia. It's really a mutation of both, as well as a bread. Start with the Italian Ring Bread Dough—the addition of commercial yeast makes it much more forgiving than other doughs; you can dimple the dough and weigh it down with sautéed onions, but it will still spring back up in the oven. This is a terrific bread to keep around for snacks or for a light lunch with a simple green salad. The anchovies—which I added because they remind me of *pissaladière*, the pizzalike tart from Nice—are optional, but I think this Onion Bread really tastes better with them.

TWO-DAY BREAD—FIRST DAY

1 recipe Italian Ring Bread Sponge (first-day directions, see page 90)

Make the sponge and let it ferment at room temperature for 8 to 12 hours, as directed for Italian Ring Bread.

SECOND DAY

HAVE READY:
2 cloth-lined baskets, lightly dusted with flour
Plastic wrap
Large skillet
Proofing cloth
Long-stemmed, instant-read thermometer
Two 12-inch circles of parchment paper
Pastry brush
Spray bottle, filled with water
Baker's peel
Cooling rack

Sponge
1 recipe Italian Ring Bread Dough (second-day directions, see page 91)
6 tablespoons extra-virgin olive oil in all
3 large onions, peeled and cut into ¼-inch slices
Sea salt
Coarsely ground fresh black pepper
4 ounces (about ½ cup) freshly grated imported Parmesan cheese for sprinkling on top
Unbleached white flour for dusting

Combine the sponge and dough ingredients, let the dough ferment, shape it into two boules, and let them proof in baskets, covered with plastic wrap, for 8 to 12 hours as directed for Italian Ring Bread.

Heat 3 tablespoons of the olive oil over medium heat in a large skillet. Add sliced onions and season to taste with salt and pepper. Cook over medium heat, stirring occasionally, until the onions are soft and well caramelized, approximately 25 minutes. Set aside to cool.

Preheat the oven to 500 degrees F 1 hour before baking.

Remove the baskets from the refrigerator, take off the plastic wrap, and cover each basket with a cloth. Let the dough continue proofing at room temperature until it reaches an internal temperature of 60 to 62 degrees F, 2 to 2½ hours. The dough should be soft and pliable.

Place parchment circles on work surface and lightly flour. Remove the cloths and lightly dust the boules with flour. Carefully run your hand around one boule to loosen it and gently invert it onto one floured parchment circle. Repeat with the second boule.

With one hand over the other, palms down, flatten each boule into a 10-inch disk. Dimple the surface of each disk at 2-inch intervals with your fingertips. Using the pastry brush, brush each round with the remaining 3 tablespoons of olive oil (1½ tablespoons per disk). Top each round with half of the onions, leaving a 1-inch rim. Sprinkle half of the Parmesan cheese. Let the dough rest, uncovered, for 20 minutes. Redimple the surface of the dough.

Open the oven door, spritz the oven heavily with water from a spray bottle, and quickly close the door. Keeping the parchment paper under the round, slide the baker's peel under one round. Open the oven door again, slide the round (and the parchment paper) directly onto the baking tiles, and quickly close the door. Spritz and load the second round in the same manner.

Reduce the oven temperature to 450 degrees F. Spritz the oven two more times during the next 5 minutes. Refrain from opening the oven door for the next 15 minutes.

After 15 minutes, slide the peel between each round and its parchment paper and remove, then discard the paper. Return the rounds to the oven and rotate if necessary to ensure even baking. Continue baking for 15 to 20 more minutes, for a total of 35 to 40 minutes.

Remove the rounds to a cooling rack. The edges of the onions will have darkened, and the rims of the rounds should have a deep brown color and be covered with fermentation bubbles.

PARMESAN CHEESE BREAD

MAKES TWO LARGE ROUNDS.

This is simply a variation of the Onion Bread, but here the Parmesan cheese not only tops the bread but goes into the dough too. Because of the extra cheese, this bread won't expand as much during proofing and baking—expect to see the dough grow only to about $1\frac{1}{3}$ times its original size.

TWO-DAY BREAD—FIRST DAY

HAVE READY:
Mixing bowl
Rubber spatula, optional
Plastic wrap

9 ounces (about 1 cup plus 1 tablespoon) cool water, 70 degrees F
2 ounces (about ¼ cup) White Starter
8 ounces (about 2 cups) unbleached white bread flour, plus extra for dusting

Make a sponge by placing water, White Starter, and flour in a mixing bowl and stirring everything with your hands or a rubber spatula. Cover the bowl tightly with plastic wrap and let it ferment at room temperature for 8 to 12 hours. If you're making this bread on a day when it is hotter than 80 degrees F, the sponge should be left at room temperature for half the fermenting time, then refrigerated for the remainder.

SECOND DAY

HAVE READY:
Mixing bowl
Mixer with attachable dough hook, optional
Proofing cloth
Rubber spatula, optional
Long-stemmed, instant-read cooking thermometer

Plastic wrap
Dough cutter
2 cloth-lined proofing baskets, lightly dusted with flour
Two 12-inch circles of parchment paper
Pastry brush
Baker's peel
Spray bottle, filled with water
Cooling rack

1¼ pounds (about 2½ cups) cold water, 60 degrees F
1 cake (.6 ounce) or 2 teaspoons packed fresh yeast
Sponge
2½ pounds (about 8 cups) unbleached white bread flour, plus extra for dusting
4 teaspoons sea salt
4 tablespoons coarsely chopped fresh marjoram, optional
6 tablespoons extra-virgin olive oil in all
1 pound (about 5½ cups) freshly grated imported Parmesan cheese
Vegetable oil

Place water and yeast in the bowl of a mixer. Uncover the sponge and add it to the yeast mixture, along with the flour. Attach the dough hook to the mixer and mix the dough on low speed for 4 minutes. The dough should feel soft and slightly sticky. (The dough may also be mixed by hand; see basic instructions on page 42.) Cover the dough with a proofing cloth and allow it to rest in the mixing bowl for about 20 minutes.

Add salt and mix on medium speed for 2 minutes, scraping the dough down the sides of the bowl as necessary with a rubber spatula. Add marjoram, 3 tablespoons of the olive oil, and 12 ounces (about 1½ cups) of the Parmesan cheese and mix on low speed just until the oil is incorporated. Turn the mixer up to medium speed and continue mixing until the dough reaches an internal temperature of 74 degrees F, about 4 minutes.

Remove the dough from the mixing bowl. The dough should feel soft. Knead the dough for a few minutes by hand on a lightly floured work surface.

Clean the mixing bowl and lightly coat it with vegetable oil. Return the dough to the oiled bowl, cover it tightly with plastic wrap, and let it ferment at room temperature until it increases in volume by half its original size, about 3 hours. The cheese will prevent the dough from rising as much as a dough without cheese.

Uncover the dough and turn it out onto a lightly floured work surface. Using a dough cutter, cut the dough into two equal pieces. Slap each piece against the work surface a few times to deflate. Tuck under the edges of each piece, cover the dough with a cloth, and let it rest for 15 minutes.

Uncover the dough and round each piece into a boule, according to the directions on page 48. Place the boules, smooth side down, into floured proofing baskets and sprinkle the surface of the dough with flour. Cover each basket tightly with plastic wrap and let the dough proof in the refrigerator for 8 to 12 hours.

Remove the baskets from the refrigerator, take off the plastic wrap, and over each basket with a cloth. Let the dough continue proofing at room temperature until it reaches an internal temperature of 58 to 60 degrees F, $1\frac{1}{2}$ to 2 hours.

Preheat the oven to 500 degrees F, 1 hour before baking.

Place parchment circles on work surface and lightly flour. Remove the cloths and lightly dust the boules with flour. Carefully run your hand around one boule to loosen it and gently invert it onto one floured parchment circle. Repeat with the second boule.

With one hand over the other, palms down, flatten each boule into a 10-inch disk. Dimple the surface of each disk at 2-inch intervals with your fingertips. Using the pastry brush, brush each round with the remaining 3 tablespoons of olive oil ($1\frac{1}{2}$ tablespoons per disk) and top each round with half of the remaining Parmesan cheese (2 cups per disk). Let the dough rest, uncovered, for 20 minutes.

Open the oven door, spritz the oven heavily with water from a spray bottle, and quickly close the door. Keeping the parchment paper under the round, slide the baker's peel under one round. Open the oven door again, slide the round (and the paper) directly onto the baking tiles, and quickly close the door. Spritz and load the second round in the same manner.

Reduce the oven temperature to 450 degrees F. Spritz the oven two more times during the next 5 minutes. Refrain from opening the oven door for the next 15 minutes.

After 15 minutes, slide the peel between each round and its parchment paper and remove, then discard the paper. Return the rounds to the oven and rotate if necessary to ensure even baking. Continue baking for 15 to 20 more minutes, for a total of 35 to 40 minutes.

Remove the rounds to a cooling rack. The cheese and the rims of the bread should be well browned.

OLIVE-ONION BREAD STICKS

MAKES APPROXIMATELY TWENTY-FOUR TO THIRTY BREAD STICKS.

These Olive-Onion Bread Sticks make great hors d'oeuvres to pass around with drinks—much better than the usual canapés. I also like them as something crisp to garnish a salad or a hot bowl of soup.

These bread sticks are another variation of the Italian Ring Bread Dough. The shaping may seem like more trouble than it's worth—essentially, shaping a bread stick is almost as complex as shaping a baguette and there are a lot more of them—but if you don't take the time to get them right, the finished sticks will not cook evenly and the interiors will be full of gaping air pockets.

TWO-DAY BREAD—FIRST DAY

1 recipe Italian Ring Bread Sponge (first-day directions, see page 90)

Make the sponge and let it ferment at room temperature for 8 to 12 hours, as directed for Italian Ring Bread.

SECOND DAY

HAVE READY:
Plastic wrap
Large skillet
Dough cutter
Proofing cloths
Spray bottle, filled with water
1 to 3 baking sheets, lined with parchment paper
Pastry brush
Cooling rack

Sponge
1 recipe Italian Ring Bread Dough (second-day directions, see page 91)

3 tablespoons extra-virgin olive oil, plus extra for brushing
3 large onions, peeled and cut into ¼-inch slices
Salt
Freshly ground pepper
Unbleached white bread flour for dusting
48 to 60 kalamata olives, pitted and left whole if possible
½ pound (about 2 cups) freshly grated imported Parmesan cheese

Follow the second-day instructions for mixing and kneading the fermented sponge and Italian Ring Bread Dough ingredients. Let the dough ferment, as directed for Italian Ring Bread, covered with plastic wrap until it doubles in volume, about 3 hours.

Heat olive oil in a large skillet over medium heat. Add the onions and season to taste with salt and pepper. Cook over low heat, stirring occasionally, until the onions are soft and caramel colored, about 20 minutes. Set aside to cool to room temperature.

Uncover the dough and turn it out onto a lightly floured surface. Slap the dough against the work surface a few times to deflate. Cut the dough into twenty-four to thirty 3-ounce pieces with a dough cutter. Tuck under the edges of each piece, cover the dough with a cloth, and let it rest for 15 minutes.

Place one to two additional proofing cloths on the work surface and lightly dust them with flour. Uncover the dough. Working with one piece at a time, smooth side down, fold in the short sides of each piece to meet in the center and press down firmly to seal. Bring the top edge of the dough to the center and seal with your fingertips. Bring the dough over again to the bottom edge and press down firmly with the heel of your hand to seal. Turn the dough seam side up and with your index and middle fingers, roll the dough to elongate it into a 5-inch cigar, one inch wide with tapering ends. Use as little flour as possible to prevent sticking. If there is not enough friction between the dough and the work surface, spritz the work surface lightly with water from a spray bottle.

Place two or three bread sticks in a vertical row on one end of the prepared proofing cloth. Pinch the cloth into a deep pleat alongside the row. Form another row of bread sticks and pleat the cloth again. Repeat with remaining sticks, making a pleat after each row.

Lightly sprinkle the sticks with flour and cover them with another cloth. Let them proof at room temperature for 1 hour.

Preheat the oven to 450 degrees F 1 hour before baking. Be sure the oven racks are placed well apart to allow plenty of air circulation.

Uncover the bread sticks. Place them seam side down, 2 inches apart, on parchment-lined baking sheets. Using a pastry brush, lightly coat each stick with olive oil and press 1 whole olive into each end of the stick, 1 inch from the tip. Cover the entire length of each stick with 2 heaping table-spoons of the caramelized onions, then press dimples into the dough with your fingertips, allowing spaces of dough to show through the onions. Sprin-kle the bread sticks with Parmesan, about 1 tablespoon per stick. Let the dough relax, uncovered, for 20 minutes. If all the baking sheets won't fit in the oven at the same time, place the extra baking sheet, uncovered, in the refrigerator until you are ready to bake it.

Open the oven door, heavily spritz the oven with water from a spray bottle, and quickly close the door. Open the oven door again, slide the baking sheets onto the baking tiles and a rack in the center of the oven, and quickly close the door. Spritz the oven two more times during the next 5 minutes. Refrain from opening the oven door for the next 15 minutes.

After 15 minutes, check the bread sticks and rotate the baking sheets if necessary to ensure even baking. Continue baking for 5 to 10 more minutes, for a total of 25 to 30 minutes.

The bread sticks should be golden brown with crisp ends. They are best eaten within a few hours after they are made—because they are narrow, the bread sticks can dry up rather quickly.

RUSTIC BREAD

— MAKES TWO APPROXIMATELY 2-POUND LOAVES.

There is one rule in bread making: The wetter the dough, the bigger the holes. And this Rustic Bread dough is so wet, it's literally a blob. What you get is a bread that Italians call *ciabatta*, or "slipper bread," because it's so flat and oval—like a slipper. (There's almost no oven spring.) Break the *ciabatta* open and you'll find an extremely porous interior. This makes Rustic Bread great for sandwiches—the bread soaks up whatever you slather onto it. My favorite way to serve Rustic Bread is to cut it into slices, brush it with olive oil, and grill it. Because this dough is really almost a batter, you don't even have to know how to shape dough to make this bread. In fact, I think the

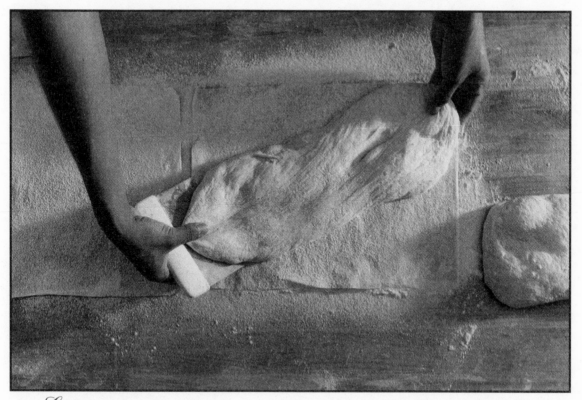

*S*TRETCHING THE RUSTIC BREAD:
"YOU DON'T EVEN HAVE TO KNOW HOW TO SHAPE DOUGH TO MAKE THIS BREAD."

more misshapen it is, the prettier it is. What you do, basically, is pick up the dough and plop it down. You form a rough oval, and that's the shape. Don't spend a lot of time pulling and tugging to get the dimensions exactly right. Be sure you have plenty of work space, because the dough gets about 2 hours of its proof time right on the counter. Handle the dough gently, to prevent it from deflating. The main thing to remember is to dimple the dough a second time just before it goes in the oven. The addition of yeast makes the dough very active. If you don't dimple it, the bread will fluff up too much during baking, and it won't come out as flat as it should.

Note: If your baking stone isn't large enough to hold two loaves at once, make one large loaf instead. If you decide to bake two loaves, one after the other, remember to turn the oven back up to 500 degrees F after removing the first loaf.

ONE-DAY BREAD

HAVE READY:
Mixing bowl
Mixer with attachable dough hook
Rubber spatula or wooden spoon
Small bowl
Plastic wrap
Proofing cloth
Parchment paper
Dough cutter
Spray bottle, filled with water
Baker's peel
Cooling rack

1 pound 6 ounces (about 2⅔ cups) cool water in all, 70 degrees F
1 pound 3 ounces (about 2 cups plus 2 tablespoons) White Starter
½ cake (.3 ounce) or 1 teaspoon packed fresh yeast
2 pounds 3 ounces (about 8¾ cups) unbleached white bread flour, plus extra for dusting
1 tablespoon sea salt
3 tablespoons cold milk
3 tablespoons extra-virgin olive oil
Semolina flour for dusting

Place I pound 3¼ ounces (about 2⅓ cups) water, White Starter, yeast, and flour in the bowl of a mixer and stir with a rubber spatula or wooden spoon just to moisten. Fit the mixer with a dough hook and mix the dough on medium speed for 6 minutes. Turn the mixer off and allow the dough to rest in the bowl for 20 minutes.

Add salt and mix on medium speed for 2 more minutes, scraping down the sides of the bowl as necessary with a rubber spatula.

Place milk, olive oil, and the remaining 2¾ ounces (about ⅓ cup) water in a small bowl and stir together. With the mixer on low speed, very gradually add the liquids to the dough. Don't add the liquids too rapidly or they'll slosh out. Continue mixing on low speed until the new ingredients are completely incorporated, then beat on high speed for 4 minutes.

Cover the bowl with plastic wrap and allow the dough to ferment at room temperature for 2 to 2½ hours, or until it reaches the top of the bowl and doubles in volume.

Sprinkle the work surface heavily with flour and pour the dough out to form a rough oval. Sprinkle the top of the dough with more flour, cover it with a cloth, and allow it to rest for 20 minutes.

Cut two pieces of parchment paper approximately 12 by 16 inches and place them side by side on the work surface. Sprinkle the parchment heavily with semolina, then with bread flour. Uncover the dough and sprinkle the top with more bread flour.

In a single continuous motion, cut the dough with a dough cutter into two equal pieces, carefully pulling the dough apart with your free hand as you go. Without pausing, carefully scoop up one piece of the dough, using the dough cutter and your free hand to hold each end, and lay the dough on a piece of the parchment paper, allowing it to stretch as it falls to form an oblong shape approximately 8 by 10 inches in area and 1½ inches thick. It's more important to get the proper thickness than the right width or length. Repeat the procedure with the second piece of dough.

Using your index fingers, dimple each piece of dough at 2-inch intervals, being sure to press all the way down to the parchment paper.

Lightly sprinkle the tops with bread flour and semolina. Cover each oval with a cloth and allow them to proof at room temperature for 2 hours. Test for readiness by lightly pressing two fingers into the dough. It should feel soft and alive, no longer sticky.

Preheat the oven to 500 degrees F I hour before baking.

Uncover the dough. Cut two additional 12-by-16-inch pieces of parchment paper and place each over the top of a proofed oval. Working with one piece of dough at a time, grab the opposite corners of the top and bottom papers and quickly flip the dough upside down. Carefully peel off the top paper, loosening any dough that may stick to it, and dimple the dough again with your fingers.

Open the oven door, spritz the oven heavily with water from a spray bottle, and quickly close the door. Keeping the parchment paper under the oval, slide the baker's peel under one oval. Open the oven door again, slide the oval (and the parchment paper) directly onto the baking tiles, and quickly close the door. Spritz and load the second oval in the same manner.

Reduce the oven temperature to 450 degrees F. Spritz the oven two more times during the next 5 minutes. Refrain from opening the door for the next 15 minutes.

After 15 minutes, slide the peel between each round and its parchment paper, then remove and discard the paper. Return the ovals to the oven and rotate if necessary to ensure even baking. Continue baking for another 5 minutes. Remove one loaf of bread from the oven and invert it onto the peel. Return it to the oven so that the bread browns evenly on both sides. Repeat with second loaf. Bake the loaves upside down for 5 to 8 minutes for a total of 30 to 33 minutes.

Remove the loaves to a cooling rack. When the bread is cooled, dust off any excess flour. The crust should be golden brown. The interior should be light and airy, with many large, well-developed holes.

RUSTIC OLIVE–HERB BREAD

1 recipe Rustic Bread (see page 105)
40 atalante or other whole green olives, pitted and left whole if possible
20 small sprigs fresh rosemary, about ½ inch long

Mix, shape, and proof the dough as directed for Rustic Bread. Just before baking, press the olives into the dimples of each loaf. Intersperse with small sprigs of rosemary inserted about ¼ inch into the dough. Bake as directed for Rustic Bread, but do not invert the bread during the last 5 minutes of baking (the olives would fall off).

When You've Become a Baker

After you've baked with this book awhile, you may feel confident enough to bake without a recipe. You may want to create your own breads in a totally different style than mine or anyone else's. This is when you know you've become a baker.

Visualize what you want your bread to look like once it's baked— imagine the oven spring, crust color, interior structure, and, of course, taste. Then use whatever method it takes to get there: Put your dough on a one-day sponge or a half-day sponge; try different shapes, different cuts, different baskets; ferment the dough at room temperature, let it proof in the refrigerator, do both—anything it takes to get the loaf you want. (Of course, you should only make one change at a time as you experiment.)

It's important to have an understanding of the ingredients and procedures that affect your bread. Too much water, for instance, will make a slack dough and a rubbery baked loaf. If you live in a humid climate, your doughs may require less water; they may ferment faster as well. If you live in a dry climate, you may have to make your doughs wetter. Increasing the water temperature or dough temperature will speed up fermentation. Heavy ingredients (for instance, nuts, dried fruit) will make a dough more dense. There are millions of possibilities. Trust your instincts.

Mushroom Bread

MAKES TWO APPROXIMATELY 2-POUND LOAVES.

My advice to bakers who want to create their own bread recipes is always the same: Start with a model you know and like, then make adjustments until you get what you're after. When I decided to make a mushroom bread, I chose my Rustic Bread as a model. I added farro, also known as spelt, to the dough; older than wheat, it's the grain that fed the Romans as they conquered their empire. With this bread, farro has a simpler task, accenting the earthiness of the porcini and dried shiitake mushrooms with its slightly nutty taste.

Note: If your baking stone isn't large enough to hold two loaves at once, make one large loaf. Farro is available at health food stores.

One-Day Bread

HAVE READY:

Saucepan
Mixing bowl
Mixer with attachable dough hook
Rubber spatula or wooden spoon
Proofing cloth
Small bowl
Plastic wrap
Parchment paper
Pastry brush
Dough cutter
Spray bottle, filled with water
Baker's peel
Cooling rack

6 cups tap water, plus extra to soak the mushrooms
2½ ounces (about ½ cups) whole farro or spelt grains
1½ ounces (about 2 cups) dried shiitake mushrooms, stems removed
5¼ ounces fresh or frozen porcini mushrooms

6 ounces (about ¾ cup) cool water, 70 degrees F

12 ounces (about 1⅓ cups) White Starter

½ cake (.3 ounce) or 1 teaspoon packed fresh yeast

1 pound 5 ounces (about 5 cups plus 1 tablespoon) unbleached white bread flour

3¼ ounces (about ¾ cup) farro or spelt flour, plus extra for dusting

1 tablespoon plus 1 teaspoon sea salt

2 tablespoons cold milk

3 tablespoons extra-virgin olive oil plus additional for brushing

Semolina flour for dusting

Place 6 cups of water in a saucepan, add the farro or spelt grains, and cook over medium heat until tender and soft, about 40 to 50 minutes. Drain, rinse to cool, and drain again thoroughly.

While the grains are cooking, place the shiitake mushrooms in a bowl and pour hot water over them to cover. Allow the mushrooms to soak until soft, about 1 hour. Drain and reserve the mushroom liquid. Slice the mushrooms into thin slices and set them aside.

If you are using frozen porcini mushrooms, remove them from the freezer and thaw for 10 minutes. Slice the mushrooms and set them aside. If you are using fresh porcini, simply wipe them clean and slice them.

Place 4 ounces (about ½ cup) water, 6 ounces (about ¾ cup) reserved mushroom liquid, White Starter, yeast, bread flour, and farro or spelt flour in the bowl of a mixer and stir with a rubber spatula or wooden spoon just to moisten. Fit the mixer with a dough hook and mix the dough on medium speed for 6 minutes. Turn the mixer off, cover the dough with a proofing cloth, and allow it to rest in the bowl for 20 minutes.

Add salt and mix on medium speed for 2 more minutes, scraping down the sides of the bowl as necessary with a rubber spatula.

Place milk, olive oil, and the remaining 2 ounces (about ¼ cup) water in a small bowl and stir together. With the mixer on low speed, very gradually add the liquids to the dough. Don't add the liquids too rapidly or they'll slosh out. Continue mixing on low speed until the new ingredients are completely incorporated, about 2 to 3 minutes. Remove the bowl from the mixer.

In a small mixing bowl stir together the whole grains and mushrooms. Add this mixture to the dough and incorporate with a rubber spatula to distribute it evenly. Return the bowl to the mixer and mix on low speed for 2 more minutes.

Cover the bowl with plastic wrap and allow the dough to ferment at room temperature until it reaches the top of the bowl and doubles in volume, 2 to 2½ hours.

Sprinkle the work surface heavily with farro or spelt flour and pour the dough out to form a rough oval. Sprinkle the top of the dough with more flour, cover it with a cloth, and allow it to rest for 20 minutes.

Cut two pieces of parchment paper approximately 12 by 16 inches and place them side by side on the work surface. Sprinkle the papers heavily with semolina, then with farro or spelt flour. Uncover the dough and sprinkle the top with more farro or spelt flour.

In a single continuous motion, cut the dough with a dough cutter into two equal pieces, carefully pulling the dough apart with your free hand as you go. Without pausing, carefully scoop up one piece of the dough, using the dough cutter and your free hand to hold each end, and lay the dough on a piece of the parchment paper, allowing it to stretch as it falls to form an oblong shape approximately 8 by 10 inches in area and 1½ inches thick. It's more important to get the proper thickness than the right width or length. Repeat the procedure with the second piece of dough.

Using your index fingers, dimple each piece of dough at 2-inch intervals, being sure to press all the way through to the parchment paper.

Lightly sprinkle the tops with farro or spelt flour and semolina. Cover each oblong with a cloth and allow them to proof at room temperature for 2 hours. Test for readiness by lightly pressing two fingers into the dough. It should feel soft and alive, no longer sticky.

Preheat the oven to 500 degrees F 1 hour before baking.

Uncover the dough. Cut two additional 12-by-16-inch pieces of parchment paper and place each over the top of a proofed oval. Working with one piece of dough at a time, grab the opposite corners of the top and bottom papers and quickly flip the dough upside down. Carefully peel off the top paper, loosening any dough that may stick to it, and brush the top of the dough with olive oil. Using a dough cutter, cut three evenly spaced horizontal lines deeply into the dough, starting 2 inches from each end of the dough and 1 inch from the sides. With your fingers, widen each cut to create a 1-inch gap.

Open the oven door, spritz the oven heavily with water from a spray bottle, and quickly close the door. Keeping the parchment paper under the oval, slide the baker's peel under one oval. Open the oven door again, slide the oval (and the parchment paper) directly onto the baking tiles, and quickly close the door. Spritz and load the second oval in the same manner.

Reduce the oven temperature to 450 degrees F. Spritz the oven two more times during the next 5 minutes. Refrain from opening the door for the next 15 minutes.

After 15 minutes, slide the peel between each round and its parchment paper, then remove and discard the paper. Return the ovals to the oven and rotate if necessary to ensure even baking. Continue baking for 5 more minutes. Remove one loaf of bread from the oven and invert it onto the peel. Return it to the oven so the bread browns evenly on both sides. Repeat with the second loaf. Bake the loaves upside down for 5 to 8 minutes for a total of 30 to 33 minutes.

Remove the loaves to a cooling rack. When the bread is cooled, dust off excess flour. The crust should be a rich brown. The interior is not quite as porous as that of the Rustic Bread and will be speckled with bits of mushrooms and grains. Although the openings may have closed a bit, the loaves should resemble the classic *fougasse* ladder shape.

FOCACCIA

— MAKES TWELVE 6-INCH-ROUND FOCACCE.

Focaccia is a fun bread to make, especially if you're not confident in your shaping skills yet. And you can top your focacce with just about anything you want, as if they were tiny pizzas. My preferences are rustic, Mediterranean-like ingredients: olives and garlic, tomatoes and anchovies. In every batch, I make each focaccia a little different. But on almost all of them, I put a thick base of greens, which wilt in the oven and form a beautiful frame for the rest of the toppings. (Each focaccia should hold about I ounce or I loosely packed cup of greens.) I also like to sprinkle the focacce with freshly grated Parmesan cheese because it gives the bread a nice browned look. You can garnish the rims of the focacce with seeds, but be sure to use just one kind at a time. Most of the ingredients you place on each focaccia should be precooked; potatoes roasted, onions sautéed. Prepared foods—marinated peppers, sun-dried tomatoes, or marinated tomatoes—work too. The toppings shouldn't be cut too small or they'll dehydrate during baking, although new potatoes should be halved or quartered. You'll also need to use greater quantities of toppings than you might at first think. The toppings should weigh down the dough, or the bread will puff up during baking and the toppings will fall off in the oven. Figure that a potato focaccia will hold about 3 quartered new potatoes, an onion focaccia will hold about 5 roasted boiling onions, and a roasted pepper focaccia will hold about ¾ of an average-size pepper.

Note: If you don't have enough baking sheets to hold all the focacce, shape what you can, then keep the remaining dough refrigerated and undivided until you're ready to use it.

ONE-DAY BREAD

HAVE READY:
2 to 4 baking sheets lined with parchment paper
Dough cutter
Proofing cloth
Pastry brush
Spray bottle, filled with water

1 recipe Rustic Bread *(see page 105)*
Semolina flour
Unbleached white bread flour for dusting
Extra-virgin olive oil
Fresh greens *(frisée, arugula, mizuna, or dandelion greens)*
Toppings of choice, such as roasted red or yellow pepper halves, roasted new potatoes (quartered), caramelized
    sliced onions or roasted boiling onions, cherry or currant tomatoes, roasted garlic cloves, pitted whole kalamata
    or green olives, anchovies, cooked bacon (not too crisp), imported Parmesan cheese or goat cheese, yellow
    mustard seeds, poppy seeds, or white or black sesame seeds
8 ounces *(about 2¾ cups) freshly grated imported Parmesan cheese*

Mix the dough and let it ferment for 2 to 2½ hours as directed for Rustic Bread.

Preheat the oven to 500 degrees F I hour before baking. Be sure the oven racks are placed well apart to allow plenty of air circulation.

Sprinkle the parchment-lined baking sheets with semolina. Pour the dough out onto a heavily floured surface. Using a dough cutter, divide the dough into twelve approximately equal pieces, placing each piece as it's cut in a single, continuous motion onto a prepared baking sheet. Figure on about three portions per baking sheet. If you have just two baking sheets, make six portions only, then cover and refrigerate the remaining dough to shape and bake later.

Form each piece of dough into a rough circle by cupping your hands around the dough and using a pushing motion. Allow the dough to rest, covered with cloth, for 20 minutes.

Brush each round with olive oil. Press a generous amount of fresh greens deeply into the perimeter of the round, I inch from the outer edge, slightly stretching the dough as you go into a 5-inch circle. Fill the centers with toppings of choice, pressing them well into the dough. Sprinkle the rim of each focaccia with seeds to garnish. Allow the focacce to rest at room temperature for 10 minutes, then press toppings down again to prevent the dough from rising too much. Sprinkle each focaccia with Parmesan cheese to taste.

Open the oven door, spritz the oven heavily with water from a spray bottle, and quickly close the door. Open the oven door again and place the baking sheets on the racks.

Reduce the oven temperature to 450 degrees F. Spritz the oven two more times during the next 5 minutes. Refrain from opening the oven door for at least the next 15 minutes.

After 15 minutes, check the focacce and rotate them if necessary to ensure even baking. Continue baking 10 to 15 more minutes, for a total of 30 to 35 minutes.

Remove the baking sheets from the oven. The focacce should be golden brown on both top and bottom.

Remember to turn the oven back up to 500 degrees F if you are baking the focacce in batches.

GRAPE FOCACCIA

Consider this more of a dessert focaccia. It's not especially sweet, and it can be eaten any time of day, plain or with rounds of goat cheese, depending on your mood. The ingredients listed here will top two focacce— I'm assuming you'll be baking several at once with different toppings on each.

Note: Turbinado sugar is coarse sugar, sometimes sold as Sugar in the Raw. Crystallized sugar, available at specialty shops, can also be used.

2 unbaked focacce, without greens
Olive oil
32 large seedless black or Concord grapes
16 small (about ½ inch) sprigs fresh rosemary
1 teaspoon anise seeds
1 tablespoon granulated sugar
1 tablespoon turbinado sugar or crystallized sugar

Brush two unbaked focacce with olive oil. Press 16 grapes deeply into the dough of each round, spacing the grapes about ¾ inch apart. Press the stem ends of the rosemary sprigs into the dough between the grapes. Sprinkle each round with anise seeds and sugars. Bake as directed for Focaccia.

ITALIAN BREAD STICKS

MAKES EIGHTEEN BREAD STICKS.

It's easy to get lost in Italy, at least if you're prone to autostrada confusion. Whoever said all roads lead to Rome was wrong: They all lead to Vercelli. A few years ago I thought I was driving to Genoa but somehow found myself in Asti, where sparkling wine comes from. No matter, I'd heard of a baker in Asti who was known as a master of hand-stretched *grissini*—the *real* version of the thin Italian bread sticks that most of us grew up thinking of as snack food on the tables at our local pizza parlors. His bread sticks, instead of the hollow, factory-made things that pass for *grissini* all over the world, were supposed to have as much integrity as a well-made French baguette, with an interior network of gluten strands as intricate as those in sourdough boules. Unfortunately, when I finally stumbled upon the address of the bakery, I found that the place had gone out of business. I ate wonderful *grissini* at a nearby restaurant, but I left Italy feeling as if I'd missed out on one of the world's great treasures. Maybe that's why I became obsessed with making *grissini* when I got back home.

After trying countless recipes, I realized the rustic dough I was already making was wet enough to give me the internal structure I was looking for. When you cut and stretch the bread sticks, don't worry about making them perfectly even and round; the more irregular, the more beautiful. As with baguettes, the quantity and length of your bread sticks will depend on the size of your oven and baking sheets. Basically, they should be as long as the largest baking sheet that will fit in your oven. If your oven requires you to use three baking sheets, don't bake all three at once. The dough is very forgiving once it's shaped, so you don't have to worry about overproofing. And you don't have to cover the bread sticks once they've been stretched—it's OK if the outside dries out a bit before they go into the oven. Plus, you're not looking for the dough to expand in the oven the way it does when you bake boules and other loaves.

ONE-DAY BREAD

HAVE READY:
Proofing cloth
2 or 3 baking sheets lined with parchment paper
Dough cutter
Spray bottle, filled with water

1 recipe Rustic Bread (see page 105)
Unbleached white bread flour for dusting
Semolina flour

Mix the dough, let it ferment, and shape it by stretching it into a rough rectangle (about $\frac{1}{2}''$ thick) on a heavily floured work surface, as directed for Rustic Bread. The shortest sides of the rectangle should be about half as long as your baking sheet. This way when you cut the strips of dough, you will be able to stretch them to the proper length. Sprinkle the top of the dough with bread flour, cover it with a cloth, and allow the dough to proof at room temperature for 2 hours. Test for readiness by lightly pressing two fingers into the dough. It should feel soft and alive, no longer sticky.

Preheat the oven to 450 degrees F 1 hour before baking. Be sure the oven racks are placed well apart to allow plenty of air circulation.

Sprinkle the parchment-lined baking sheets with semolina. Remove the cloth from the dough. Lightly flour the dough to make cutting more manageable.

With a dough cutter, cut strips no more than 1 inch wide from a shorter side of the dough. Tuck your fingers under the center of each strip and gently lift it onto the baking sheet, allowing the dough to stretch to twice its length as it falls.

Continue cutting one strip at a time, placing them parallel on the baking sheets, about $1\frac{1}{2}$ inches apart. You should have about eighteen strips.

Open the oven door, spritz the oven heavily with water from a spray bottle, and quickly close the door. Open the oven door again, place the baking sheets on the oven racks, and quickly close the door. Spritz the oven two more times during the next 5 minutes. Refrain from opening the oven door for the next 15 minutes.

After 15 minutes, check the bread sticks and rotate if necessary to ensure even baking. Continue baking for 5 to 10 more minutes, for a total of 25 to 30 minutes.

The bread sticks are done when their ends begin to lift off the parchment and are crisp and brown.

VARIATION
6 fresh rosemary sprigs about 6 inches long

Before baking, break sprigs of rosemary into small pieces and press the stem ends into each bread stick about every 3 inches. When baked, the rosemary chars nicely.

RAISIN BRIOCHE

—— MAKES TWO APPROXIMATELY 2¼-POUND LOAVES.

I love raisin toast, and this bread makes the best. I call it a brioche because it's made with eggs and butter, but it's not as airy as a true French brioche. It's more of a light panettone. At the bakery, this Raisin Brioche is made as a pan bread (slices from a regular loaf fit better in a toaster), but it works beautifully shaped into a boule. I actually like it better as a boule—it's a lot more rustic looking, and you get a great crust.

THREE-DAY BREAD—FIRST DAY

HAVE READY:
Mixing bowl
Rubber spatula, optional
Plastic wrap

6 ounces (about ¾ cup) cool water, 70 degrees F
½ cake (.3 ounce) or 1 teaspoon packed fresh yeast
6½ ounces (about ¾ cup) White Starter
4 ounces (about ¼ cup) milk
10 ounces (about 2¼ cups) unbleached white bread flour

Make a sponge by placing water, yeast, White Starter, milk, and flour in a mixing bowl and stirring with your hands or a rubber spatula. Cover the bowl tightly with plastic wrap and leave it at room temperature for 10 to 12 hours.

Check the sponge. Bubbles should have formed on the surface. Resecure the plastic wrap, and place the bowl in the refrigerator for 10 to 12 hours.

SECOND DAY

HAVE READY:
Small bowl
Fork

Mixing bowl
Mixer with attachable dough hook
Rubber spatula, optional
Long-stemmed, instant-read cooking thermometer
Plastic wrap

5 large eggs, room temperature
Sponge
1 pound (about 4 cups) unbleached white bread flour, plus extra for dusting
3 ounces (about ⅓ cup) sugar
1 tablespoon sea salt
9 ounces (2 sticks plus 2 tablespoons) unsalted butter, cut into tablespoon-size pieces, room temperature
1 pound (about 3 cups) golden raisins
Vegetable oil

Place eggs in a small bowl and whisk them with a fork just to break apart. Set aside.

Remove the sponge from the refrigerator and take off the plastic wrap. Place sponge, half the whisked eggs, flour, and sugar in the bowl of a mixer fitted with a dough hook. Mix on medium speed for 2 minutes. The dough should be wet and sticky.

Add salt and continue mixing on low for 2 minutes, scraping the dough down the sides of the bowl as necessary with a rubber spatula. With the mixer still running on low, add the remaining eggs, a little at a time, being sure they are incorporated into the dough each time before the next addition. When the eggs are completely incorporated, turn the mixer to medium-high and continue mixing until the dough is smooth and satiny, wraps itself around the dough hook, and cleans itself from the sides of the bowl, about 8 more minutes. Hold on to your mixer—it may jump around the counter at this point.

Turn the mixer down to medium speed and add the butter one piece at a time, making sure each piece is semi-incorporated before you add the next. When all the butter has been added, turn the mixer back up to medium-high and allow the dough to mix until it is smooth and shiny (but not greasy), wraps itself around the dough hook, cleans itself from the sides of the bowl, and reaches an internal temperature of 76 degrees F, 3 to 4 minutes. You may have to add a few pinches of flour to encourage the dough to wrap itself around the dough hook.

If the raisins are clumped together, break them apart. Add them with the mixer running and mix on low just until they are incorporated into the dough, about 1 minute.

Remove the dough from the mixing bowl, place it on a lightly floured work surface, and knead it by hand for a few minutes.

Clean the mixing bowl and lightly coat it with vegetable oil. Return the dough to the oiled bowl, cover it tightly with plastic wrap, and place it in the refrigerator to continue fermenting 12 to 24 hours.

THIRD DAY

HAVE READY:
Proofing cloth
Dough cutter
Two 3½ × 12-inch, 10-cup-capacity loaf pans
Pastry brush
Small bowl
Fork
Spray bottle, filled with water
Cooling rack

Dough
Unbleached white bread flour for dusting
2 tablespoons melted unsalted butter
2 egg yolks

Remove the dough from the refrigerator and take off the plastic wrap. The dough should have almost doubled in volume and feel slightly sticky. If it hasn't risen enough, leave the dough out at room temperature covered with a cloth until it has, an extra hour or so.

Turn the dough out onto a lightly floured work surface and cut it into two equal pieces with a dough cutter. Slap each piece against the work surface a few times to deflate. Tuck under the edges of each piece, cover them with a cloth, and let the dough rest for 15 minutes.

Brush each loaf pan with melted butter and set it aside.

Uncover one piece of dough. Flatten it into a 4 by 12-inch rectangle by placing one hand over the other, palms down, in the center of the dough and patting it to an even thickness (working outward). With the longer edges parallel to the edge of the work surface, fold the top edge of the dough in half and seal it with the heel of your hand. Fold the top edge over to meet at the bottom edge and seal. Tuck in and seal the ends. Place one hand on top of the other, palms down, in the center of the dough and start rolling it into a cylinder the length of your loaf pan. As the dough begins to stretch, uncross your hands and continue rolling with even pressure, moving your hands to the ends of the cylinder. Do not taper the ends. Shape the second loaf in the same manner.

Place the loaves seam side down in the loaf pans. With one hand formed into a fist, knock down the dough with the flat side of your knuckles, beginning at one end of the loaf pan and ending at the opposite end so that the dough spreads to an even layer and fills the pans. Cover the pans with cloth and let the dough proof at room temperature for approximately 5 hours total. After about 4 hours, check the dough. If the dough is near the tops of the pans, remove the cloth.

Place egg yolks in a small bowl and stir them with a fork just to break apart. Brush each loaf with this egg wash and let the dough continue rising, uncovered, to 1 inch above the rims of the pans, and until it reaches an internal temperature of 72 degrees F, about 1 hour.

Preheat the oven to 500 degrees F 1 hour before baking. Place one oven rack on the bottom rung and remove all the others.

Open the oven door, spritz the oven heavily with water from a spray bottle, and quickly close the door. Open the oven door again, place both loaf pans on the rack, spaced well apart, and quickly close the door.

Reduce the oven temperature to 450 degrees F. Spritz the oven two more times during the next 5 minutes. Refrain from opening the oven door for the next 20 minutes.

After 20 minutes, check the loaves and rotate them if necessary to ensure even baking. Continue baking for 15 to 20 more minutes, for a total of 40 to 45 minutes.

Remove one pan from the oven and immediately turn out the loaf by knocking the side of the pan on a countertop to loosen the bread. (If necessary, run a knife around the inside edge to help release it.) The sides of the loaf should feel firm, otherwise they will cave in as they cool. If the bread is not quite done, return the loaf to the pan and continue baking for another 5 minutes or so. Repeat this test with the second loaf.

When the loaves are done, remove them to a cooling rack. The bread should be dark brown on top and have risen 2 to 3 inches above the rims of the pans.

HAMBURGER BUNS

✎ MAKES TWELVE LARGE HAMBURGER BUNS.

Hamburgers are among my favorite things to eat, and I have specific ideas about what makes a good one. Beyond the perfect patty and supercrisp iceberg lettuce, the bun is crucial. I don't like most people's ideas of "fancy" hamburgers—I don't like hamburgers on grilled bread or on rustic baguettes, even ones from my own bakery. My perfect burger is more of a junk-food burger—there *was* a time when fast-food burgers were actually good. The bun should be soft, but not so soft it falls apart. It should smoosh into the burger as you bite in.

When I decided to bake hamburger buns for the bakery, I chose a dough similar to the one I use for the Raisin Brioche. The high fat content keeps the bread moist. It's not the ideal junk-food bun of my youth, but it's close.

THREE-DAY BREAD—FIRST AND SECOND DAYS

1 recipe Raisin Brioche Dough, minus raisins (see page 120)

Follow the first-day and second-day directions for Raisin Brioche dough, without the raisins.

THIRD DAY

HAVE READY:
Proofing cloth
Dough cutter
Spray bottle, filled with water
2 baking sheets lined with parchment paper
Long-stemmed, instant-read cooking thermometer
Pastry brush

Raisin Brioche dough
Unbleached white bread flour for dusting
¾ cup sesame seeds, optional

Remove the dough from the refrigerator and take off the plastic wrap. The dough should have almost doubled in size. If it hasn't doubled, leave the dough out at room temperature covered with a cloth until it has.

Turn the dough out onto a lightly floured work surface and cut it into twelve $4\frac{1}{2}$-ounce pieces with a dough cutter. Tuck under the edges of each piece, cover them with a cloth, and let the dough rest for 15 minutes.

Working with one piece at a time, and keeping the rest covered with a cloth, shape the dough into balls by cupping your hand lightly around the dough and rounding it against the friction of the work surface to form a smooth bun. Begin slowly and increase speed as the ball becomes tighter and smoother. Use as little flour as possible to prevent sticking. If there is not enough friction between the work surface and the dough, spritz the work surface lightly with water from a spray bottle.

As each bun is shaped, check to be sure it is smooth and taut and the surface of the dough is not torn, which would indicate overrounding. Place the buns at least 2 inches apart, smooth side up, on parchment-lined baking sheets. Press down gently on each bun to flatten it into a disk. Cover the buns with a cloth and let them proof at room temperature until they nearly double in size and reach an internal temperature of 68 degrees F, approximately 3 hours.

Preheat the oven to 500 degrees F 1 hour before baking. Be sure the oven racks are placed well apart to allow plenty of air circulation.

Brush the tops of the buns with water and sprinkle each with 2 teaspoons of sesame seeds.

Open the oven door, spritz the oven heavily with water from a spray bottle, and quickly close the door. Open the oven door again, load both baking sheets onto the racks, and quickly close the door.

Reduce the oven temperature to 400 degrees F. Spritz the oven two more times during the next 5 minutes. Refrain from opening the oven door for the next 10 minutes.

After 10 minutes, check the buns and rotate them if necessary to ensure even baking. Continue baking until the buns are golden brown and nicely puffed, 10 to 15 more minutes, for a total baking time of 25 to 30 minutes. Remove the buns from the oven and allow to cool.

VARIATION:

Instead of sprinkling the buns with sesame seeds, try using poppy seeds, black sesame seeds, sprigs of herbs such as fresh chervil or thyme, or cracked black pepper.

GEORGE'S SEEDED SOUR

⁓ MAKES TWO APPROXIMATELY 1½-POUND LOAVES.

This is a great bread-and-butter bread. I love the way the crunch of the seeds combines with the bite of the sour; with a little butter you have the makings of a perfect food. The bread, developed by my head baker, George Erasmus, is one of our newest additions. We wanted something similar to our Multigrain Bread but lighter—some people want the health qualities of a grain bread but don't like its dense texture. This bread contains white, whole-wheat, and rye flours, poppy and sesame seeds, and the grains quinoa, amaranth, and millet, which are available in most health food stores. The seeds and grains, with the addition of anise and fennel seeds, go on top of the dough, where they toast and develop a wonderfully nutty crunch from the heat of the oven during baking. And the bread can stand up to a lot more than butter—it's terrific for sandwiches, including my favorite, turkey.

TWO-DAY BREAD—FIRST DAY

HAVE READY:
2 mixing bowls
Rubber spatula, optional
Plastic wrap
Mixer with attachable dough hook, optional
Long-stemmed, instant-read cooking thermometer

SPONGE
1¾ pounds (about 2¼ cups) White Starter
2 ounces (about ¼ cup) cold milk
3½ ounces (about ⅔ cup) whole-wheat flour
1⅓ ounces (about ½ cup) dark rye flour
2 tablespoons unbleached high-gluten flour or unbleached white bread flour

Make a sponge by placing White Starter, milk, and flours in a mixing bowl and stirring with your hands or a rubber spatula. Cover the bowl tightly with plastic wrap and leave it at room temperature until it has doubled in volume and is covered with small bubbles, 3 to 3½ hours.

DOUGH

10 ounces (about 1½ cups) cool water, 70 degrees F
Sponge
2½ tablespoons quinoa
2½ tablespoons millet
4 tablespoons amaranth
1 tablespoon poppy seeds
1 pound 5½ ounces (about 5 cups plus 2 tablespoons) unbleached white bread flour, plus extra for dusting
1 tablespoon sea salt
Vegetable oil

Place water, sponge, grains, poppy seeds, and bread flour in the bowl of a mixer fitted with a dough hook. Mix on low speed for 4 minutes. (The dough may also be mixed by hand; see basic instructions on page 42.) Cover the dough with a proofing cloth and allow it to rest in the mixing bowl for 20 minutes. The dough should be wet and sticky.

Add salt and continue mixing on medium speed, scraping the dough down the sides of the bowl as necessary with a rubber spatula, until the dough reaches an internal temperature of 78 degrees F, 4 to 5 more minutes.

Remove the dough from the mixing bowl, place it on a well-floured work surface, and knead it for a few minutes by hand.

Clean the mixing bowl and coat it lightly with vegetable oil. Return the dough to the oiled bowl, cover it tightly with plastic wrap, and place the bowl in the refrigerator for 6 to 7 hours. The dough should double in volume. Check the dough after 1½ to 2 hours. If it is growing too quickly and has already doubled in volume, remove the plastic wrap and turn the dough out onto a lightly floured work surface. Knead it once to deflate. Return the dough and let it continue fermenting until it doubles again.

SECOND DAY

HAVE READY:
Proofing cloth
Dough cutter
Small bowl
Baking sheet
Spray bottle, filled with water
*Wood board or baking sheet covered with a large, flour-dusted proofing cloth or 2 oval (2-pound-capacity)
    proofing baskets*
Plastic wrap
Plastic trash can liner, optional
Long-stemmed, instant-read cooking thermometer
Baker's peel
Single-edged razor blade
Cooling rack

Dough
Unbleached white bread flour for dusting
2 tablespoons amaranth
½ cup sesame seeds
3 tablespoons poppy seeds
3½ tablespoons anise seeds
3 teaspoons fennel seeds

Remove the dough from the refrigerator and take off the plastic wrap. If the dough hasn't risen enough, leave the dough out at room temperature covered with a cloth until it has.

Turn the dough out onto a lightly floured work surface and cut it into two equal pieces with a dough cutter. Slap each piece against the work surface a few times to deflate. Tuck under the edges of each piece, cover them with a cloth, and let the dough rest for 15 minutes.

Place the amaranth and seeds in a small bowl and mix. Spread them in an even layer on one baking sheet. Set aside.

Uncover the dough and round each piece into a boule, according to the directions on page 48. Then elongate each boule by placing one hand on top of the other, palms down, in the center of the dough and simultaneously rolling and molding it into a football shape, about 10 inches long. As the dough begins to stretch, uncross your hands and continue rolling with light, even pressure, moving your hands slowly all the way to the ends of the dough as it tapers.

Lightly spritz the tops of the loaves (smooth side up) with water from a spray bottle. Gently roll the wet side of each loaf from side to side in the mixed seeds to coat it as heavily as possible.

If you are using proofing baskets, invert each loaf, seed side down, into a basket. Sprinkle the surface of the dough with flour and cover each basket tightly with plastic wrap.

If you are proofing on a cloth-covered board or baking sheet, invert one loaf, seed side down, onto the cloth. Pinch the cloth into a deep pleat alongside the dough. (This will separate the loaves, help them hold their shape, and prevent them from sticking together as they proof.) Place the second loaf on the proofing surface in the same manner, pinching the cloth around it. Cover with a flour-dusted proofing cloth, slide the board into a plastic trash can liner, and close the bag securely.

Let the loaves proof at room temperature until they have doubled in size and reached an internal temperature of 62 degrees F, 3 to 4 hours.

Preheat the oven to 500 degrees F 1 hour before baking.

Remove the plastic wrap and cloth and lightly dust the loaves with flour. Invert the loaves, seeded side up, spaced well apart, on a lightly floured baker's peel. Holding a single-edged razor blade at a 45-degree angle, slash the top of the dough, making a gentle arch cut to one side of the center of the dough. Begin the cut 1 inch away from one tip of the dough and end it 1 inch away from the opposite tip.

Open the oven door, spritz the oven heavily with water from a spray bottle, and quickly close the door. Open the oven door again, place the loaves directly on the baking tiles, and quickly close the door. Reduce the oven temperature to 450 degrees F. Spritz the oven two more times during the next 5 minutes. Refrain from opening the oven door for the next 20 minutes.

After 20 minutes, check the loaves and rotate them if necessary to ensure even baking. Continue baking for 10 to 15 more minutes, for a total of 35 to 40 minutes.

Remove the loaves to a cooling rack. The bread should be a deep burnished brown with a crust of toasted seeds. The interior should be moist with a fairly open texture.

Sesame-Semolina Sandwich Rolls

➤ MAKES TWELVE SANDWICH ROLLS.

My favorite kind of salami sandwich is the Italian deli–style one on a soft roll, as opposed to the Jewish deli–style one on rye. There's a thin, crisp crust on this roll, but when you bite into the sandwich, the whole thing compresses in your mouth, forming a singular, perfect bite. I love the beautiful pale yellow of the interior, which comes from the durum wheat.

    Note: Be sure to have plenty of counter space to work; Sesame-Semolina Sandwich Rolls spend a short time proofing right on the work surface.

One-Day Bread

HAVE READY:
Mixing bowl
Mixer with attachable dough hook
Rubber spatula, optional
Long-stemmed, instant-read cooking thermometer
Plastic wrap
Dough cutter
2 floured proofing cloths
1 to 3 baking sheets
1 or 2 shallow plates with edges, optional
Spray bottle, filled with water
Parchment paper
Single-edged razor blade

5½ ounces (about ⅔ cup) cool water, 70 degrees F
½ cake (.3 ounce) or 1 teaspoon packed fresh yeast
6 ounces (about ⅔ cup) White Starter
12½ ounces (about 3 cups) unbleached white bread flour, plus extra for dusting
14 ounces (about 2½ cups) semolina flour, plus extra for coating rolls
10 ounces (about 2 cups plus 2 tablespoons) durum flour

1 tablespoon sea salt
Vegetable oil
¾ cup natural sesame seeds, untoasted

Place water, yeast, White Starter, and flours in the bowl of a mixer fitted with a dough hook. Mix on low speed until the ingredients are combined, about 3 minutes, scraping the dough down the sides of the bowl as necessary with a rubber spatula. The dough should be soft but not sticky. (The dough may also be mixed by hand; see basic instructions on page 42.)

Add salt and mix on medium speed until the dough is smooth and elastic and reaches an internal temperature of 74 degrees F, about 7 minutes.

Remove the dough from the mixing bowl, place it on a lightly floured work surface, and knead it for a few minutes by hand.

Clean the mixing bowl and lightly coat it with vegetable oil. Return the dough to the oiled bowl, cover it tightly with plastic wrap, and let it ferment at room temperature until it doubles in volume, about 2 hours.

Uncover the dough and turn it out onto a lightly floured surface. Using a dough cutter, cut it into twelve equal pieces. Slap each piece against the work surface a few times to deflate. Tuck under the edges of each piece, cover the dough with a cloth, and let it rest for 15 minutes.

Uncover the dough. Working with one piece at a time, and keeping the rest covered with a cloth, flatten the dough into a rectangle by placing one hand over the other, palms down, and patting the dough to an even thickness of about 1 inch. Fold the short ends in to meet in the center and press down firmly with the heel of your hand to seal. With the shorter edges parallel to the edge of the work surface, fold the bottom edge of the dough to the center. Pat across the whole seam firmly with the heel of your hand. Fold the top edge of the dough over the seam, to about 1 inch from the bottom. Seal the seam in the same manner. Fold the dough once more so that the top and bottom edges meet. Seal the seam. Tuck in the loose dough at each end and press firmly to get a clean seal.

Turn the dough seam side up. Place one hand on top of the other, palms down, in the center of the dough and start rolling it into a cylinder about 7 inches long. As the dough begins to stretch, uncross your hands and continue rolling with light, even pressure, moving your hands slowly to each end. Do not taper the ends. Shape the remaining pieces of dough in the same manner.

Place a flour-dusted proofing cloth directly on the work surface.

Place extra semolina flour in an even layer on a baking sheet or shallow plate. Fill an additional baking sheet or shallow plate with tap water, about 1 inch deep. Set the baking sheets or plates side by side in assembly-line fashion: water closest to you, semolina flour in the middle, and the floured cloth at the end.

Spritz the smooth side of one roll with water from a spray bottle and sprinkle it with one tablespoon of sesame seeds. Pick up the roll and dip it, seam side down, into the water and then into the semolina flour, rolling it back and forth to coat. Place the roll, semolina side down, on the floured cloth. Repeat with the remaining rolls, placing them in vertical rows, two to three to a row. As each row is formed, pinch the cloth into a deep pleat alongside the rolls (this will keep the rolls separate, help them hold their shape, and prevent them from sticking together as they proof). Cover the rolls with a proofing cloth to prevent them from drying out.

Let the rolls proof at room temperature until they double in volume, about 1 hour.

Preheat the oven to 400 degrees F 1 hour before baking. Be sure the oven racks are placed well apart to allow plenty of air circulation.

Line two baking sheets with parchment paper. Uncover the rolls and transfer them, seed side up, about 2 inches apart, onto the lined sheets. With a single-edged razor blade held at a 45-degree angle, make two straight cuts on top of each roll, the first beginning ½ inch from the end and continuing halfway down the roll. The second cut should begin about ¼ inch below the center of the first cut and end ½ inch from the opposite end of the roll.

Open the oven door, spritz the oven heavily with water from a spray bottle, and quickly close the door. Open the oven door again, place the baking sheets on the racks, and quickly close the door. Spritz the oven two more times during the next 5 minutes. Refrain from opening the oven door for the next 15 minutes.

After 15 minutes, check the rolls and rotate the baking sheets if necessary to ensure even baking. Let the rolls continue baking until they are golden brown, 5 to 10 more minutes, for a total of 25 to 30 minutes.

Remove the baking sheets from the oven and let the rolls cool before serving. The bottom and top crusts should be thin and crisp and the interior soft, with evenly distributed small holes.

CHOCOLATE–SOUR CHERRY BREAD

MAKES TWO APPROXIMATELY 1-POUND BOULES.

This isn't a completely weird idea—the Italians have been making chocolate bread for years. I started making Chocolate–Sour Cherry Bread a few months after the bakery opened, when people in the neighborhood were still getting used to my style of bread. They'd come in, look around, and say, "Do you have anything besides bread? Anything sweet?"

To them a bakery meant a place to buy cake. This bread is my compromise. It's on the sweet side, but it's definitely not a cake. I make the bread with a sourdough starter, though there is some commercial yeast—without it, the cocoa powder would make the bread too dense. The only real trick to this bread is to buy good ingredients—especially chocolate, such as Valrhona. I've given the recipe to people who tried to make the bread with less expensive chocolate, and the results were disappointing. Also, you need to use an imported dark cocoa powder, otherwise the color will be grayish, not as rich and appealing as it should be.

Note: Dried sour cherries are available in health food stores, gourmet markets, and specialty shops. They're sold sweetened or unsweetened. I prefer unsweetened, though sweetened are OK too.

TWO-DAY BREAD—FIRST DAY

HAVE READY:
Mixing bowl
Mixer with attachable dough hook
Rubber spatula, optional
Long-stemmed, instant-read cooking thermometer
Plastic wrap

4 ounces (about ½ cup) cool water, 70 degrees F
1 cake (.6 ounce) or 2 teaspoons packed fresh yeast
6 ounces (about ⅔ cup) White Starter
1 ounce (about 5½ tablespoons) unsweetened imported dark cocoa powder
2 ounces (about ¼ cup) sugar

10½ ounces (about 2 cups plus 2 tablespoons) unbleached white bread flour, plus extra for dusting
2 ounces (4 tablespoons) unsalted butter, cut into tablespoon-size pieces, softened
1½ teaspoons sea salt
3 ounces (about ⅔ cup) dried sour cherries, preferably unsweetened
4 ounces imported bittersweet chocolate, chopped into ½-inch chunks
Vegetable oil

Place water, yeast, White Starter, cocoa powder, sugar, and flour in the bowl of a mixer fitted with a dough hook. Mix on low speed for 3 minutes. Adjust the speed to medium and, with the mixer running, gradually add butter, 1 tablespoon at a time, scraping the dough down the sides of the bowl as necessary with a rubber spatula.

When the butter is completely incorporated, add the salt and continue mixing on medium speed until the dough reaches an internal temperature of 75 degrees F, about 9 more minutes. The dough should be soft and sticky. Add the cherries and chopped chocolate and mix on low speed just to incorporate, 1 to 2 minutes.

Remove the dough from the mixing bowl and place it on a lightly floured work surface. Clean the mixing bowl and lightly coat it with vegetable oil. Return the dough to the oiled bowl, cover it tightly with plastic wrap, and let it ferment at room temperature just until it shows signs of movement, about 2 hours.

Check the dough, resecure the plastic wrap, and place the bowl in the refrigerator 8 to 12 hours.

SECOND DAY

HAVE READY:
Proofing cloth
Dough cutter
Wood board or baking sheet covered with a large flour-dusted proofing cloth or two 1-pound-capacity proofing baskets
Plastic trash can liners, optional
Long-stemmed, instant-read cooking thermometer
Baker's peel
Single-edged razor blade

Spray bottle, filled with water
Cooling rack

Dough
Unbleached white bread flour for dusting

Remove the dough from the refrigerator and take off the plastic wrap. The dough should have almost doubled in volume and feel spongy and sticky. If it hasn't doubled, leave the dough out at room temperature covered with a cloth until it has.

Turn the dough out onto a lightly floured work surface and cut it into two equal pieces with a dough cutter. Slap each piece against the work surface a few times to deflate. Tuck under the edges of each piece, cover them with a cloth, and let the dough rest for 15 minutes.

Uncover the dough and round each piece into a boule, according to the directions on page 48. The boules will not be completely smooth because of the chunks of chocolate.

If you are using proofing baskets, invert each boule, smooth side down, into a floured basket and sprinkle the surface of the dough with flour. Cover each basket tightly with plastic wrap.

If you are proofing on a cloth-covered board or baking sheet, invert one boule, smooth side down, onto the flour-dusted cloth. Pinch the cloth into a deep pleat alongside the boule. (This will separate the boules, help them hold their shape, and prevent them from sticking together as they proof.) Repeat with the remaining boule. Dust the boules lightly with flour and cover them with a cloth. Slide the board or baking sheet into a clean plastic trash can liner and close the bag securely.

Let the boules proof at room temperature until they almost double in size and reach an internal temperature of 64 degrees F, 3 to 4 hours.

Preheat the oven to 500 degrees F 1 hour before baking.

Remove the plastic wrap and cloth and lightly dust the boules with flour. Invert the boules, spaced well apart, onto a lightly floured baker's peel.

With a single-edged razor blade held perpendicular to the boule, slash an *X* about 2 inches long in the center of each boule, keeping the ends of the cuts ¾ inch away from the edges. Put four short, straight cuts in the center of each *V* created by the *X*.

Open the oven door, spritz the oven heavily with water from a spray bottle, and quickly close the door. Open the oven door again, slide the boules onto the baking tiles, and quickly close the door.

Reduce the oven temperature to 450 degrees F. Spritz the oven two more times during the next 5 minutes. Refrain from opening the oven door for the next 20 minutes.

After 20 minutes, check the boules and rotate them if necessary to ensure even baking. Continue baking for 10 to 15 more minutes, for a total of 35 to 40 minutes.

Remove the boules to a cooling rack. The outside of this bread becomes very dark, almost black, and has no visible signs of fermentation bubbles. Because the dough is soft, even when it is tapped on the bottom it won't sound hollow. Be careful not to overbake; the bread will dry out. The interior should have a more evenly distributed, smaller hole structure than those of other breads because of the butter and chocolate.

CHALLAH

MAKES TWO APPROXIMATELY 1¾-POUND LOAVES.

Challah is traditionally a braided bread, one of the hardest shapes to make. But if the technique seems frightening to you, the bread also looks beautiful formed into a rope and simply tied in a knot. You can also bake this dough in a loaf pan, as you would the Raisin Brioche. If you're up to it, though, the braid makes the best-looking shape.

The interior is pale yellow—this color is as traditional as the braided shape. But where the bread once got its color from the yolks of fresh farm eggs, many challah bakers now cheat with food coloring. I prefer to cheat with a more natural ingredient: Since I can't always get great eggs, I use saffron for color. I also like the play of the saffron flavor against the egginess of the bread. I found out from a Jewish baker friend that his grandmother used to put saffron in her challah—so there is precedent. One other trick: I add apples to help keep the bread moist.

Note: When you braid the dough, you want to make it snug but not too tight because tight braids will tear as the bread expands in the oven. Also, it may take a couple of tries to get the braid close to looking like what you see at your local deli. But it's better to have a rough braid than to keep redoing it and risk overworking the dough or letting it overproof. It will still come out pretty, just gnarled.

TWO-DAY BREAD—FIRST DAY

HAVE READY:
2 small saucepans
Aluminum foil
Fork
Mixing bowl
Rubber spatula, optional
Plastic wrap

14 ounces (about 1¾ cups) water in all
⅛ teaspoon saffron threads

1 large (about 5 ounces) tart green apple, such as Granny Smith, peeled, cored, and cut into eighths
4½ ounces (about ½ cup) White Starter
4 ounces (about 1 cup) unbleached high-gluten flour or unbleached white bread flour, plus extra for dusting
3 ounces (about ½ cup) semolina flour
3 ounces (about ¾ cup) durum wheat flour

Boil 12 ounces (about 1½ cups) of water in a small saucepan. Add the saffron, boil for another 30 seconds, and set aside to cool to room temperature.

Add the remaining 2 ounces (about ¼ cup) water and apple pieces to a separate saucepan and cover it tightly with aluminum foil. Bring it to a boil over high heat. As soon as the foil swells up, turn off the heat and allow the apples to steep until they are completely cooked and without color, 15 to 20 minutes. Allow the apples to cool, then mash them with a fork until the mixture resembles applesauce.

Make a sponge by placing the saffron water, apple puree, White Starter, and flours in a mixing bowl. Mix with your hands or a rubber spatula. Cover the sponge tightly with plastic wrap and let it ferment at room temperature 8 to 12 hours.

SECOND DAY

HAVE READY:
Small bowl
Fork
Mixing bowl
Mixer with attachable dough hook, optional
Rubber spatula, optional
Long-stemmed, instant-read cooking thermometer
Plastic wrap
Proofing cloth
Dough cutter
2 baking sheets
Spray bottle, filled with water
Cooling rack

3 large eggs, room temperature

4 egg yolks in all
Sponge
1 cake (.6 ounce) or 2 teaspoons packed fresh yeast
3 tablespoons vegetable oil plus extra for oiling the bowl
1 tablespoon barley malt syrup
8 ounces (about 2 cups) unbleached high-gluten flour or unbleached white bread flour
6½ ounces (about 1 cup plus 1 tablespoon) semolina flour
5 ounces (about 1 cup) durum flour, plus extra for dusting
2 ounces (about ¼ cup) sugar
1 tablespoon sea salt
2 tablespoons sesame or poppy seeds

Place whole eggs and 2 egg yolks in a small bowl and stir with a fork just to break apart. Set aside.

Place sponge, yeast, 3 tablespoons oil, malt syrup, flours, and sugar in the bowl of a mixer fitted with a dough hook. Mix on low speed for 4 minutes. The dough should be soft but not sticky. (The dough may also be mixed by hand; see basic instructions on page 42.)

Add salt and continue mixing on low for 2 minutes, scraping down the sides of the bowl with a rubber spatula as necessary. With the mixer still running on low, add the whisked eggs, a little at a time, being sure each portion is incorporated into the dough before you add the next. When the eggs are completely incorporated, turn the mixer to medium-high and continue beating until the dough is smooth and elastic and reaches an internal temperature of 78 degrees F, about 6 minutes.

Remove the dough from the mixing bowl, place it on a lightly floured work surface, and knead it for a few minutes by hand.

Clean the mixing bowl and lightly coat it with vegetable oil. Return the dough to the oiled bowl, cover it tightly with plastic wrap, and let it ferment in the refrigerator until it doubles in volume, 5 to 6 hours.

Remove the dough from the refrigerator and take off the plastic wrap. Turn the dough out onto a work surface lightly dusted with durum flour. Cover it with cloth and let the dough continue fermenting until it reaches an internal temperature of 60 degrees F, 30 to 60 minutes.

Uncover the dough and cut it into two equal pieces with a dough cutter. Cut each piece into six equal pieces with a dough cutter, for a total of twelve pieces. Slap each piece once against the work surface to deflate. Tuck under the edges of each piece, cover with a cloth, and let the dough rest for 15 minutes.

Working with one piece at a time and keeping the rest covered with a cloth, shape, fold, and roll into a cylinder with tapered ends according to the directions for baguettes on page 64. The only difference is that the cylinder shape of a baguette should be even for most of its length; ropes for challah should be more like old-fashioned cigars, with a slightly fatter belly in the middle. The ropes should be 8 to 9 inches long and $\frac{3}{4}$ to 1 inch thick.

Lightly dust the ropes with flour to prevent them from sticking together when the dough proofs; the dusting also keeps the ropes from tearing when they bake.

Lay six shaped pieces lengthwise on one semolina-dusted baking sheet, about 1 inch apart. Place the remaining six ropes on the second baking sheet. Cover one baking sheet with cloth and place it in the refrigerator (this will ensure that the dough won't overproof as you braid the first challah).

To braid, join all six pieces at one end by pinching the tips together to hold firm. Spread the remaining lengths of the ropes about 1 inch apart in a tepeelike pattern. Working from left to right, mentally number the ropes 1 through 6. Pick up rope 3 and bring it to the top right so that it becomes almost an extension of rope 1. Take rope 6 and bring it to the top left so that it becomes an extension of rope 5. Bring rope 3 back down to the middle, crossing over rope 6. Bring rope 1 across all the strips to the top right (rope 3's previous position). Move ropes 4 and 5 slightly to the right. Bring rope 6 down to the middle to take the place of rope 4. Pull rope 5 up to the top left so it becomes an extension of rope 4. Move ropes 2 and 3 slightly to the left and bring rope 1 down to the middle to take the place of rope 3.

From now on, take the rope on the lower left and bring it to the top right. Slide the two ropes on the bottom right over a bit and bring down the rope on the upper left to the space you made by moving the ropes over. Repeat this procedure, starting on the lower right, using opposite ropes. Braid all the way to the end. Pinch the ends together and tuck them under slightly.

You'll probably be braiding about six to eight times back and forth. You will end up with a challah that is raised in the center with tapered ends. A three-rope challah braid would be just flat.

Cover the challah with cloth, remove the second baking sheet from the refrigerator, and braid the second challah in the same manner.

If you don't want to braid the challah, cut the dough in two equal pieces, then shape and bake according to the directions for Raisin Brioche, pages 122–23.

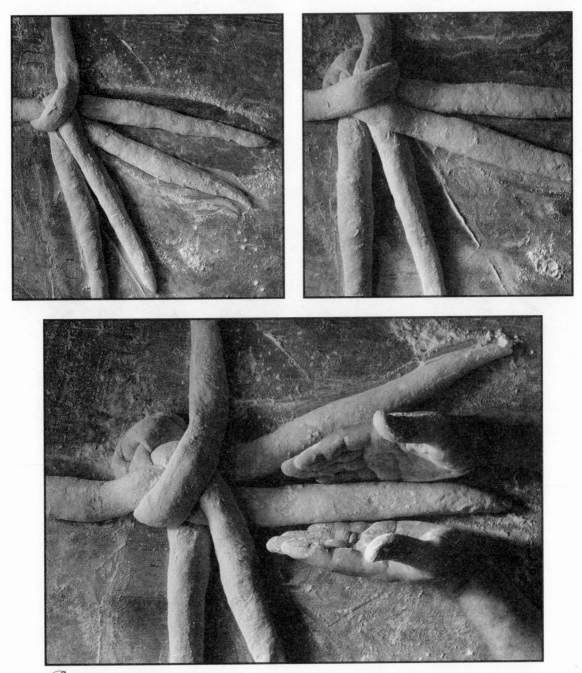

*B*RAIDING A CHALLAH:

"ROPES FOR CHALLAH SHOULD BE MORE LIKE OLD-FASHIONED CIGARS,
WITH A SLIGHTLY FATTER BELLY IN THE MIDDLE."

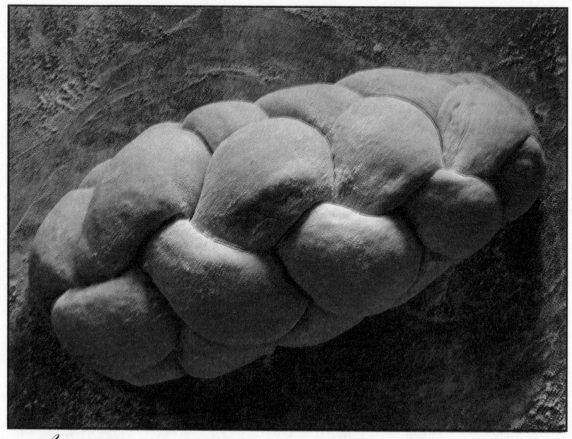

A SHAPED CHALLAH

Allow both challahs to proof at room temperature until they reach an internal temperature of 72 to 74 degrees F and double in volume, about 1 hour.

Preheat the oven to 500 degrees F 1 hour before baking. Be sure the oven racks are placed well apart to allow plenty of air circulation.

When the dough has doubled in volume, whisk the remaining egg yolks in a small bowl, brush the challah tops with the egg, and sprinkle them with sesame seeds.

Open the oven door, spritz the oven heavily with water from a spray bottle, and quickly close the door. Open the oven door again, load the baking sheets onto the racks, heavily spritz the oven with water, and quickly close the door. Reduce the oven temperature to 450 degrees F. Spritz the oven three more times during the next 5 minutes. Refrain from opening the oven door for the next 15 minutes.

After 15 minutes, check the challahs and rotate the baking sheets if necessary to ensure even baking. Continue baking 10 to 15 more minutes, for a total of 30 to 35 minutes.

Remove the baking sheets from the oven. Transfer the challah to a cooling rack.

The top of the challah should be evenly brown and firm to the touch. This is a soft-textured bread with a "pulled" or ropy look to the interior.

PUMPKIN BREAD

MAKES THREE APPROXIMATELY 1-POUND LOAVES.

There are no pumpkins in this Pumpkin Bread. There were when I first started making the bread, but I didn't think they gave it enough flavor or color. Instead I started relying on Garnet or Jewel yams, and sometimes Kabosha squash. I thought the taste, slightly sweet and nutty, was worth the deception. Why keep the old name? *Pumpkin bread* sounds much more appealing than *yam bread*.

I do, however, use toasted pumpkin seeds (*pepitas*) in this bread to give it a crunchy texture. You can find the seeds packaged in most supermarkets. Or try looking in a Latino grocery store or a health food store. This bread makes a welcome addition to a Thanksgiving meal.

Note: Like the Potato-Dill Bread, this recipe makes smaller loaves than many of the other breads in this book—and it is football shaped instead of round like a boule. This means the proofing baskets you may have used for the Country White and other basic breads will be too large for this dough. (Remember, if a dough is given too much proof space, it will expand horizontally instead of vertically.) At the bakery, we use smaller, oval-shaped baskets for this bread, but unless you are a completely dedicated bread maker, you probably have only one size basket, for the basic 2-pound boules. One solution: Proof the bread on a pleated cloth, or *couche*.

TWO-DAY BREAD—FIRST DAY

HAVE READY:
2 mixing bowls
Fork
Baking sheet
Mixer with attachable dough hook, optional
Rubber spatula, optional
Long-stemmed, instant-read cooking thermometer
Plastic wrap

2 pounds Garnet or Jewel yams (1 or 2 yams)

7 ounces (1⅓ cups) shelled raw pumpkin seeds (pepitas)

12 ounces (1½ cups) cold water, 55 degrees F

8 ounces (about 1 cup) White Starter

5 tablespoons raw wheat germ

1 teaspoon ground cumin

1 pound 2 ounces (about 3¼ cups) unbleached white bread flour, plus extra for dusting

7 ounces (about 1¼ cups) whole-wheat flour

1 tablespoon sea salt

Vegetable oil

Preheat the oven to 400 degrees F. Place the yams directly on an oven rack and bake them until they are very soft, about 1 hour. Remove the yams and chill them in a refrigerator until they are cold, about 30 minutes. Peel the yams and mash the pulp in a bowl with a fork. Measure out 10 ounces (about 1¼ cups) pulp and set it aside.

Reduce the oven temperature to 350 degrees F. Place the pumpkin seeds on a baking sheet and toast in the oven until they are puffed and very lightly browned, about 15 minutes, shaking the sheet once during baking. Remove the seeds and let them cool to room temperature.

Place water, White Starter, wheat germ, cumin, yam pulp, and flours in the bowl of a mixer fitted with a dough hook. Mix on low speed for 4 minutes, scraping the dough down the sides of the bowl with a rubber spatula as necessary. The dough should be wet and sticky. (The dough may also be mixed by hand; see basic instructions on page 42.)

Add salt and mix on medium speed for 7 minutes. Add the toasted pumpkin seeds and mix on low speed just until the ingredients are incorporated and the dough reaches an internal temperature of 70 to 72 degrees F, about 2 minutes.

Remove the dough from the mixing bowl, place it on a lightly floured work surface, and knead it for a few minutes by hand.

Clean the mixing bowl and lightly coat it with vegetable oil. Return the dough to the oiled bowl, cover it tightly with plastic wrap, and let it ferment in the refrigerator 6 to 10 hours.

SECOND DAY

HAVE READY:
Dough cutter
Proofing cloth
3 oval-shaped proofing baskets or wood board
Plastic trash can liners, optional
Long-stemmed, instant-read cooking thermometer
Baker's peel
Single-edged razor blade
Spray bottle, filled with water
Cooling rack

Dough
Unbleached white bread flour for dusting

Remove the dough from the refrigerator and take off the plastic wrap. The dough should feel moist and should have grown half its original size. If the dough hasn't grown, cover it with a cloth and leave the dough at room temperature for about an hour.

Turn the dough out onto a lightly floured work surface. Cut the dough with a dough cutter into three equal pieces. Slap each piece against the work surface a few times to deflate. Tuck under the edges of each piece, cover them with a cloth, and let them rest for 15 minutes.

Uncover the dough and round each piece into a boule according to the directions on page 48. Then elongate each boule by placing one hand on top of the other, palms down, in the center of the dough and simultaneously rolling and molding the dough into a football shape, about 8 inches long. The shape should be similar to that of a sweet potato. As the dough begins to stretch, uncross your hands and continue rolling with light, even pressure, moving your hands slowly all the way to the ends of the dough as it tapers.

If you are using proofing baskets, invert each oval, smooth side down, into a floured basket, sprinkle the surface of the dough with flour, and cover each basket tightly with plastic wrap.

If you are proofing on a cloth-covered board, invert one oval, smooth side down, onto the flour-dusted cloth. Pinch the cloth into a deep pleat alongside the oval. (This will separate the ovals, help them hold their shape, and prevent them from sticking together as they proof.) Repeat with the other two ovals. Cover the loaves with a flour-dusted cloth. Slide the board into a plastic trash can liner and close the bag securely.

Place the baskets or board in the refrigerator and let the dough proof for 6 to 10 hours.

Preheat the oven to 500 degrees F at least 1 hour before baking.

Remove the dough from the refrigerator, take off the plastic wrap, and cover each basket with a cloth. Let the dough continue proofing at room temperature until it grows half its original size and reaches an internal temperature of 60 to 62 degrees F, up to 1 hour. (*Note:* Test the dough's temperature as soon as it comes out of the refrigerator; sometimes it's ready right away.)

Remove the cloth and lightly dust the ovals with flour. Invert one to three loaves spaced well apart onto a lightly floured baker's peel. If the baker's peel will not accommodate all three loaves, work with one at a time.

Holding a single-edged razor blade perpendicular to the first loaf, slash an elongated *X* across the top of the dough, ¹/₂ inch deep, keeping the ends of the cuts ³/₄ inch from the ends of the dough. Then make one long, straight cut in the center of the *V* created at each end of the *X* (start the cut at least ¹/₄ inch from the intersection of each *V* and end it ¹/₄ inch away from the end of the dough).

Open the oven door, spritz the oven heavily with water from a spray bottle, and quickly close the door. Open the oven door again, slide the loaves onto the baking tiles, and quickly close the door. If you are loading each loaf separately, cut, spritz, and load the second and third loaves in the same manner.

Reduce the oven temperature to 450 degrees F. Spritz the oven two more times during the next 5 minutes. Refrain from opening the oven door for the next 20 minutes.

After 20 minutes, check the loaves and rotate them if necessary to ensure even baking. Continue baking for 10 more minutes, for a total of 35 minutes.

Remove the loaves to a cooling rack. The crust should have a burnished brown color, and the interior should have more of an even texture than most other loaves made with White Starter—you won't see the open, airy structure of Country White Bread.

FIG–ANISE BREAD

MAKES TWO APPROXIMATELY 1-POUND-2-OUNCE BOULES.

This bread bakes dark, almost black, so don't confuse it with burnt bread— it's just the figs. I use dried black mission figs for the strength of their flavor and their color. I leave some of them whole to make the interior of the bread darker and to help make the bread slightly chewy when you take a bite. I puree the rest so that the figs become part of the character of the dough.

I like Fig-Anise Bread toasted for breakfast, but it's also great to eat with a strong goat cheese after dinner.

Note: To get the best possible texture, it's important that the dried figs be soft and chewy. Dried fruit hardens with age, and when it's too hard it doesn't puree well. Don't use fresh figs—they're too watery.

TWO–DAY BREAD—FIRST DAY

HAVE READY:
Blender
Mixing bowl
Mixer with attachable dough hook
Rubber spatula, optional
Long stemmed, instant-read cooking thermometer
Plastic wrap

10 ounces (1½ cups, packed) soft, dried black mission figs, stems removed
4 tablespoons hot tap water
4 ounces (about ½ cup) cool water, 70 degrees F
1 cake (.6 ounce) or 2 teaspoons packed fresh yeast
9 ounces (about 1 cup) White Starter
12¾ ounces (about 3 cups) unbleached white bread flour
3¾ ounces (about 6 tablespoons) sugar
1½ teaspoons sea salt
½ teaspoon anise seeds
2 tablespoons polenta or cornmeal
Vegetable oil

Cut the figs into halves (if large, into quarters). Measure 3 ounces or ½ cup packed figs and place them in the blender with hot tap water. Puree them and set aside.

Place 4 ounces cool water, yeast, White Starter, flour, and sugar in the bowl of a mixer fitted with a dough hook. Mix on low speed for 2 minutes.

Add salt and mix on medium speed for 6 minutes, scraping the dough down the sides of the bowl as necessary with a rubber spatula.

Add the pureed figs, anise seeds, and polenta and mix on medium speed until the puree is completely incorporated and the dough reaches an internal temperature of 75 degrees F, about 2 minutes. Add remaining fig pieces and mix on low just until they are incorporated in the dough, about 2 minutes.

Remove the dough from the mixing bowl, place it on a lightly floured work surface, and knead it for a few minutes by hand. Clean the mixing bowl and lightly coat it with vegetable oil. Return the dough to the oiled bowl, cover it tightly with plastic wrap, and place it in the refrigerator for 24 hours.

SECOND DAY

HAVE READY:
Proofing cloth
Dough cutter
Two 1-pound-capacity cloth-lined proofing baskets or wood board or baking sheet
Plastic wrap
Plastic trash can liner, optional
Long-stemmed, instant-read cooking thermometer
Baker's peel
Single-edged razor blade
Spray bottle, filled with water
Cooling rack

Dough
Unbleached white bread flour for dusting

Remove the dough from the refrigerator and take off the plastic wrap. The dough should have almost doubled in volume and feel spongy and sticky. If it hasn't doubled, leave the dough out at room temperature covered with a cloth until it has.

Turn the dough out onto a lightly floured work surface and cut it into two equal pieces with a dough cutter. Slap each piece against the work surface a few times to deflate. Tuck under the edges of each piece, cover them with a cloth, and let the dough rest for 15 minutes.

Uncover the dough and round each piece into a boule, according to the directions on page 48. The boules will not be completely smooth because of the figs.

If you are using proofing baskets, invert each boule, smooth side down, into a floured basket and sprinkle the surface of the dough with flour. Cover each basket tightly with plastic wrap.

If you are proofing on a cloth-covered board or baking sheet, invert one boule, smooth side down, onto the flour-dusted cloth. Pinch the cloth into a deep pleat alongside the boule. (This will separate the boules, help them hold their shape, and prevent them from sticking together as they proof.) Repeat with the remaining boule. Cover the loaves with a flour-dusted cloth. Slide the board or baking sheet into a plastic trash can liner and close the bag securely.

Let the boules proof at room temperature until they almost double in size and reach an internal temperature of 64 degrees F, 3 to 4 hours.

Preheat the oven to 500 degrees F 1 hour before baking.

Remove the plastic wrap and cloth and lightly dust the boules with flour. Invert the boules, spaced well apart, onto a lightly floured baker's peel.

With a single-edged razor blade held perpendicular to the boule, slash an *X* about 2 inches long in the center of each boule, keeping the ends of the cuts ¾ inch away from the edges. Then cut four small *X*s in the centers of each *V* created by the first *X*.

Open the oven door, spritz the oven heavily with water from a spray bottle, and quickly close the door. Open the door again, slide the boules onto the baking tiles, and quickly close the door.

Reduce the oven temperature to 450 degrees F. Spritz the oven two more times during the next 5 minutes. Refrain from opening the oven door for the next 20 minutes.

After 20 minutes, check the boules and rotate them if necessary to ensure even baking. Continue baking for about 10 more minutes, for a total of 35.

Remove the boules to a cooling rack. The crust should be dark brown, almost black, and the interior should be soft and tan colored from the pureed figs.

LEVAIN BÂTARD

levain is simply the French word for "leaven," but to bakers it refers to the French "old dough" system in which a nugget from each day's dough is held back and used as the leavening in the next day's baking.

That nugget, called a *chef*, or "seed," does the same job as the liquid starter I use in most of the breads at the bakery—and in this book.

There are a lot of appealing aspects about the *levain* system of sourdough baking. For one thing, it perpetuates a complete bread cycle—yesterday's dough literally becomes tomorrow's loaf. It's also a very visual method; each time the *levain* is fed or refreshed—in stages called *builds*—you can see it grow because the consistency is much thicker than that of a liquid starter.

But when I first opened the bakery, the *levain* process confused me. How could I determine how much dough to hold back each day? What if I needed more bread than usual one day? Would I have enough *levain* on hand?

A liquid starter seems so much easier to maintain—and the results are nearly identical. For me and the style of bread I eventually developed, a liquid starter worked best. Still, I was curious. I decided to try using a *levain* when I started making *bâtards* at the bakery.

The *bâtard* I make is essentially a fat baguette. Like a baguette, it's mostly crust. But the added girth of a *bâtard* makes it better for sandwiches. And it's the perfect size for *bruschetta*.

You start by saving a piece of *aged* white sourdough about the size of a Ping-Pong or golf ball. Some bakers make this initial seed or *chef* from scratch by mixing flour and water and leaving it out to ferment, wrapped in cloth or sometimes buried in a sack of flour. But if you're going to make a loaf of Country White anyway—and you should—I think it's easier to steal a piece of dough for your *levain*. After you make the *Levain Bâtard*, save a piece of its dough instead.

Refresh the seed each time before you make a dough by doing a series of *builds*, the equivalent of feedings for a liquid sourdough starter. Each time you do a build, you have to transfer the dough to a container that is barely 3 inches larger than the ball of dough; there should be only enough room in the bowl for the dough to increase in volume 2½ times. A closed space is necessary to trap the fermentation gases as the dough grows.

As the builds ferment, they actually rise the way a dough does. When the seed is ready to be refreshed again, the dough should be domed; ideally you need to do the next build before the dough deflates.

THREE-DAY BREAD
(plus a 24- to 36-hour step to get one piece of aged dough)

TO FORM THE SEED
HAVE READY:
One 1-cup bowl, with optional sealable lid
Plastic wrap, optional
1 recipe Country White Bread (see page 40)

Follow the recipe for Country White Bread. But just before shaping, tear off one 1.2-ounce piece of dough, about the size of a Ping-Pong ball or golf ball. (Shape and bake the remaining dough as directed in Country White recipe.) Roll the dough into a ball and place it in a small bowl. Cover the bowl tightly with a sealable lid or plastic wrap secured tightly around the rim. Place the dough in the refrigerator to age for 24 to 36 hours.

If you'll be making the *Levain Bâtard* on a regular basis, save the dough from your previous batch of *Levain Bâtard* dough and age it in the same manner.

FIRST DAY

LEVAIN: FIRST BUILD
HAVE READY:
One 1½-cup bowl, with optional sealable but not airtight lid
Plastic wrap, optional

1.2 ounces (about 3 tablespoons) lukewarm water, 80 degrees F
One 1.2-ounce piece Country White dough or Levain Bâtard dough, aged 24 to 36 hours
1.2 ounces (about 5 tablespoons) unbleached high-gluten or unbleached white bread flour

Place water and the aged dough in a bowl with just enough room for the mixture to increase 2½ times in volume. Break apart the dough with your hands until it dissolves in the water.

Add flour and incorporate it into the mixture with your hands. Cover the bowl with a sealable lid or plastic wrap secured tightly around the rim. Let the mixture ferment at room temperature until it doubles in volume, about 12 hours.

SECOND DAY

LEVAIN: SECOND BUILD

HAVE READY:
One 4-cup bowl, with optional sealable but not airtight lid
Plastic wrap, optional

First-build dough
2.5 ounces (about ⅓ cup) lukewarm water, 80 degrees F
3 ounces (about ½ cup plus 2 tablespoons) unbleached high-gluten or unbleached white bread flour

Remove the lid or plastic wrap from the first-build dough. Transfer the mixture to a 4-cup bowl. Add water. Break apart the dough with your hands until it dissolves in the water.

Add flour and incorporate it into the mixture with your hands until a stiff, elastic dough forms. Cover the bowl with a sealable lid or plastic wrap secured tightly around the rim. Let the mixture ferment at room temperature until it doubles in volume and is bubbly on the surface, 5 to 6 hours.

LEVAIN: THIRD BUILD

HAVE READY:
One 8-cup bowl, with optional sealable but not airtight lid
Plastic wrap, optional

Second-build dough
6 ounces (about ¾ cup) lukewarm water, 80 degrees F
6½ ounces (about 1½ cups) unbleached high-gluten or unbleached white bread flour

Remove the lid or plastic wrap from the second-build dough. Transfer the mixture to an 8-cup bowl. Add water. Break apart the dough with your hands until it dissolves in the water.

Add flour and incorporate it into the mixture with your hands until a stiff, elastic dough forms. Cover the bowl with a sealable lid or plastic wrap secured tightly around the rim. Let the mixture ferment at room temperature until it doubles in volume and is bubbly on the surface, 4 to 5 hours.

At this point you have an active leaven that could be used to make several kinds of breads in this book, including ones made with rye and wheat flours. If you prefer this method and want to experiment, keep in mind that you'll need to add extra water to each recipe—enough to match the amount of water from the liquid starter called for in a recipe.

This *chef* can be kept refrigerated for 24 but not more than 36 hours.

THE *BÂTARD*

HAVE READY:

Mixing bowl
Mixer with attachable dough hook
Spray bottle, filled with water
Long-stemmed, instant-read cooking thermometer
Rubber spatula, optional
Plastic wrap
Dough cutter
Proofing cloth
French baguette pan or cloth-lined wood board or baking sheet
Plastic trash can liner

14 ounces (about 1¾ cups) lukewarm water, 80 degrees F
Levain
1 pound 11½ ounces (about 5½ cups) unbleached white bread flour, plus extra for dusting
½ cup raw wheat germ
4½ teaspoons sea salt
Vegetable oil

Place water, *levain,* flour, and wheat germ in the bowl of a mixer fitted with a dough hook. Mix on low speed for 5 minutes. (The dough may also be mixed by hand; see basic instructions on page 42.) Cover the dough with a proofing cloth and let it rest in the mixing bowl for 20 minutes. The dough should be sticky and pliable.

Add salt and mix on low speed until the dough reaches an internal temperature of 78 degrees F, about 6 minutes, scraping the dough down the sides of the bowl as necessary with a rubber spatula. The dough should be smooth and resilient.

Remove the dough from the mixing bowl, place it on a lightly floured work surface, and knead it for a few minutes by hand.

Clean the mixing bowl and lightly coat it with vegetable oil. Return the dough to the oiled bowl, cover it tightly with plastic wrap, and let it ferment at room temperature until it doubles in volume, about 4 hours.

Turn the dough out onto a lightly floured work surface and cut it into two equal pieces with a dough cutter. Tuck under the edges of each piece, cover them with a cloth, and let the dough rest for 15 minutes.

Uncover the dough. Working with one piece at a time, flatten the dough into a 6 by 8-inch rectangle by placing one hand over the other, palms down, and patting the dough to an even thickness. (Begin in the center and work outward.) This gives you more control and ensures evenness—the top hand works as a guide.

Fold in the short ends to meet in the center and press down firmly with the heel of your hand to seal the seam. With the shorter edges parallel to the edge of the work surface, fold the bottom edge of the dough to the center. Pat across the whole seam firmly with the heel of your hand. Fold the top edge of the dough over the seam, to about 1 inch from the bottom. Seal the seam in the same manner as before. Fold the dough once more so that the top and bottom edges meet. Seal the seam as before. Tuck in each end and press firmly to get a clean seal.

Turn the dough seam side up. Place one hand on top of the other, palms down, in the center of the dough and start rolling the dough into a cylinder shape. As the dough begins to stretch, uncross your hands and continue rolling with light, even pressure, moving your hands slowly all the way to the ends of the *bâtard*. (It may be necessary to repeat this motion, starting in the center, hand over hand, to get the proper *bâtard* shape.) Do not taper the ends as you would with a baguette; leave them rounded. Use as little flour as possible to prevent sticking. If there is not enough friction between the dough and the work surface, spritz the work surface lightly with water from a spray bottle.

When the *bâtard* is long enough to fit the baguette pan, board, or baking sheet (and not longer than the depth of your oven), cup your hands around the ends of the dough to make sure they're smooth and reseal if necessary. Make sure the dough is the same thickness throughout its length.

If you are using a baguette pan, lightly dust the pan with flour and invert each *bâtard*, seam side down, onto the pan.

If you are using a cloth-covered board or baking sheet, place one *bâtard*, seam side up, on the proofing surface. Pinch the cloth into a deep pleat alongside the *bâtard*. (This will separate the *bâtards*, help them hold their shape, and prevent them from sticking together as they proof.) Place the second *bâtard* alongside the pleat, then pleat the cloth on the exposed side of the *bâtard*.

Dust the tops of the *bâtards* lightly with flour. Cover them with a cloth, slide the pan into a plastic trash can liner, and close the bag securely. Place the *bâtards* in the refrigerator and let them proof 12 to 24 hours.

THIRD DAY

HAVE READY:
Long-stemmed, instant-read cooking thermometer
Baker's peel, optional
Single-edged razor blade
Spray bottle, filled with water
Cooling rack

Shaped bâtard *dough*
Unbleached white bread flour for dusting

Take the shaped *bâtards* out of the refrigerator and remove the plastic bag. Keep the *bâtards* covered with the proofing cloth and set them out at room temperature to continue proofing until they reach an internal temperature of 62 degrees F, 2 to 2½ hours.

Preheat the oven to 500 degrees F 1 hour before baking.

Remove the cloth when the dough is the proper temperature and lightly dust the *bâtards* with flour.

If the *bâtards* proofed on a board or baking sheet, place a lightly floured baker's peel on the work surface. Carefully lift the ends and flip one *bâtard* at a time, spaced well apart, seam side down, onto the peel.

Make sure the *bâtards* are parallel to the edge of the work surface. Hold a single-edged razor blade at a 45-degree angle and, beginning about ½ inch from the end of the *bâtard*, just to the left of center, make a straight cut about

5 inches long and $\frac{1}{2}$ inch deep. The next cut should begin about $\frac{1}{4}$ inch below the center of the first cut and as close to the center of the *bâtard* as possible. The last cut should end just to the right of the center, $\frac{1}{2}$ inch from the end. The cuts should be not curved but straight and parallel to one another. All the cuts should be the same length. *Note:* If you hold the razor at the correct angle, the flaps you've cut should be very thin. If you are using a baguette pan, simply make the cuts directly on the *bâtards* without removing them from the pan.

Open the oven door, spritz the oven heavily with water from a spray bottle, and quickly close the door. Open the oven door again, slide the *bâtards* onto the baking tiles, spritz the oven heavily with water, and quickly close the door.

Reduce the oven temperature to 450 degrees F. Spritz the oven three more times during the next 5 minutes. Refrain from opening the oven door for the next 20 minutes.

After 20 minutes, check the *bâtards* and rotate them if necessary to ensure even baking. Continue baking until the *bâtards* are medium golden brown, about 15 more minutes, for a total of 40 minutes.

Remove the *bâtards* to a cooling rack. They should have a golden brown crust with plenty of fermentation bubbles and a porous interior.

PAIN DE MIE

MAKES TWO APPROXIMATELY 2-POUND SANDWICH LOAVES.

I have to say in all honesty that, besides my rolls, *Pain de Mie* is the only bread I make that my kids actually like. It looks more like a "normal" loaf of bread. It's in this chapter because it's a white bread, but it's the only bread in this book made without a sourdough starter. It's ideal for sandwiches, for spreading with jam, and especially for French toast. Most of all, I think it's the perfect bread for a radish and butter sandwich.

The name means "bread of the *mie*," which is how the French refer to the crumb or interior of a loaf of bread. The opposite of a baguette, which is all crust, this bread is all interior. The effect comes in part from baking the loaf in a lidded pullman pan, a confining, straight-edged pan that forms a perfectly rectangular loaf with a much tighter crumb than loaves baked free form. You can also bake this bread in a more traditional loaf pan, or in a pullman pan without the lid; those loaves will have a slightly more open interior and a crisper crust.

ONE-DAY BREAD

HAVE READY:
Mixing bowl
Mixer with attachable dough hook, optional
Long-stemmed, instant-read cooking thermometer
Plastic wrap
Dough cutter
Proofing cloth
Two (3½ × 12-inch, 10-cup-capacity) lidded pullman pans
Pastry brush
Cooling rack

1 pound 12 ounces (about 3½ cups) lukewarm water, 80 degrees F
2½ cakes (1.5 ounces) or 5 teaspoons packed fresh yeast
3 pounds (about 12 cups) unbleached white bread flour, plus extra for dusting
1 tablespoon milk powder

2½ tablespoons sugar
1 tablespoon sea salt
1 ounce (2 tablespoons) unsalted butter, room temperature
Vegetable oil
2 tablespoons melted butter

Place water, yeast, flour, milk powder, and sugar in the bowl of a mixer fitted with a dough hook. Mix on low speed just until the ingredients are incorporated, a few seconds. (The dough may also may be mixed by hand; see basic instructions on page 42.) Mix on medium speed for 2 minutes. The dough should come together and clean the sides of the bowl. With the mixer still running, add salt and softened butter and continue mixing until the dough is smooth and elastic and reaches an internal temperature of 78 degrees F, about 10 minutes.

Remove the dough from the mixing bowl, place it on a lightly floured work surface, and knead it for a few minutes by hand.

Clean the mixing bowl and lightly coat it with vegetable oil. Return the dough to the oiled bowl, cover it tightly with plastic wrap, and let it ferment at room temperature until it doubles in volume, 45 to 60 minutes.

Uncover the dough and turn it out onto a lightly floured work surface. Using a dough cutter, cut the dough into two equal pieces. Slap each piece against the work surface a few times to deflate. Tuck under the edges of each piece, cover them with a proofing cloth, and let them rest for 15 minutes.

Brush each pan and the underside of the lid with melted butter and set aside.

Uncover one piece of dough. Flatten it into a 4-by-12-inch square by placing one hand over the other, palms down, in the center of the dough and patting the dough to an even thickness (begin in the center and work outward). With the longer edges parallel to the edge of the work surface, fold the top edge of the dough in half and seal the seam with the heel of your hand. Fold the top edge over to meet the bottom edge and seal. Tuck in the ends and seal them. Place one hand on top of the other, palms down, in the center of the dough and begin rolling it into a cylinder the length of your pans. As the dough begins to stretch, uncross your hands and continue rolling with light, even pressure, moving your hands to the ends of the cylinder. Do not taper the ends. Shape the second loaf in the same manner.

Place the loaves, seam side down, in the prepared pans. With one hand formed into a fist, knock down the dough with the flat side of your knuckles, from end to end so that it spreads evenly and covers the surface of the pan. Slide the lid onto the pan to within 1 inch of the end, to allow you to see how high the dough has risen.

Let the dough proof at room temperature until it almost touches the tops of the pans, about 1½ hours. Slide the lids closed. When the dough just begins to poke out of the pans, about 20 minutes more, you are ready to bake. (If the 20 minutes have passed and the dough has not poked through, carefully slide the lid back to make sure the dough is sticking to the top of the pan before you bake.)

Preheat the oven to 500 degrees F 1 hour before baking. Place one oven rack on the bottom rung and remove all the others.

Open the oven door, place both pans, lids closed, on the rack, spaced well apart, and close the door. (It's not necessary to steam the oven if you are using lidded pans.)

Reduce the oven temperature to 475 degrees F and let the bread bake for 50 minutes. Rotate the pans after 20 minutes if your oven doesn't heat evenly.

After 50 minutes, remove one pan from the oven. Some dough may have seeped out the ends and corners of the pan during baking. Break off and discard these pieces.

Slide the lid off the pan and immediately turn out the loaf by knocking the side of the pan on a countertop to loosen. (If necessary, slide a knife around the inside edge to help release it.) The loaf should be light brown, the edges should be perfectly squared, and the sides should feel firm to the touch, otherwise they will cave in as they cool. If it is not quite done, return the loaf to the pan and continue baking for another 5 minutes or so. Repeat this test with the second loaf. If they are done, place the loaves on a cooling rack.

WHITE SANDWICH BREAD

To make a more traditional sandwich loaf with a rounded top crust, prepare the *Pain de Mie* as directed, but instead of baking it in a lidded pullman pan, use a regular loaf pan (or a pullman pan without the lid) and steam the oven as you would for the Country White and most other breads in this book. The bread will rise above the top of the pan and form a browned, rounded top. Because the top crust is exposed directly to the heat, the bread will need about 5 minutes *less* baking time.

Cleaning Up

I don't want to sound too much like your mom here, but in cooking—and especially in baking—it's easier to clean up after yourself as you go. One tip: Rinse first with cold water, then switch to warm. Why? Warm water melts the dough and makes it sticky and hard to clean off. Also, avoid using plastic scour pads—once dough gets caught in the holes, and it will, the pads will never come clean again.

DECORATED BREAD

MAKES ONE 4-POUND OR TWO 2-POUND LOAVES.

Some breads are meant to be seen, not eaten. These are the huge center-piece loaves decorated with clusters of grapes, wheat stalks, or autumn leaves placed proudly on holiday tables or in the display windows of boutique bakeries. They're almost too beautiful to eat. And they last for months.

Bread can be decorated with almost anything—pasta, beans, colored hard-boiled eggs. But even though decorated breads aren't likely to be eaten, I think it's important to stick to toppings that are edible. The most common decoration is, of course, dough. Some bakers simply use leftover dough; many use a dough specially designed for decorating. In French, this dough is called *pâte morte*, or "dead dough," because it contains no yeast.

This recipe is for a classic *pâte morte* and includes instructions for making grape clusters, grape leaves, and wheat stalks. Since the dough contains no leavening, it's ideal for decorating. This is one dough you don't want to rise; if it did, the shapes would distort during baking—you'd end up with a lot of funny-looking grapes. If you do use leavened dough, bake the bread before the decorating dough has a chance to proof so it will maintain the shape you give it.

Except for last-minute touches—grape tendrils, for instance—it's important that the decorations be shaped well ahead of the time you plan to bake the base loaf. Keep in mind that it will probably take about 30 minutes to make the decorations. Start working at least 2 hours before the base dough is fully proofed and use as little flour during shaping as possible. The decorations may also be shaped days ahead of time and frozen; this is a good idea if you want to be sure the decorations are ready as soon as the base loaf is proofed. Once the loaf is proofed and ready to put in the oven, you can quickly place the frozen decorations and bake the bread.

Timing is important. If the base dough is underproofed, there will be too much oven spring and the decorations will pop off all over the place during baking. If it's overproofed, the base loaf will be too soft, and the decorations will sink into the dough.

Consider the size of the bread you will be decorating and the surface area to be covered when you decide on the scale of the decorations.

Traditionally, base loaves for decorated breads are 4 pounds, but you

*D*ECORATED BREADS:
"SOME BREADS ARE MEANT TO BE SEEN, NOT EATEN.
THEY'RE ALMOST TOO BEAUTIFUL TO EAT."

can decorate a 2-pound loaf or even a 6-pound loaf, which is beautiful. I think the Rosemary–Olive Oil Bread works best as a base dough; it has less oven spring than other breads because of the olive oil. If you want a more plain-tasting dough, omit the rosemary.

Note: If you plan to use the decorations the same day, always keep them covered, and on a hot day keep them refrigerated.

HAVE READY:
Proofing cloth
Long-stemmed instant-read thermometer
Mixing bowl
Mixer with paddle attachment
Plastic wrap
4-inch scissors
1 piece of paper or cardboard

Dough cutter
Paring knife
Pastry brush
Baker's peel
Cooling rack

Shaped and proofed dough for one 4-pound base loaf or two 2-pound loaves, such as Country White or
   Rosemary—Olive Oil
14 ounces (about 3½ cups) unbleached white bread flour, plus extra for dusting
1 teaspoon sea salt
1½ ounces (3½ tablespoons) unsalted butter, softened
1 cup cold water, 60 degrees F, plus extra as needed

Remove base dough from the refrigerator, take off the plastic wrap, and cover with a cloth. Let the dough continue proofing at room temperature until it reaches an internal temperature of 58 to 60 degrees F, about 2 hours.

Preheat the oven to 500 degrees F 1 hour before baking.

Place flour, salt, and butter in the bowl of a mixer fitted with a paddle attachment. Mix on medium-low speed until the mixture has a fine, crumbled texture. Reduce the mixing speed to low and, with the mixer running, slowly add 1 cup cold water. Mix until the dough comes together. (The dough may also be mixed by hand; see basic instructions on page 42.) It should be soft. Add 1 to 2 more tablespoons water, if necessary.

Mix on high speed for 5 minutes. Remove the dough from the mixing bowl, wrap it tightly in plastic wrap, and let it relax at room temperature for 1 hour. (If it's an extremely hot day, let it relax in the refrigerator for 1 hour.) The dough may also be refrigerated for 2 to 3 days or frozen to be used another time. (If it has been frozen, let the dough thaw before rolling it out.)

Use the dough to make one or all of the following shapes. Consider the size of the base loaf or loaves as you plan and try to visualize or sketch the final look before you begin shaping.

GRAPE LEAF

To make the grape leaf, cut a paper or cardboard template in the shape you desire. Remember to keep the size of the boule in mind. The leaf should be at least twice and up to three times the size of the grape cluster.

Cut a 1½-ounce piece of dough with a dough cutter and roll it out to be about ⅛ inch thick. Keep remaining dough covered as you work. Put the template over the dough and cut around the form with a paring knife. With the tip of the knife, score the leaf to simulate leaf veins. Set aside.

GRAPE CLUSTER

To make a grape cluster that is ideal for a 2-pound boule, use a dough cutter to cut off a 1-ounce portion of dough, about the size of a plum. Cover the remaining dough with a proofing cloth. Using as little flour as possible, flatten the 1-ounce portion with the heel of your hand into a rough triangle (with rounded points), about ¼ inch thick and 3 inches long. Brush the triangle lightly with water (if it dries out as the grapes are formed, brush the triangle again).

Keeping most of the remaining dough covered, break off a tiny bit, about the size of a fat raisin, to make a grape. Work the dough bit around the tip of your thumb, smoothing and rounding as you go. Pull your thumb out, pinch the ends together, then twist and pinch off one end. Repeat about fifty times for fifty grapes, placing the grapes on the triangle as each is shaped, using the pattern described in the following paragraph. This may seem like a tedious shaping method, but if you instead roll the dough with the palm of your hand against the work surface, the balls won't be smooth and they'll crack open during baking. Besides, the process goes very quickly.

With one point of the triangle facing you, lay the grapes in rows touching each other, starting at the wide end of the triangle and working toward the point. Add a second layer with the grapes placed randomly to form a realistic-looking bunch. Place a few other grapes on the bunch wherever you think they belong to make a good-looking cluster. Brush with water as necessary to help the grapes adhere. Set aside.

Remove the cloth from the base loaf (or loaves) and lightly dust the boule with flour. Carefully run your hand around the boule to loosen it and gently invert it onto a heavily floured baker's peel.

Brush the underside of the reserved leaf with water and place it on the boule, slightly off center. Then brush the bottom of the grape cluster and place it off center over the leaf so that it is partially on the dough and partially on the leaf. If you like, sprinkle a few pinches of flour over the grapes; this gives a nice look once the loaf is baked.

WHEAT STALKS

To make wheat stalks, pinch off one piece of dough at a time and fold and roll each as if you were shaping an Olive-Onion Bread Stick (see page 103).

Be sure to vary the lengths of the stalks, between 4 and 8 inches long and ¼ inch round. A good combination is two 8-inch, four 6-inch, and three 4-inch stalks.

With sharp scissors, nip the top of the entire stalk. Do this by placing the scissors horizontally and as close to the dough as possible, then snip the surface. Be careful not to cut all the way through the dough. Each successive cut should begin halfway into the *V* created by the first cut. Flip the stalk on one side and repeat the snipping process.

Choose a spot on the boule for the wheat stalks and brush it with water. Carefully place the stalks on the boule (these are the most fragile of all the shapes described here), overlapping at irregular angles.

GRAPE TENDRILS

To make a few grape tendrils, pinch off a little dough and roll it out with your fingers until it is half the diameter of a pencil (with the dough this thin, there is no need to fold it before rolling). Curl this piece into a coil and place it randomly on the grape leaf. Repeat with as many tendrils as you like.

BAKING

When all the decorations are in place, open the oven door, spritz the oven heavily with water from a spray bottle, and quickly close the door. Open the door again, slide the boule onto the baking tiles, and quickly close the door. Repeat process if baking more than one loaf.

Reduce the oven temperature to 400 degrees F. Spritz the oven with water one more time. Do not spritz more than a total of two times: You don't need as much oven spring as usual for these loaves because you don't want the bread to expand and cause the decorations to fall off. Refrain from opening the oven door for the next 30 minutes.

After 30 minutes, check the bread and rotate if necessary to ensure even baking. Cover the decorations with foil if they're browning too quickly. Continue baking for 15 to 25 more minutes, for a total of 45 minutes, if you plan to eat the bread, 50 to 55 minutes if the bread is intended for decoration only. Add 30 to 35 minutes baking time if you are making one 4-pound loaf instead of two 2-pound loaves. The bread needs to be completely baked; if it's not, it may shrink as it cools, causing the decorations to fall off.

Remove the bread to a cooling rack. The loaves should be well browned, and the decorations should be raised above the surface.

BREADS
MADE
with
WHOLE-
WHEAT
STARTER

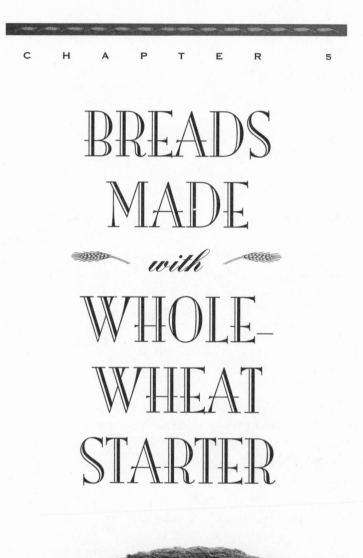

ALL STARTERS ARE NOT ALIKE. A simple change in flour—white to whole wheat, for instance—transforms a hearty, frothy mixture into a thinner, more sour liquid that is more perishable. It is more perishable because the wheat germ (which is high in natural oils) left in the flour from the whole kernel can turn rancid if the starter isn't maintained properly.

Instead of making a whole-wheat starter from scratch, I begin the process with a fully developed white starter—called the *mother* because it gives birth to new generations—then feed it whole-wheat flour. This saves two weeks. Besides, I never had any luck raising a whole-wheat starter using whole-wheat flour—it went rancid before it had a chance to become a working culture. If you think you will bake only whole-wheat bread—and you will bake it frequently—you should maintain this starter every day. My preference is to match a starter with a bread: whole-wheat starter for whole-wheat. But you can always make a whole-wheat bread with White Starter and add a small amount of extra whole wheat to your dough. (Don't use rye starters for this, however.)

If you think you'll only make whole-wheat bread occasionally, plan on starting the three-day process of building up a whole-wheat starter each time you want to bake. Unlike White Starter, which can stay dormant in the refrigerator for up to several months, a whole-wheat starter should be kept dormant no longer than two weeks. After that, it will probably spoil.

Don't be alarmed when your starter separates between feedings; this is natural with a liquid starter, especially with coarse-ground whole wheat—the flour doesn't incorporate the same way as it does in a white starter.

*R*YE STARTER (ABOVE) AND WHOLE-WHEAT STARTER (BELOW)

Whole-Wheat Starter

Three-Day Build–First Day

First Feeding

HAVE READY:

One 2-quart plastic, ceramic, or glass container with optional lid
Rubber spatula, optional
Plastic wrap, optional

9 ounces (about 1 cup) White Starter
4 ounces (about ½ cup) lukewarm water, 78 degrees F
1½ ounces (about ¼ cup) whole-wheat flour

Pour White Starter into the container. Stir in water and flour, using your hands or a rubber spatula. Cover the container with a sealable but not airtight lid or with plastic wrap secured tightly around the rim and leave the starter at room temperature for 4 hours or up to 6 hours.

Second Feeding

Starter
6 ounces (about ¾ cup) lukewarm water, 78 degrees F
3 ounces (about ½ cup) whole-wheat flour

Uncover the starter. Stir in water and flour. Cover the container and leave the starter at room temperature for 4 to 6 hours.

Third Feeding

Starter
12 ounces (about 1½ cups) lukewarm water, 78 degrees F
6 ounces (about 1 cup) whole-wheat flour

Uncover the starter. Stir in water and flour. Be sure to incorporate all the flour and scrape the sides of the container clean as you stir. Cover the container and leave the starter at room temperature for 8 to 12 hours, no more than 15 hours.

Second and Third Days

First Feeding

Starter
4 ounces (about ½ cup) lukewarm water, 78 degrees F
1½ ounces (about ¼ cup) whole-wheat flour

Uncover the starter. Measure out 1 cup. Discard or give away the remainder. Place the measured cup of starter back in the container. Stir in water and flour. Cover the container and leave the starter at room temperature for 4 hours or up to 6 hours.

Second Feeding

Starter
6 ounces (about ¾ cup) lukewarm water, 78 degrees F
3 ounces (about ½ cup) whole-wheat flour

Uncover the starter. Stir in water and flour. Cover the container and leave the starter at room temperature for 4 to 6 hours.

Third Feeding

Starter
12 ounces (1½ cups) lukewarm water, 78 degrees F
6 ounces (about 1 cup) whole-wheat flour

Uncover the starter. Stir in water and flour. Cover the container and leave the starter at room temperature for 8 to 12 hours, no more than 15 hours.

Repeat this feeding schedule on the third day. After three days the starter should be ready to be used in a bread recipe. You may choose to follow the flour-saving instructions for White Starter on page 37.

You may place the covered starter container in the refrigerator for up to 7 days. To reactivate, bring the starter to room temperature and give it three daily feedings for 2 days before baking.

Note: I have found that this starter tends to thin down over time. Trust your instincts and give your starter a few extra tablespoons of flour every once in a while for an energizing snack.

WHOLE-WHEAT BOULE

MAKES TWO APPROXIMATELY 2-POUND BOULES.

It surprises nonbakers that my whole-wheat breads are made with a portion of white bread flour. But as I mentioned in the "Whole-Wheat Flour" section of Chapter I (page 7), 100 percent whole-wheat bread is extremely dense. The trick in making whole-wheat bread is getting the right balance of white and whole-wheat flours. Some people add so much white flour that they might as well be making white bread.

This Whole-Wheat Boule is a nice compromise. It has a lot of volume, but there's plenty of whole-wheat flavor.

If you want an even more substantial loaf, experiment by gradually increasing the proportion of whole-wheat to white flour. It's important that you do this in small increments so you don't get a superdense loaf the first time you improvise.

I use a very coarsely ground whole-wheat flour plus additional bran, giving the loaf a good crunchy texture. You can use a fine-ground whole-wheat flour, but know that your bread may turn out extremely light in color, almost white.

TWO-DAY BREAD—FIRST DAY

HAVE READY:
Mixing bowl
Mixer with attachable dough hook, optional
Proofing cloth
Long-stemmed, instant-read cooking thermometer
Rubber spatula, optional
Plastic wrap
Dough cutter
2 cloth-lined proofing baskets, lightly dusted with flour

1 pound (about 2 cups) cool water, 70 degrees F
1 pound 1 ounce (about 1¾ cups) Whole-Wheat Starter
1 tablespoon barley malt syrup

1 pound 11 ounces (about 5⅔ cups) unbleached high-gluten flour or unbleached white bread flour, plus extra
 for dusting
6 ounces (about 1½ cups) coarse-ground whole-wheat flour
4 tablespoons wheat bran
1 tablespoon sea salt
Vegetable oil

Place water, Whole-Wheat Starter, malt syrup, flours, and wheat bran in the bowl of a mixer fitted with a dough hook. Mix on low speed for 4 minutes. The dough should be wet and slightly sticky. (The dough may also by mixed by hand; see basic instructions on page 42.) Cover the dough with a proofing cloth and allow it to rest in the mixing bowl for 20 minutes.

Add salt and mix on medium speed until the dough reaches an internal temperature of 76 degrees F, about 6 minutes, scraping the dough down the sides of the bowl as necessary with a rubber spatula.

Remove the dough from the mixing bowl and place it on a lightly floured work surface. It should feel soft and resilient. Knead the dough a few times by hand.

Clean the mixing bowl and lightly coat it with vegetable oil. Return the dough to the oiled bowl, cover it tightly with plastic wrap, and let it ferment at room temperature until it doubles in volume, 3 to 4 hours.

Uncover the dough and turn it out onto a lightly floured work surface. Using a dough cutter, cut it into two equal pieces. Slap each piece against the work surface a few times to deflate. Tuck under the edges of each piece, cover them with a cloth, and let the dough rest for 15 minutes.

Uncover the dough and round each piece into a boule, according to the directions on page 48. Place the boules, smooth side down, into floured proofing baskets and sprinkle the surface of the dough with white bread flour. Wrap each basket tightly in plastic wrap and let the dough proof in the refrigerator for 8 to 12 hours.

SECOND DAY

HAVE READY:
Proofing cloth
Long-stemmed, instant-read cooking thermometer
Baker's peel

2 ounces (about ¾ cup) wheat bran
1 teaspoon sea salt

  Make a sponge by placing water, Whole-Wheat Starter, milk, flours, bran, and salt in a mixing bowl and stirring with your hands or a rubber spatula. Cover the bowl tightly with plastic wrap and leave it at room temperature until bubbles begin to break on the surface, about 3 to 4 hours. Check the sponge, resecure the plastic wrap, and place the bowl in the refrigerator for 8 to 12 hours.

SECOND DAY

HAVE READY:
1 or 2 saucepans
Baking sheet
Mixing bowl
Mixer with attachable dough hook
Rubber spatula
Long stemmed, instant-read cooking thermometer
Pastry brush
Two 3½ × 12-inch, 10-cup-capacity loaf pans
Dough cutter
Proofing cloth
Spray bottle, filled with water
Plastic wrap
Cooling rack

4½ cups tap water, in all
2 ounces (about ¾ cup) wheat berries
7 ounces (about 1½ cups) raw sunflower seeds
Sponge
½ pound (about 1 cup) cool water, 70 degrees F
4 cakes (2.4 ounces total) or 8 teaspoons packed fresh yeast
¼ cup honey
9½ ounces (about 1½ cups) whole-wheat flour
9½ ounces (about 2 cups) unbleached high-gluten flour or unbleached white bread flour, plus a little extra for dusting

2 teaspoons sea salt
1 ounce (½ tablespoon) unsalted butter, room temperature
1½ ounces (about ½ cup) cracked wheat
1½ ounces (about ¼ cup) poppy seeds, plus 2 tablespoons for sprinkling
Vegetable oil
2 tablespoons melted butter

Place 3 cups of water in a saucepan, add wheat berries, and cook until completely tender, about 45 minutes. Add more water if necessary. Drain, rinse to cool, and drain thoroughly again. Bring 1½ cups water to a boil. Place cracked wheat in a bowl and moisten with boiling water. Let stand 1 to 2 minutes. Drain, rinse to cool, and drain thoroughly again.

Preheat the oven to 350 degrees F. Spread the sunflower seeds in an even layer on a baking sheet and bake them until they are lightly toasted, about 15 minutes. Set them aside to cool.

Remove the sponge from the refrigerator and take off the plastic wrap. Place ½ pound (1 cup) water, yeast, sponge, honey, and flours in the bowl of a mixer fitted with a dough hook. Mix on low speed for 2 minutes, scraping the dough down the sides of the bowl as necessary with a rubber spatula.

Add salt and softened butter and mix on medium speed until the dough reaches an internal temperature of 75 degrees F, about 8 minutes. The dough should be wet and sticky. Add wheat berries, cracked wheat, sunflower seeds, and poppy seeds and mix on low speed just until incorporated, about 2 minutes.

Remove the dough from the mixing bowl, place it on a lightly floured work surface, and knead it for a few minutes by hand.

Clean the mixing bowl and lightly coat it with vegetable oil. Return the dough to the oiled bowl, cover it tightly with plastic wrap, and let it ferment at room temperature until it doubles in volume, about 1½ hours.

Using a pastry brush, brush the loaf pans with melted butter.

Turn the dough out onto a lightly floured surface. Slap it against the work surface a few times to deflate. Using a dough cutter, cut the dough into forty-two 1-ounce pieces. As you cut, tuck under the edges of each roll. Cover the rolls with a cloth and let the dough rest for 15 minutes.

Preheat the oven to 450 degrees F 1 hour before baking. Place one oven rack on the bottom rung and remove all the others.

Working with one piece of dough at a time, keeping the remainder covered, shape by cupping your hand lightly around the ball and rounding it

2½ ounces (about ¼ cup) Whole-Wheat Starter
13½ ounces (about 3 cups) unbleached white bread flour, plus extra for dusting
2 tablespoons whole-wheat flour
1 tablespoon polenta or cornmeal
1 tablespoon wheat bran
1½ teaspoons sea salt
2 medium (8-ounce) sweet red bell peppers, cut into 1-inch chunks
6 green onions, including 2 inches of the dark green, cut into ¼-inch slices
Dark rye or white rye or rice flour for dusting
Vegetable oil

Place water, yeast, Whole-Wheat Starter, flours, polenta, and bran in the bowl of a mixer fitted with a dough hook. Mix on low speed for 2 minutes, scraping the dough down the sides of the bowl with a rubber spatula as necessary.

Add salt and mix on medium speed until the dough reaches an internal temperature of 75 degrees F, about 8 minutes. Add the red peppers and green onions and mix on low speed for 2 more minutes, until the vegetables are almost incorporated. The dough should be soft, wet, and sticky.

Remove the dough from the mixing bowl, place it on a work surface lightly dusted with bread flour, and knead it by hand for a few minutes, making sure the vegetables are thoroughly incorporated.

Clean the mixing bowl and lightly coat it with vegetable oil. Return the dough to the oiled bowl, cover it tightly with plastic wrap, and refrigerate it for 12 to 24 hours.

SECOND DAY

HAVE READY:
Proofing cloth
Long-stemmed, instant-read cooking thermometer
Dough cutter
Rolling pin
Baker's peel
Spray bottle, filled with water
Cooling rack

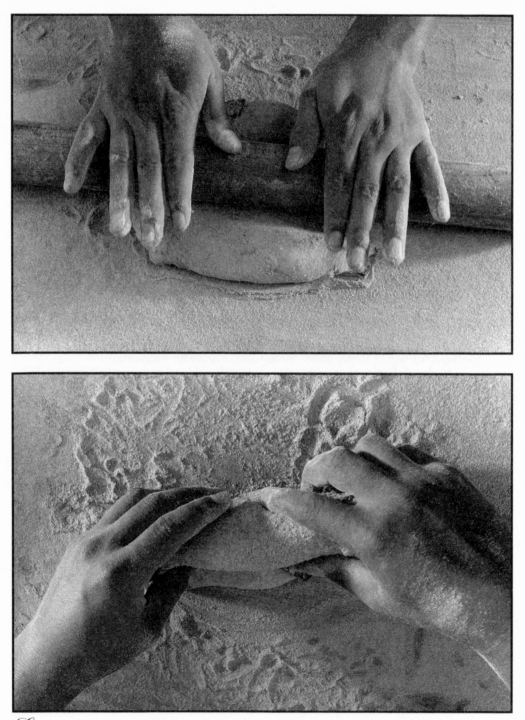

*S*HAPING THE RED PEPPER–SCALLION BREAD:
"THE KIND OF BREAD THAT MAKES A NICE, SIMPLE MEAL,
MAYBE A SLICE OR TWO WITH CHEESE AND A NOT-TOO-FANCY GREEN SALAD."

RYE FLOUR IS TRICKY TO WORK WITH, and rye starter is the trickiest of all the starters in this book to make. There's poor gluten in rye flour, which makes starter and doughs made from it less elastic—and stickier—than ones made from other flours. Then I make things even more difficult by using dark rye flour instead of white rye—dark rye flour contains all of the bran from the kernel and if incorrectly made will produce a very dense loaf. But I can't help it—I like the more rustic characteristics of the bread you get when you use dark rye. Remember, it's very important not to let rye doughs overproof. The weak gluten from the flour makes for a very unforgiving dough. Rye breads can be made with white starter and rye flour just in the dough, a short-cut used by many bakers to avoid maintaining several starters—but they don't have depth of flavor for me.

Still, I did make one compromise in this starter. Instead of building the starter from scratch with rye flour, I began with a white mother starter, as I did with my Whole-Wheat Starter. I put the starter on a three-times-a-day feeding schedule, with dark rye flour and water as the meal. The starter needs to be on this regimen for at least three full days before it's made the transition from a white starter to a rye starter and is ready to be used in baking.

If you're not going to make rye bread on a regular basis, it's best to build a new rye starter every time you want to bake bread. Why feed a starter three times a day if you're going to use it only twice a year? And unlike white starter, which is easy to maintain in both active and dormant states, you shouldn't keep a rye starter dormant in the refrigerator for more than a week. The reason: Rye ferments much faster than any other flour, so a starter made with it will get way too sour if it's left unused for too long.

All that said, a rye starter is definitely the most fun to watch. Its fast fermentation means it bubbles and seethes much more than a white starter. It's more of a paste than a liquid starter—it looks almost like a mud slide. You can actually see the difference each feeding makes, and that the recommended 4 hours between meals is not arbitrary. Watch the starter as it nears its fourth hour without food. It will crack on top when it's ready to be fed, then dome over and collapse on itself if it's not fed on time. Ideally, you want to feed it before the dome falls.

Note: If the starter becomes too difficult to mix when you feed it, add a little more water. The consistency should be pasty and thick, but not impossible to stir. You need to be able to incorporate the flour.

NORMANDY RYE

MAKES TWO APPROXIMATELY 1-POUND-12-OUNCE OVALS.

Most rye breads are best suited to sandwiches. But Normandy Rye works as well with oysters as it does with pastrami.

I call it Normandy Rye because it's common to find fermented apple cider in many of the breads that come from Normandy. I love the contrast between the strong flavor of the sour from the rye and the sweetness from the cider.

Consider yourself lucky if you are one of the two people who get to eat one of the heels of the bread—the crust is the best part of the Normandy Rye. The sugar from the cider causes the crust to become caramelized (almost black), and the concentration of flavor in the crust is more pronounced in this bread than in any other that I make.

Note: Fermented apple cider is available at most wine shops.

TWO-DAY BREAD—FIRST DAY

HAVE READY:
Mixing bowl
Rubber spatula, optional
Plastic wrap

½ pound (about 1 cup) cool water, 70 degrees F
1 tablespoon barley malt syrup
13½ ounces (1½ cups) Rye Starter
3 ounces (about ¾ cup) unbleached high-gluten flour or unbleached white bread flour
3 ounces (about 1 cup) dark rye flour

Make a sponge by placing water, malt syrup, Rye Starter, and flours in a mixing bowl and stirring with your hands or a rubber spatula. Cover the bowl tightly with plastic wrap and leave the sponge at room temperature for 24 hours. If you're making this bread on a day when it is hotter than 80 degrees F, leave the sponge at room temperature for 8 to 12 hours and then refrigerate for the remaining time.

SECOND DAY

HAVE READY:
Mixing bowl
Mixer with attachable dough hook
Proofing cloth
Long-stemmed, instant-read cooking thermometer
Rubber spatula
Plastic wrap
Dough cutter
Two 2-pound-capacity unlined oval or round proofing baskets
Baker's peel
Single-edged razor blade
Spray bottle, filled with water
Cooling rack

Sponge
½ pound (about 1 cup) cool water, 70 degrees F
8 ounces (about 1 cup) fermented apple cider (alcohol content 5.8 percent)
1 pound 13 ounces (about 7¼ cups) high-gluten flour, plus extra for dusting
1 ounce (⅓ cup) dark rye flour
1 tablespoon sea salt
Vegetable oil

Uncover the sponge. It should look soft and expanded, with a pebbly surface.

Place water, cider, the sponge, and flours in the bowl of a mixer fitted with a dough hook. Mix on low speed for 2 minutes. Cover the dough with a proofing cloth and let the dough rest in the bowl for 20 minutes.

Add salt and continue mixing on medium-low speed until the dough reaches an internal temperature of 78 degrees F, about 8 minutes, scraping the dough down the sides of the bowl as necessary with a rubber spatula. The dough should be soft and a bit sticky.

Remove the dough from the mixing bowl, place it on a lightly floured work surface, and knead it for a few minutes by hand.

Clean the mixing bowl and lightly coat it with vegetable oil. Return the dough to the oiled bowl, cover it with plastic wrap, and let it ferment at room temperature until it nearly doubles in volume, approximately 2 hours.

Turn the dough out onto a lightly floured work surface and with a dough cutter cut it into two equal pieces. Slap each piece against the work surface a few times to deflate. Tuck under the edges of each piece, cover them with a cloth, and let the dough rest for 15 minutes.

Preheat the oven to 500 degrees F 1 hour before baking.

Uncover the dough and round each piece into a boule according to the directions on page 48. Elongate each boule into an oval by placing one hand on top of the other, palms down, in the center of the dough and simultaneously rolling and molding the dough into an oval shape that will just fit inside a proofing basket.

Place each loaf, smooth side down, in a floured proofing basket. Sprin-

NORMANDY RYE, READY TO GO INTO THE OVEN:
"CONSIDER YOURSELF LUCKY IF YOU ARE ONE OF THE TWO PEOPLE WHO GET TO EAT ONE OF THE HEELS OF THE BREAD."

kle the surface of the dough with flour, cover with a cloth, and let the dough proof at room temperature until it shows some signs of movement and reaches an internal temperature of 72 degrees F, approximately 1 to 2 hours. Check the surface of the dough carefully during the last half hour of proofing. Either when the surface just begins to crack or when a bubble bursts on the dough, the loaves are ready.

Remove the cloth and lightly dust the ovals with flour. Carefully run your hand around one oval to loosen it and gently invert it onto a lightly floured baker's peel. Holding a single-edged razor blade perpendicular to the oval, make a ¼-inch-deep vertical cut down the center of the oval, ¾ inch away from each end. Then make six curved slashes, three on each side of the vertical cut, evenly spaced. Start the cuts on the side of the dough, ¾ inch away from the bottom of the oval (halfway up the sides). End the cuts ¾ inch away from the center vertical slash.

Open the oven door, spritz the oven heavily with water from a spray bottle, and quickly close the door. Open the oven door again, slide the oval onto the baking tiles, and quickly close the door. Cut, spritz, and load the second oval in the same manner.

Reduce the oven temperature to 475 degrees F. Spritz the oven two more times during the next 5 minutes. Refrain from opening the oven door for the next 20 minutes.

After 20 minutes, check the ovals and rotate them if necessary to ensure even baking. If the bread looks too dark, reduce the oven temperature to about 450 degrees F and leave the door ajar. (You're far enough along in the baking at this point that the steam effect won't be ruined.) Continue baking for another 10 minutes, for a total of 35 minutes.

Remove the ovals to a cooling rack. The crust should have a deep brown color, close to black, and should have risen by about a third. The interior should have small, evenly distributed holes and a strong sourdough taste.

Izzy's New York Rye

➤ MAKES TWO APPROXIMATELY 2-POUND LOAVES.

Izzy is Izzy Cohen, a fellow baker who started dropping by when I first opened the bakery. Without him, I doubt I would have ever considered making a Jewish-style rye bread. I figured there were enough bakeries in Los Angeles where you could get a fine-enough Jewish rye bread. But Izzy kept nagging, and we finally decided to work on it together.

We disagreed a fair bit in the beginning. I wanted to make what I thought of as a New York–style rye or corn rye. We agreed that a corn rye called for those little black seeds called *chernushka* (or *kalonji* at Indian stores or *habbet baraka* at Middle Eastern stores). We agreed that a corn rye bread contains a larger percentage of rye flour than a traditional Jewish rye bread, but then our argument began. I insisted on using ice-cold water (because of the amount of Rye Starter in the recipe, I was afraid that the dough would ferment too quickly). He insisted on hot water. (I won!) I'd always visualized a corn rye darker than the traditional light Jewish rye, so I wanted to make the bread with a dark rye starter and dark rye flour in the dough. He objected, insisting on a white rye starter and white rye flour. We compromised. His version did have more volume and was truer to traditional Jewish ryes; mine was a bit too dense for a pastrami sandwich. But I figured, why simply duplicate the bread you could buy in any good deli? In the end, we were both happy using a dark rye starter and white rye flour in the dough.

Notice that each loaf is brushed with a cornstarch mixture immediately after it comes out of the oven. This is what gives the bread its deli-like sheen.

One-Day Bread

HAVE READY:
Mixing bowl
Mixer with attachable dough hook
Rubber spatula
Long-stemmed, instant-read cooking thermometer
Plastic wrap
Dough cutter

Proofing cloth
2 large, shallow containers (square Pyrex ideal)
Pastry brush
Baker's peel
Spray bottle, filled with water
Small saucepan
Whisk or wooden spoon
Cooling rack

1 pound (about 2 cups) cold water, 40 degrees F
2 cakes (1.2 ounces total) or 4 teaspoons packed fresh yeast
1 pound 4 ounces (about 2 cups) Rye Starter
1 pound 3 ounces (about 5 cups) unbleached high-gluten flour or unbleached white bread flour
13 ounces (about 4 cups) white rye flour, plus extra for dusting
3 tablespoons caraway seeds, plus extra for sprinkling
1½ teaspoons chernushka *seeds, plus extra for sprinkling*
1 tablespoon sea salt
Vegetable oil
4½ ounces (about ¾ cup) polenta or cornmeal plus extra for dusting
2 cups plus 1 teaspoon tap water in all, plus extra for brushing
½ teaspoon cornstarch

Place cold water, yeast, Rye Starter, flours, caraway seeds, and *chernushka* seeds in the bowl of a mixer fitted with a dough hook. Mix on low speed for 3 minutes, scraping the dough down the sides of the bowl as necessary with a rubber spatula. The dough should be wet and sticky.

Add salt and continue mixing on medium speed until the dough reaches an internal temperature of 70 degrees F, about 8 minutes.

Remove the dough from the mixing bowl and place it on a lightly floured work surface.

Clean the bowl and lightly coat it with vegetable oil. Gather the dough into a ball and return it to the oiled bowl, cover it tightly with plastic wrap, and let it ferment at room temperature until it doubles in size, about 1¼ hours.

Turn the dough out onto a well-floured work surface and cut it into two equal pieces with a dough cutter. Slap each piece against the work surface a few times to deflate. Tuck under the edges of each piece, cover them with a cloth, and let the dough rest for 15 minutes.

PUMPERNICKEL BREAD

MAKES TWO APPROXIMATELY 2-POUND BOULES.

It took about two years for me to get this recipe right—maybe that's why it's the bread I'm proudest of perfecting. Sliced superthin and toasted, Pumpernickel Bread is exactly right as a crouton for soups, it's great with oysters, and it's wonderful with smoked fish.

The trick in developing this bread was getting the interior moist but not gummy, the crust crisp but not so rock hard that you can't cut through it, the flavor *strongly* sour, and the color a gorgeous dark brown without adding the coffee, cocoa powder, or caramel coloring that some bakers use.

This dough is probably the stickiest in this book. It's difficult to work with but absolutely worth the trouble. This is one bread that works best if you don't rely on your intuition. Don't let the bread set out proofing any longer than the recipe says. There's so much rye in it that the dough is not strong enough to ferment for very long. Also, you won't see the growth in volume with pumpernickel that you do with other breads. You have to be vigilant to prevent overproofing.

Unlike most of the breads you'll bake from this book, there are no directions for cutting this dough just before it's put in the oven (though you can slash it as you would any other loaf if you like). I prefer to set aside a little of the dough to make a disk, which bakes into a crisp crust. The shape you get is an oversize version of the *Chapeau* Rolls—you're essentially making a big *chapeau*, or hat.

TWO-DAY BREAD—FIRST DAY

HAVE READY:
Large mixing bowl
Rubber spatula, optional
Plastic wrap

1 pound (about 2 cups) cold water, 60 degrees F
18 ounces (about 2 cups) Rye Starter

1 pound 5 ounces (about 5¼ cups) rye chops or flakes
1 teaspoon sea salt

        Make a sponge by placing water, Rye Starter, rye chops, and salt in a mixing bowl and stirring with your hands or a rubber spatula. Cover the bowl tightly with plastic wrap and set the dough out at room temperature for 24 hours.

SECOND DAY

HAVE READY:
Mortar and pestle or spice grinder
Mixing bowl
Mixer with attachable dough hook and optional paddle attachment
Long-stemmed, instant-read cooking thermometer
Plastic wrap
Dough cutter
Proofing cloth
Rolling pin
One 4- or 5-inch-round biscuit cutter
2 unlined (2-pound-capacity) proofing baskets, heavily dusted with flour
Baker's peel
Spray bottle, filled with water
Cooling rack

1 tablespoon caraway seeds
4 ounces (about ½ cup) dark beer
Sponge
1 tablespoon barley malt syrup
2 ounces (about ½ cup) dark rye flour plus extra for dusting
1 pound (about 4 cups) unbleached high-gluten flour or unbleached white bread flour, plus extra for dusting
2 teaspoons sea salt
Vegetable oil

        Grind the caraway seeds to a fine powder using a mortar and pestle or spice grinder.

Place beer, sponge, malt syrup, caraway powder, and flours in the bowl of a mixer fitted with a dough hook. (A paddle attachment may be necessary during the first 2 to 3 minutes of mixing because this dough is so sticky.) Mix on low speed until the ingredients are combined, 2 to 3 minutes.

Add salt and continue mixing on medium speed until the dough reaches an internal temperature of 76 to 78 degrees F, about 8 minutes. (Use the dough hook for this mixing.) The dough will be extremely wet and sticky and will appear almost as if no kneading has been done.

Remove the dough from the mixing bowl and place it on a work surface heavily dusted with white flour.

Clean the mixing bowl and lightly coat it with vegetable oil. Gather the dough into a ball and return the dough to the oiled bowl, cover it tightly with plastic wrap, and let it ferment for exactly 1 hour.

Uncover the dough. It should have risen only slightly and begun to show tiny cracks on the surface.

Turn the dough out onto a heavily floured surface. Using a dough cutter, cut off one 8-ounce piece. Cover this piece with a proofing cloth. Cut the remaining dough into two equal pieces with a dough cutter. Turn under the edges of each piece, cover them with a cloth, and let the dough rest for 15 minutes.

Preheat the oven to 500 degrees F 1 hour before baking.

Heavily flour the work surface. Roll out the 8-ounce piece of dough into a $\frac{1}{4}$-inch-thick sheet large enough to accommodate two 5-inch circles. Cut out two circles with a biscuit cutter and place each on the bottom of a floured proofing basket. Heavily dust the tops of the dough circles with rye flour. These will form the "hats" of the finished loaves. The rye flour will prevent the "hat" and the boule from melding together when the loaf is baked.

Round each remaining piece of dough into a boule, according to the directions on page 48. It may not be easy to shape this dough because of its sticky consistency. Place the boules smooth side down onto each floured circle of dough. Sprinkle the surface of the dough with flour, cover each basket with a cloth, and let the dough proof no more than 50 minutes. The dough will not expand much. Check the surface of the dough carefully during the last 10 minutes of proofing. When the surface just begins to crack or when a bubble bursts on the dough, the boules are ready.

Remove the cloth. Carefully run your hand around one boule to loosen it and gently invert it onto a heavily floured baker's peel.

Open the oven door, spritz the oven heavily with water from a spray bottle, and quickly close the door. Open the oven door again, slide the boule onto the baking tiles, and quickly close the door. Spritz and load the second boule in the same manner.

Reduce the oven temperature to 475 degrees F. Spritz the oven heavily with water two more times during the next 5 minutes. Refrain from opening the oven door for the next 20 minutes.

After 20 minutes, check the boules and rotate them if necessary to ensure even baking. Continue baking for 25 to 30 more minutes, for a total of 50 to 55 minutes. If the bread looks too dark, reduce the oven temperature to about 450 degrees F and leave the door ajar (you're far enough along in the baking at this point that the steam effect won't be ruined).

Remove the boules to a cooling rack. The crust should be extremely dark brown and may have formed cracks just beneath the "hat." Refrain from slicing until the bread is completely cooled—as long as 2 hours. True pumpernickel eaters never eat their bread until it has been out of the oven for a full day, allowing the complex flavors to mingle.

FRUIT-NUT BREAD

MAKES TWO APPROXIMATELY 2-POUND LOAVES.

This is a beautiful bread to look at—somewhere between a bread and a fruitcake. There are so many flavors, so much fruit, yet the essence of the bread still comes across. I use pecans because I think they have a flavor that can stand up to the fruit. Both Rye Starter and White Starter go into this dough, and I mix in rye chops for texture. My favorite way to eat Fruit-Nut Bread is sliced thin and toasted. And it's really delicious with a smear of goat cheese.

Note: The recipe calls for candied orange peel, which is usually available in specialty stores or can easily be made at home by cooking the rind in a sugar syrup.

ONE-DAY BREAD

HAVE READY:
Baking sheet
Mixing bowl
Mixer with attachable dough hook
Rubber spatula
Long-stemmed, instant-read cooking thermometer
Plastic wrap
Dough cutter
Proofing cloth
Two 2-pound-capacity unlined oval proofing baskets, optional
Baker's peel
Single-edged razor blade
Spray bottle, filled with water
Cooling rack

10 ounces (about 2¾ cups) pecan halves
12 ounces (about 1½ cups) cold water, 60 degrees F
1 cake (.6-ounce) or 2 teaspoons packed fresh yeast
2 ounces (about ¼ cup) White Starter

2½ ounces (about ¼ cup) Rye Starter

1 tablespoon barley malt syrup

13 ounces (about 3 cups) unbleached high-gluten flour or unbleached white bread flour, plus extra for dusting

5½ ounces (about 1 cup) whole-wheat flour

6 tablespoons rye chops or coarsely chopped rye flakes

3 tablespoons sugar

1 tablespoon sea salt

¼ cup coarsely chopped candied orange peel, optional

3 ounces (about ¾ cup) dried sour cherries

8½ ounces (about 1½ cups) currants

3 ounces (about ⅔ cup) golden raisins

4½ ounces (about 1 cup) jumbo (if available) black raisins

Vegetable oil

Preheat the oven to 325 degrees F.

Spread the pecans in a single layer on a baking sheet and bake them until they are lightly toasted, about 10 minutes. Set aside to cool.

Place water, yeast, starters, malt syrup, flours, rye chops, and sugar in the bowl of a mixer fitted with a dough hook. Mix on low speed for 2 minutes, scraping the dough down the sides of the bowl as necessary with a rubber spatula. The dough should be wet and sticky.

Add salt and continue mixing on medium-low speed until the dough reaches an internal temperature of 64 degrees F, about 6 minutes. Add orange peel and dried fruits, and mix on low speed just until these ingredients are incorporated, about 2 minutes. Add the toasted pecans and mix on low speed just until the nuts are incorporated, about 1 minute.

Remove the dough from the mixing bowl and place it on a lightly floured work surface. Clean the mixing bowl and lightly coat it with vegetable oil. Gather the dough into a ball and return the dough to the oiled bowl, cover it tightly with plastic wrap, and let it ferment at room temperature for 1 to 1½ hours, until the dough just begins to rise. (Because this dough is so packed with fruit and nuts, it will barely increase in volume.)

Uncover the dough and place it on a floured work surface. Cut the dough into two equal pieces with a dough cutter. Cover the dough with a cloth and let it rest for 15 minutes.

Flatten each piece of dough into a rectangle by placing one hand over the other, palms down, and patting the dough to an even thickness (begin in the center and work outward). Roll each piece of dough into an oblong by folding the top edge of the dough to the middle. Pat across the whole seam firmly with the heel of your hand to seal it. Fold the top edge of the dough over the seam to the bottom edge and seal as before. The folding will not be as easy to do as it is with a dough that doesn't have any chunky fruit.

Turn the dough seam side down. Place one hand on top of the other, palms down, in the center of the dough and simultaneously rock the dough back and forth and mold it into an oblong 8 inches long and 4 inches wide, moving your hands to the ends of the loaf as you work. When your hands reach the ends, cup them around the ends to keep the edges slightly rounded.

Invert the dough, seam side up, into floured proofing baskets or directly onto a floured work surface. Sprinkle the surface of the dough with flour, cover with a cloth, and let the dough proof at room temperature until it reaches an internal temperature of 68 degrees F, about 2 hours. The dough will still feel dense and will not show much sign of movement.

Preheat the oven to 500 degrees F 1 hour before baking.

Carefully run your hand around one loaf to loosen it and gently invert it onto a lightly floured baker's peel.

Holding a single-edged razor blade perpendicular to the loaf, slash an elongated X across the top of the dough, $1/2$ inch deep, keeping the ends of the cuts $3/4$ inch from the ends of the dough. Then make one long, straight cut in the center of the V created at each end of the X (start the cut at least $1/4$ inch from the intersection of each V; end it $1/4$ inch away from the end of the dough).

Open the oven door, spritz the oven heavily with water from a spray bottle, and quickly close the door. Open the oven door again, slide the loaf onto the baking tiles, and quickly close the door. Cut, spritz, and load the second loaf in the same manner. Reduce the oven temperature to 450 degrees F.

Spritz the oven two more times during the next 5 minutes. Refrain from opening the oven door for 20 minutes.

After 20 minutes, check the loaves and rotate them if necessary to ensure even baking. Continue baking for 20 to 25 more minutes, for a total of 45 to 50 minutes.

Remove the loaves to a cooling rack. The crust should be bumpy and almost black. No cheating here; you will not be able to get a clean slice of bread if you don't wait until it's absolutely cold.

Rye-Currant Bread

MAKES TWO APPROXIMATELY 1-POUND-4-OUNCE BOULES.

A bread packed with currants (tiny raisins) may seem like a frivolous, special occasion sort of thing, but this is a substantial loaf that I think works as an everyday bread. It's based on the classic French bread that is often served in fine restaurants as part of the cheese course—the slight sweetness of the bread plays off nicely against the pungency of great aged cheese. It's a wonderful breakfast bread too.

Rye Starter gives the bread a good sour structure, but there's no rye flour mixed into the dough itself. Instead, I use whole-wheat flour and high-gluten white bread flour. Rye chops are added for texture.

At the bakery, we shape the bread into two sizes of boules and also into rolls—Rye-Currant is among our best-selling breads. To make rolls using this dough, follow the shaping directions for rolls on pages 70–71.

One-Day Bread

HAVE READY:
Mixing bowl
Mixer with attachable dough hook
Rubber spatula
Long-stemmed, instant-read cooking thermometer
Plastic wrap
Dough cutter
Proofing cloth
Two 1-pound-capacity proofing baskets or wood board or baking sheet covered with large flour-dusted proofing cloth
Plastic trash can liner, optional
Baker's peel
4-inch scissors
Spray bottle, filled with water
Cooling rack

12 ounces (about 1½ cups) cool water, 70 degrees F

½ cake (.3 ounce) or 1 teaspoon packed fresh yeast

1 tablespoon barley malt syrup

5 ounces (about ½ cup) Rye Starter

13 ounces (about 2¾ cups) unbleached high-gluten flour or unbleached white bread flour, plus extra for dusting

6 ounces (about 1 cup) whole-wheat flour

1½ ounces (about 6 tablespoons) rye chops or coarsely chopped rye flakes

2 teaspoons sea salt

11 ounces (about 2 cups) currants

Vegetable oil

Place water, yeast, malt syrup, Rye Starter, flours, and rye chops in the bowl of a mixer fitted with a dough hook. Mix on low speed until the ingredients are incorporated, about 2 minutes, scraping the dough down the sides of the bowl as necessary with a rubber spatula. The dough should be fairly wet and sticky.

Add salt and continue mixing on medium-low speed until the dough reaches an internal temperature of 70 degrees F, about 6 minutes.

Break up the currants if they're stuck together. With the mixer running on low speed, gradually add the currants and continue to mix just until they are incorporated, about 2 minutes.

Remove the dough from the mixing bowl and place it on a lightly floured work surface. Clean the bowl and lightly coat it with vegetable oil. Gather the dough into a ball and return the dough to the oiled bowl, cover it tightly with plastic wrap, and let it ferment at room temperature for about 1 to 1½ hours. Check the surface of the dough carefully during the last 15 minutes of proofing. When the surface just begins to crack or when a bubble bursts on the dough, the boules are ready. The dough should have increased in volume by one third and feel slightly sticky.

Preheat the oven to 500 degrees F 1 hour before baking.

Turn the dough out onto a lightly floured work surface and cut it into two equal pieces with a dough cutter. Slap each piece against the work surface a few times to deflate. Tuck under the edges of each piece, cover them with a cloth, and let the dough rest for 15 minutes.

Uncover the dough and round each piece into a boule, according to the directions on page 48.

If you are using proofing baskets, invert each boule, smooth side down, into a floured basket. Sprinkle the surface of the dough with flour and cover each basket tightly with plastic wrap.

If you are proofing on a cloth-covered board or baking sheet, invert one boule, smooth side down, onto the flour-dusted cloth. Pinch the cloth into a deep pleat alongside the dough. (This will separate the pieces of dough, help them hold their shape, and prevent them from sticking together as they continue to proof.) Repeat with the remaining boule. Dust the boules lightly with flour and cover them with a cloth. Slide the board or baking sheet into a plastic trash can liner and close the bag securely.

Let the boules proof at room temperature until the dough expands by about a third, the surface of the dough just begins to crack, and the dough reaches an internal temperature of 72 degrees F, about 1 hour.

If you are using proofing baskets, remove the plastic and lightly dust the boules with flour. Carefully run your hand around one boule to loosen it and gently invert it onto a lightly floured baker's peel. Using the same method, invert the second boule onto the peel, spaced well apart from the first boule (both should fit). If you are using a board or sheet, remove the bag and cloth, dust the boules with flour, and invert them onto the peel.

With scissors held horizontally, make seven deep snips in a circle all the way around the edge of one boule. Then hold the scissors at a 45-degree angle and make another circle inside the first by cutting four deep snips, each between two snips of the outer circle.

Open the oven door, spritz the oven heavily with water from a spray bottle, then quickly close the door. Open the oven door again, slide the boule onto the baking tiles, and quickly close the door. Cut, spritz, and load the second boule in the same manner.

Reduce the oven temperature to 450 degrees F. Spritz the oven twice more during the next 5 minutes. Continue baking for 30 more minutes, for a total of 35 minutes.

Remove the bread to a cooling rack. The crust should be very dark, almost black, and the cuts should have opened to form a star pattern around the top circumference of the boules.

MULTIGRAIN BREAD

MAKES TWO APPROXIMATELY 2-POUND BOULES.

Y ou can't get the open structure of a white bread when you mix a dough with lots of gluten-slashing grains. Some people try to solve this problem by basically making a white bread with just a few bits of grain for looks. I wanted a bread of substance, something crunchy to bite into. But using only whole-wheat flour and grains results in an unacceptably dense loaf—a brick. My compromise for this Multigrain Bread is to use just enough unbleached white or high-gluten flour to make the loaf lighter. Rye Starter and a multigrain cereal go into the dough, and I add extra flax seeds and millet for crunch. The dough is made using the sponge method to allow the bread to benefit from a long, slow fermentation without letting it fall apart. When it's first mixed, the dough will feel pretty sticky; it will become easier to handle as it's shaped. The final result is a wonderful bread full of fiber.

Note: I use Guisto's multigrain cereal (see Bob's Red Mill, "Sources," page 254), which is similar to the ones available in most health food stores. Cracked wheat, barley, corn, millet, oats, rye, triticale, brown rice, soya, and flax seeds go into the mix. If you can't find an acceptable blend, you can make your own. Buy the grains separately at a health food store and grind them together. The texture should be a little coarser than sand. Don't confuse grain mix with grain flour, which is too fine and won't give you the best quality of this bread, the crunch.

TWO-DAY BREAD—FIRST DAY

HAVE READY:
Mixing bowl
Rubber spatula, optional
Plastic wrap

11 ounces (about 1⅓ cups) cool water, 70 degrees F
1 tablespoon barley malt syrup
13 ounces (about 1⅓ cups) Rye Starter

11½ ounces (about 2⅓ cups) unbleached high-gluten or unbleached white bread flour
1 teaspoon sea salt

> Make a sponge by placing water, malt syrup, Rye Starter, flour, and salt in a mixing bowl and stirring with your hands or a rubber spatula. Cover the bowl tightly with plastic wrap and leave it at room temperature for 2 hours, then refrigerate 8 to 12 hours.

SECOND DAY

HAVE READY:
Mixing bowl
Mixer with attachable dough hook
Rubber spatula
Long-stemmed, instant-read cooking thermometer
Plastic wrap
Dough cutter
Proofing cloths
2 unlined proofing baskets
Baker's peel
Single-edged razor blade
Spray bottle, filled with water
Cooling rack

10 ounces (about 1¼ cups) cool water, 70 degrees F
½ cake (.3 ounce) or 1 teaspoon packed fresh yeast
Sponge
12½ ounces (about 3 cups) unbleached high-gluten or unbleached white bread flour, plus extra for dusting
7 ounces (about 1¼ cups) whole-wheat flour
9 ounces (about 1⅔ cups) multigrain cereal
3½ ounces (about ½ cup) flax seeds
1¾ ounces (about ¼ cup) millet
2 teaspoons sea salt
Vegetable oil

Place water, yeast, sponge, flours, cereal, flax seeds, and millet in the bowl of a mixer fitted with a dough hook. Mix on low speed for 2 minutes, scraping the dough down the sides of the bowl with a rubber spatula to help incorporate the flour. The dough should be very wet and sticky.

Add salt and continue mixing on medium-low speed until the dough reaches an internal temperature of 65 degrees F, about 8 minutes.

Remove the dough from the mixing bowl and place it on a lightly floured work surface. Clean the mixing bowl and lightly coat it with vegetable oil. Gather the dough into a ball and return the dough to the oiled bowl, cover it tightly with plastic wrap, and let it ferment at room temperature for $1\frac{1}{2}$ hours. The dough should rise in the bowl by half its original volume and begin to show tiny cracks on the surface.

Preheat the oven to 500 degrees F 1 hour before baking.

Turn the dough out onto a floured work surface and cut it into two equal pieces with a dough cutter. Slap each piece against the work surface a few times to deflate. Turn under the edges of each piece, cover them with a cloth, and let the dough rest for 15 minutes.

Uncover the dough. Using as little flour as possible, round each piece into a boule, according to the directions on page 48. Place each boule, smooth side down, into a floured proofing basket. Sprinkle the surface of the dough with flour and cover each basket tightly with plastic wrap. Let the dough proof at room temperature until it grows by half its original volume and reaches an internal temperature of 70 degrees F, about 1 hour. Check the surface of the dough carefully during the last 15 minutes of proofing. When the surface just begins to crack or when a bubble bursts on the dough, the boules are ready.

Remove the plastic and lightly dust the boules with flour. Carefully run your hand around one boule to loosen it and gently invert it onto a lightly floured baker's peel. Holding a single-edged razor blade perpendicular to the boule, cut a 2-inch vertical cross on the top of the boule, starting and ending 1 inch away from the edges.

Open the oven door, spritz the oven heavily with water from a spray bottle, and quickly close the door. Open the oven door again, slide the boule onto the baking tiles, and quickly close the door. Cut, spritz, and load the second boule in the same manner.

Reduce the oven temperature to 475 degrees F. Spritz the oven two more times during the next 5 minutes. Refrain from opening the oven door for the next 20 minutes.

After 20 minutes, check the boules and rotate them if necessary to ensure even baking. If the bread looks too dark, reduce the oven temperature to about 450 degrees F and leave the door ajar. (You're far enough along in the baking at this point that the steam effect won't be ruined.) Continue baking for 25 more minutes, for a total of 50 minutes.

Remove the boules to a cooling rack. The boules should have increased in volume by about one third of their size. The crust should be dark and the interior fine grained, with coarse particles of cereal and seeds visible.

SOURDOUGH
SPECIALTIES

ANY BAKER WHO MAINTAINS A SOURDOUGH STARTER always has leftovers. Think of the zucchini problem many gardeners encounter every year—there's just too much of a good thing. Instead of throwing out your excess starter, use it up in the following recipes. Most are fairly simple to make, perfect for those *rare* moments when you're not quite in the mood to make a loaf of bread. Remember to use your starter the same way you do when you make a loaf of bread—8 to 12, no more than 15 hours after the last feeding.

PRETZELS

I'm very particular about pretzels. For one thing, I like them with both thick and thin sections; this prevents pretzel boredom. The crust should have a nice snap when you bite in, and the interior shouldn't be too doughy.

The instructions for shaping these pretzels may seem complicated when you first read them, but with a little practice it will all make sense.

These pretzels are dipped in a food-grade lye to give them extra color and a pretzel-like flavor, something you won't get with the baking soda dips that many other recipes call for. Of course, lye is a bit tricky to work with. First, you have to be sure you buy edible lye, *not* the stuff to clear drains. Many pharmacies carry the right type. And it's essential that you wear rubber gloves as you work. If you want to be supercautious, you might even wear eye goggles. If all this makes you nervous, you can brush the pretzels with an egg wash. They won't have the same flavor, but they will have a nice golden shine.

Note: Lye can be reused as long as it's kept covered, although it gets weaker with time. If your pretzels don't come out as dark as they should, it's probably time to buy new lye.

TWO-DAY BREAD—FIRST DAY

HAVE READY:
Mixing bowl
Mixer with attachable dough hook, optional
Long-stemmed, instant-read cooking thermometer
Dough cutter
Proofing cloth
Spray bottle, filled with water
1 or 2 parchment-lined (or Magic Baking Sheet—lined) baking sheets plus an additional baking sheet for dipping,
    optional
1 or 2 plastic trash can liners

6 ounces (about ¾ cup) cool water, 70 degrees F
9 ounces (about 1 cup) White Starter

1 pound 4 ounces (about 5 cups) unbleached white bread flour, plus extra for dusting
1 tablespoon barley malt syrup
2 teaspoons fine sea salt

Place water, White Starter, flour, malt syrup, and salt in the bowl of a mixer fitted with a dough hook. Mix on low speed for 1 to 2 minutes to combine ingredients. (The dough may also be mixed by hand; see basic instructions on page 42.) Turn the mixer up to medium and mix until the dough is smooth, elastic, and firm and reaches an internal temperature of 75 to 76 degrees F, about 8 minutes.

Turn the dough out onto an unfloured work surface and knead it for a few minutes by hand. Cut the dough with a dough cutter into eighteen 3-ounce pieces. Tuck under the edges of each piece, cover them with a cloth, and let the dough rest for 45 minutes.

Working with one piece of dough at a time and keeping the rest covered, shape a rope 9 inches long by placing one hand on top of the other, palms down, in the center of the dough and rolling it into a cylinder shape. Avoid using flour. If there is not enough friction between the dough and the work surface, spritz the work surface lightly with water from a spray bottle. As the rope begins to stretch, uncross your hands and continue rolling with light, even pressure, moving your hands slowly to the ends of the rope without tapering the ends. Leaving a center belly 3 inches long, place the palms of your hands on each side of the belly, and roll and stretch again to elongate the cylinder to about 20 inches. Lay your hands on top of each end and taper the ends by alternately rolling each one toward and away from you (think of the arm motions of a cross-country skier).

Cross your arms and grab opposite ends of the dough by pinching it between your thumbs and forefingers. Without letting go of the dough, uncross your arms and cross the ends of the dough to make a twist with a 4-inch tail on each side. Lift the left end and press it firmly into the left top of the belly just where the belly begins to taper, leaving a ¼-inch overhang. Repeat with the right end.

Transfer the pretzel to a parchment-lined baking sheet. Adjust shape if necessary. Repeat this shape with the remaining pieces of dough, placing them 2 inches apart on the baking sheet. Cover the pretzels with a cloth and allow them to sit at room temperature just until they begin to show signs of movement, about 1 hour.

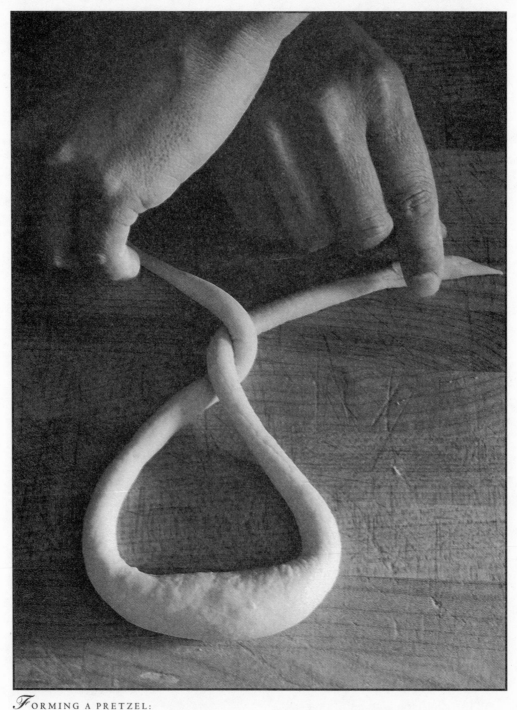

*F*ORMING A PRETZEL:

"I'M VERY PARTICULAR ABOUT PRETZELS. THE CRUST SHOULD HAVE A NICE SNAP
WHEN YOU BITE IN, AND THE INTERIOR SHOULDN'T BE TOO DOUGHY."

Place each baking sheet into a plastic trash can liner and refrigerate for 12 to 24 hours.

SECOND DAY

HAVE READY:

Nonreactive mixing bowl (plastic or ceramic)
Wooden spoon
Rubber gloves
Eye goggles, optional
Baking sheets
Cooling rack

1 quart water
1 ounce (1 tablespoon) food-grade lye or 2 egg yolks mixed with a teaspoon of water
Pastry brush, optional
Vegetable oil
Coarse sea salt for sprinkling

Preheat the oven to 400 degrees F 1 hour before baking. Be sure the oven racks are placed well apart to allow plenty of air circulation.

If you are going to dip the pretzels in a lye solution, they need to be dipped as soon as they are removed from the refrigerator. Otherwise they will lose their shape and be too difficult to dip. Have plenty of counter space available to set up a dipping and draining assembly line.

Mix water and lye in a plastic or ceramic (nonreactive) mixing bowl and stir with a wooden spoon to combine. Set the solution aside. Place a cooling rack on top of a baking sheet and set it next to the lye solution.

Lightly oil another 1 or 2 baking sheets and set these next to the first baking sheet.

Remove the dough from the refrigerator and take off the plastic trash can liner. Wearing rubber gloves, and goggles if desired, dip the pretzels one at a time in the lye solution for 15 to 30 seconds. Transfer each pretzel to the cooling rack and allow it to drain before putting it on the oil-coated baking sheet. Dip and drain the remaining pretzels, placing them on the baking sheet about 2 inches apart.

If you are going to use an egg wash, simply remove the dough from the refrigerator, take off the plastic wrap, and brush the pretzels with the egg wash. (It is not necessary to bake the pretzels on an oiled baking sheet.)

After all the pretzels have been dipped or brushed with egg, sprinkle each with a large pinch of sea salt. The pretzels must be baked immediately after they have been topped with salt or the salt will dissolve.

Place the pretzels in the oven and bake for 20 to 25 minutes. It may be necessary to rotate the baking sheets to ensure even baking.

The pretzels are done when they turn a rich, mahogany brown.

BAGELS

MAKES EIGHTEEN 4-OUNCE BAGELS.

This is what Izzy Cohen says about a bagel he doesn't respect: "Where's the sugar?" He means it might as well be a doughnut.

Izzy, a baker for most of his seventy-eight years (and the inspiration for Izzy's New York Rye), is my bagel adviser. He shows up at the bakery almost every Saturday morning to make bagels, and there is no one I trust more on the subject.

"I've been through a bit of the hinterlands," he says. "I stop at places and look for bagels. A lot of nothing passes for bagels. They're round. They have a hole."

There are many things that Izzy insists on when it comes to bagels. High-gluten flour might be the most important ingredient. "Without high-gluten," Izzy says darkly, "you can't make a bagel. One week I came to the bakery and walked out five minutes later—no high-gluten flour." And no bagels that week.

Izzy is also particular about the proper boiling of a bagel. "Some of these cookbooks," he says, "I don't know, you read the instructions and they say, 'Boil the bagels for two minutes on each side.' Two minutes! You should barely cook them twenty seconds."

But those twenty seconds are important. "Cooking the dough serves a useful function," Izzy explains. "It kills off some of the yeast on the outside layer of dough and makes a tight skin. It also cooks the starch on the outside layer, which gives a bagel its shine. If you put two bagels in an oven, one boiled, one not boiled, the one that's cooked will be smaller because the cooked skin inhibits growth. Of course, the longer you boil it, the thicker that skin gets." Boiling also makes steaming the oven unnecessary.

Naturally, Izzy doesn't approve of the shortcuts other bakers use to develop flavor in bagels: "You can put sugar in there, you can put flour in there, but if you don't have fermentation, all the flavor will be on the tongue, not in the chew. And the real flavor of a bagel comes in the chewing." Of course, this exactly meshes with my bread philosophy, which in practical terms means that this bagel is made with sourdough starter.

There are, however, a few Izzy-approved tricks in this recipe to develop flavor. Malt syrup goes into the dough, and there's a 10-minute rest period between mixing and cutting the dough to help boost the fermentation.

One big don't: *Don't* dust the work surface with flour as you cut and shape the dough. Bagels shouldn't have *any* contact with extra flour. None. This is a firm dough, and extra flour will only prevent the ends of the bagel from sticking together when they're shaped.

Note: If you can't find high-gluten flour, see the "Unbleached High-Gluten Flour" section of Chapter I (page 6) for instructions on how to combine bread flour with vital wheat gluten to make a stronger flour.

Two-Day Bread—First Day

HAVE READY:
Mixing bowl
Mixer with attachable dough hook, optional
Long-stemmed, instant-read cooking thermometer
Proofing cloth
Dough cutter
Parchment paper
1 to 3 baking sheets, dusted with semolina flour

12 ounces (about 1½ cups) cool water, 70 degrees F
1 cake (.6 ounce) or 2 teaspoons packed fresh yeast
13½ ounces (about 1½ cups) White Starter
2 pounds (about 6½ cups) unbleached high-gluten flour or unbleached white bread flour
2 ounces (about ¼ cup) sugar
1 tablespoon sea salt
2 tablespoons barley malt syrup
6 tablespoons milk powder
Semolina flour for dusting

Place water, yeast, White Starter, flour, sugar, salt, malt syrup, and milk powder in the bowl of a mixer fitted with a dough hook. Mix on low speed 1 to 2 minutes to combine the ingredients. Turn the mixer up to medium and mix until the dough is smooth, elastic, and firm and has reached an internal temperature of 75 degrees F, about 8 minutes.

Turn the dough out onto a flour-free work surface and knead it for a few minutes by hand. Cover the dough with a flour-free cloth and let it rest for 10 minutes.

Cut the dough into eighteen 4-ounce pieces with a dough cutter. Tuck under the edges of each piece, cover them with a flour-free cloth, and let the dough rest for 15 minutes.

Working with one piece of dough at a time and keeping the rest covered, shape a rope 6 inches long by placing one hand on top of the other, palms down, in the center of the dough and rolling it into a cylinder shape. As the rope begins to stretch, uncross your hands and continue rolling with light, even pressure, moving your hands slowly to the ends of the rope without tapering the ends.

Take one end between your thumb and forefinger and wrap the dough around the back of your hand so that the opposite end overlaps the first by 1½ inches. With the overlapped ends joined at the center of your palm and the dough still encircling your hand, seal the ends by rolling the rope back and forth on the work surface, palm down, to a thickness even with the rest of the dough.

Place the bagel on a parchment-lined baking sheet dusted with semolina flour. Repeat this shape with the remaining pieces of the dough, placing them 2 inches apart on the baking sheet. Cover the bagels with a cloth and refrigerate them for 12 to 24 hours.

SECOND DAY

HAVE READY:
Large stockpot or roasting pan
Wooden spoon
Strainer
Baker's peel, optional

Shaped bagels
Water

Preheat the oven to 450 degrees F 1 hour before baking. The bagels may be baked on parchment paper either directly on baking tiles or a stone, or on baking sheets. If they are to be baked on baking sheets, make sure the oven racks are placed well apart to allow plenty of air circulation.

$\mathscr{S}$HAPING A BAGEL:

IZZY COHEN SAYS, "THE REAL FLAVOR OF A BAGEL COMES IN THE CHEWING."

Remove the bagels from the refrigerator. Place water at least 4 inches deep in a large pot and bring it to a rapid boil. Uncover the bagels and check to make sure they are slightly puffy and light. To test for readiness, throw one bagel in the boiling water. If it rises immediately to the surface and floats, it is ready. If it stays at the bottom of the pan, it is not. If the bagels are not ready, cover them and allow them to sit at room temperature until they are. (But don't let the bagels get too warm or flabby or they will lose their shape when boiled.)

When the bagels are ready, drop three at a time into the boiling water, pressing on them lightly with a wooden spoon just to submerge the tops for 10 seconds. Dust the baking sheet with more semolina as bagels are removed. Lift the spoon, let the bagels cook just 10 seconds more, then remove them with a strainer, allowing the excess water to drain off. Immediately set them rounded side up on a semolina-dusted baking sheet, about 2 inches apart. Make sure the water comes back up to a boil before adding the next batch of bagels.

If your baker's peel is large enough, slide it under the bagel-topped parchment paper and place the bagels and the paper directly on the baking tiles. Or just bake the bagels on the baking sheets, but make sure you rotate them halfway through to ensure even baking.

Bake for 20 minutes. If necessary, rotate the bagels halfway through the cooking time to ensure even baking. The bagels should be golden brown.

SEEDED BAGELS

HAVE READY:
Small bowl
Baking sheet or large plate
1 or 2 parchment-lined baking sheets

½ cup shelled sunflower seeds
½ cup poppy seeds
½ cup sesame seeds
1 scant tablespoon coarse sea salt
Semolina flour
Boiled bagels

Place seeds and salt in a small bowl and combine. (You can also use 1½ cups of a single seed.) Spread the mixture in an even layer on a baking sheet or large plate.

Lightly dust 1 or 2 parchment-lined baking sheets with semolina flour.

Immediately after boiling the bagels as directed in the main recipe, press each one, rounded side down, into the topping mixture. Then place the bagel, seeded side up, on a parchment-lined baking sheet. Bake as directed for Bagels.

and mix until all the ingredients are well combined, 4 to 5 minutes. The dough should come together and clean the sides of the bowl.

Remove the dough from the mixing bowl, place it on a lightly floured work surface, and knead it by hand until it is smooth, about 1 minute.

Wrap the dough tightly in plastic wrap and let it rest at room temperature for 2 hours.

Remove the plastic wrap and place the dough on a lightly floured work surface. Roll out the dough with a rolling pin until it is about 1/3 inch thick. Cut biscuits out of the dough with a cookie cutter and place them on a parchment-lined baking sheet, about 1/2 inch apart. Knead together the scraps, reroll the dough to the same thickness as before, and cut more biscuits with the cookie cutter, placing them on the baking sheet. Repeat this process as many times as necessary for the remaining dough.

Brush the tops of the biscuits with beaten egg.

Place the baking sheets on the oven racks and bake for 15 minutes. Rotate the sheets if necessary and continue baking for another 15 minutes, for a total of 30 minutes. The biscuits should be nicely browned.

Turn off the heat, leave the oven door ajar, and keep the biscuits in the oven for an additional 15 minutes to dry out.

Remove the biscuits from the oven and let them cool completely before serving to Fido (or Baby).

ENGLISH MUFFINS

MAKES FIFTEEN MUFFINS.

It's fairly easy to buy good English muffins at the grocery store. So when the restaurant opened for breakfast, we decided to make ours more substantial than traditional muffins. I gave the project to Pammy Sue Fitzpatrick, who worked at the bakery a few years back. She came up with a wonderful muffin in which rye chops, sunflower seeds, wheat germ, and bran add texture and flavor. And of course there are plenty of the required nooks and crannies to catch lots of butter and jam.

Note: English muffin rings are available at gourmet cooking specialty shops. But you can also open both ends of a tuna fish can, rinse it out, and use the ring as your mold.

ONE-DAY BREAD

HAVE READY:
2 mixing bowls
Rubber spatula, optional
Plastic wrap
Mixer with paddle attachment
Pastry brush
15 English muffin rings, 3¼ inches in diameter × 1 inch high, or 15 tuna fish cans
1 or 2 baking sheets
Parchment paper
Dough cutter
Knife

SPONGE
18 ounces (about 2 cups) White Starter
2 cups milk
8 ounces (about 2 cups) unbleached white bread flour
3½ ounces (about 1 cup) dark rye flour

Place White Starter, milk, and flours in a mixing bowl and stir with your hands or a rubber spatula. Cover the bowl tightly with plastic wrap and let the sponge ferment at room temperature for about 1½ hours.

DOUGH

Sponge
10 ounces (about 1¼ cups) warm water, 85 degrees F
1½ cakes (.9 ounce) or 3½ teaspoons packed fresh yeast
¼ cup wheat bran
¼ cup wheat germ
¼ cup flax seeds
¼ cup rye chops or coarsely chopped rye flakes
¼ cup raw sunflower seeds (untoasted)
8 ounces (about 2 cups) unbleached white bread flour
4 tablespoons barley malt syrup
4 tablespoons vegetable oil
1 tablespoon sea salt
Rice flour for dusting
2 tablespoons unsalted butter, melted
Semolina flour for dusting, optional

Uncover the sponge. It should look bubbly on the surface. Place the sponge, water, yeast, wheat bran, wheat germ, flax seeds, rye chops, sunflower seeds, flour, malt syrup, and vegetable oil in the bowl of a mixer fitted with a paddle attachment.

Mix on low speed until the ingredients are combined, 1 to 2 minutes. Turn the mixer up to medium and continue mixing until the dough looks elastic and starts to pull away from the sides of the bowl, about 6 minutes. Add salt and mix on medium speed for about 2 minutes.

Cover the bowl tightly with plastic wrap and let the dough ferment at room temperature until it doubles in volume, about 1½ hours.

Uncover the dough and transfer it to a work surface heavily dusted with rice flour. The dough should be extremely wet and sticky and may not hold its shape. Sprinkle the surface of the dough with a thin, even layer of rice flour or semolina and let it rest, uncovered, for 20 minutes.

Using a pastry brush, coat the insides of the English muffin rings with melted butter and place the rings 2 inches apart on parchment-lined baking sheets that have been dusted with semolina or rice flour.

Using a dough cutter, cut and scoop up the wet dough in portions roughly the size of your ring. (If the dough is too sticky to work with, dip your hand in water.) Place the dough inside the ring. It should reach almost to the top of the ring. Press the dough gently to spread it into an even but not necessarily smooth layer.

Let the dough proof uncovered in the muffin rings at room temperature for 1 hour. It is more important for this dough to relax than for it to grow in volume.

Preheat the oven to 400 degrees F 1 hour before baking. Be sure the oven racks are placed well apart to allow plenty of air circulation.

Just before baking, sprinkle the tops of the muffins with additional rice or semolina flour.

Place the baking sheets on the oven racks and bake for 20 minutes. Remove the sheets from the oven, flip the muffins upside down, still inside the rings, and rotate the baking sheets. Bake for 20 more minutes, for a total of 40 minutes.

Remove the baking sheets from the oven. Remove the rings when the muffins are cool. Both the tops and bottoms of the muffins should be lightly browned.

Split in half with a fork, toast, and slather with butter.

CROISSANTS

MAKES TWELVE LARGE CROISSANTS.

Too often, croissants are nothing more than crescent-shaped rolls. My vision of a great croissant, the kind you usually see only in great French bakeries, is swollen in the center, with bubbly, flaky layers and a blistered crust. Instead of being dry and bready on the inside, it has an almost stretchy core. You should be able to dismantle the layers into feathery sheets.

With this in mind, I gave Martha Fousse the project of getting the bakery's croissants as close to this ideal as possible. I think she came through with a textbook-perfect croissant.

The initial batch can contain a small portion of aged Country White Bread Dough, which not only enhances the leavening, texture, and flavor of the croissants but helps them stay fresh longer. Once you've made a batch, do as we do at the bakery and save a portion of the croissant dough, just as you would for *Levain Bâtard.* Then use the reserved, refrigerated croissant dough in place of the aged Country White Dough for each subsequent batch.

One hint: Use the best—richest—butter you can find. Often, for instance, you can find imported Normandy butter in specialty cheese shops. With it you'll notice a big difference in the flavor of your croissants.

ONE-DAY BREAD

(Plus an optional one-time, 24- to 36-hour step to get one piece of aged Country White Dough. See under Levain Bâtard, page 151, for how to form the seed.)

HAVE READY:
1 or 2 baking sheets
Parchment paper
Mixing bowl
Mixer with attachable dough hook
Plastic wrap
2 linen towels
Rolling pin

Large chef's knife
Spray bottle, filled with water

2½ pounds (about 10 cups) unbleached white bread flour, plus extra for dusting
2⅔ cups whole milk
4½ cakes (2.5 ounces) or 3 tablespoons packed fresh yeast
2 teaspoons sea salt
3 ounces (about 6 tablespoons) light brown sugar, packed
One 4-ounce piece Country White Dough or one 4-ounce piece aged croissant dough, optional
1½ pounds (3 cups) unsalted butter, chilled

Line the baking sheets with parchment paper, lightly dust with flour, and set them aside.

Place milk, yeast, salt, brown sugar, flour, and optional aged Country White Dough or aged croissant dough in the bowl of a mixer fitted with a dough hook. Mix on low speed until the dough is smooth, about 8 minutes.

Remove the dough from the mixing bowl, place it on a lightly floured work surface, and knead it for a few minutes by hand. Press the dough into a rectangle, roughly 1½ inches thick. Wrap it tightly with plastic wrap and refrigerate it for 1 hour.

Meanwhile, place the cold butter between two linen towels and beat it with a rolling pin to flatten into a rectangle measuring 10 by 16 inches. Refrigerate it for ½ hour.

Remove the dough from the refrigerator and take off the plastic wrap. Transfer the dough to a lightly floured work surface. Roll it with a rolling pin into a rectangle measuring 16 by 20 inches, being sure to keep the short end parallel to the edge of the work surface. Remove the butter from the refrigerator and take off the linen towels. Ideally, the butter and the dough should be the same temperature. If the butter is too cold, it will break through the surface of the dough when the dough is rolled out. If the butter is overchilled, leave it out at room temperature and keep the dough in the refrigerator or vice versa, until both are the same temperature.

Place the rectangle of butter on the upper two thirds of the dough rectangle.

Fold the dough as you would a business letter: the bottom third up to the middle and the top edge down to the bottom edge.

Enlarge the rectangle by rolling out the dough until it is ½ inch thick.

Doughnuts

~~~ MAKES THIRTY SMALL DOUGHNUTS, THREE OR FOUR DOUGHNUTS PER SERVING.

This recipe came about as the result of an occasional doughnut urge that I couldn't seem to satisfy. I ended up with sackfuls of the mass-produced version—artificially flavored, made from packaged mixes, and fried in old oil. Ultimately, I came to the conclusion that the doughnut flavor of my imagination would never be found at a chain store. My European customers often tell me that these light, briochelike doughnuts are reminiscent of the type sold at village festivals. This may seem like a lot of doughnuts to make, but because I make these in a 5-quart freestanding mixer, the quantity of dough required to knead properly yields thirty small doughnuts.

ONE-DAY RECIPE

HAVE READY:

Mixing bowl
Mixer with attachable dough hook
Plastic wrap
1 or 2 baking sheets
Parchment paper
Rolling pin
Doughnut cutter or a 2-inch-round cookie cutter plus a ¾-inch-round cutter or the wide end of a metal pastry nozzle
Large heavy-bottom skillet
Deep-fat frying thermometer
Small mixing bowl
Slotted spoon
Powdered sugar dredger or fine-mesh strainer, optional

SPONGE

6 ounces (about ¾ cup) White Starter
2 cakes (1.2 ounces) or 4 teaspoons packed fresh yeast
½ cup plus 2 tablespoons buttermilk
⅓ cup milk powder

8 ounces (about 2 cups) unbleached white pastry flour or all-purpose flour, plus extra for dusting
Vegetable oil

Place White Starter, yeast, buttermilk, milk powder, and flour in the bowl of a mixer fitted with a dough hook. Mix on medium-low speed until the dough is smooth and comes together in a ball, about 2 to 3 minutes. (The dough may also be mixed by hand; see basic instructions on page 42.)

Remove the dough from the mixing bowl, place it on a lightly floured work surface, and knead it for a few minutes by hand.

Clean the mixing bowl and lightly coat it with vegetable oil. Return the dough to the oiled bowl, cover it tightly with plastic wrap, and let it ferment at room temperature until it doubles in volume, about 30 to 40 minutes.

TO MAKE THE DOUGH
Sponge
5 tablespoons buttermilk
7 ounces (1½ cups) unbleached pastry flour or all-purpose flour, plus extra for dusting
3 ounces (⅓ cup) granulated sugar
2 teaspoons sea salt
5 ounces (10 tablespoons) unsalted butter, room temperature
2 whole nutmegs, freshly grated
5 teaspoons ground cinnamon
13 egg yolks
¾ cup dried sour cherries, coarsely chopped
vegetable oil

FOR FRYING
3 cups peanut, canola, or vegetable oil

FOR GARNISHING
1 cup granulated sugar
1 teaspoon ground cinnamon
Confectioners' sugar, optional

Remove the plastic wrap from the sponge mixing bowl. Add buttermilk, flour, sugar, salt, butter, nutmeg, cinnamon, and 8 egg yolks. Fit the mixer with a dough hook and mix on low speed just to combine. Turn the mixer up to medium speed and continue mixing until the ingredients are well incorporated, about 4 to 5 minutes. Turn off the mixer. Add the remaining egg yolks and dried cherries. Turn the mixer up to high speed and mix until well blended, about 1 minute.

Transfer the dough to a heavily floured work surface and knead for a few minutes by hand until smooth. (*Note:* If the dough is sticky, you may need to add up to 1½ ounces, about ⅓ cup, more flour.)

Clean the mixing bowl and lightly coat it with vegetable oil. Return the dough to the oiled bowl, cover it tightly with plastic wrap, and let it ferment at room temperature until it doubles in volume, about 1½ hours.

Remove the dough from the mixing bowl and knead it by hand on a lightly floured work surface a few times to deflate. Return the dough to the mixing bowl, cover it tightly with plastic wrap, and let it rise again until it doubles in bulk, about 1½ hours.

Lightly dust the parchment-lined baking sheets with flour and set them aside.

Uncover the dough and transfer it to a lightly floured work surface. Roll the dough into a rectangle, about ½ inch thick. Cut it with a doughnut cutter or round cookie cutter. Don't forget to save the doughnut holes and trimmings. Fry them, after you've cooked the doughnuts, for those people who love the flavor but don't care about the shape of their doughnut. (*Note:* If you are using a round cookie cutter, cut out the center of each doughnut with the wide end of a metal pastry nozzle.) Place the doughnuts on parchment-lined baking sheets 1 inch apart. Lightly dust the tops of the doughnuts with flour. Cover them with plastic wrap. (*Note:* At this point, the doughnuts can be refrigerated for up to 4 hours. Afterward, continue with the following proofing instructions.)

Allow the doughnuts to proof at room temperature until they've grown by one third of their size—about ½ hour. Meanwhile, 5 to 10 minutes before you will be ready to use it, heat 2 to 3 inches of oil in skillet over high heat to 375 degrees F. Toss granulated sugar and cinnamon together in a small mixing bowl and set aside. Drop the doughnuts into the hot oil a few at a time and cook them until their undersides are brown—about 1 minute. Carefully turn the doughnuts over with a slotted spoon. Cook until both sides are equally brown. Be sure to maintain the cooking temperature by raising or lowering the heat.

When the doughnuts are cooked, immediately dip one side of each into the sugar mixture and allow it to cool on the undipped side. Sprinkle with confectioners' sugar and serve.

WARM SOURDOUGH CHOCOLATE CAKE

MAKES EIGHT INDIVIDUAL CAKES.

The sourdough starter is integral to this soufflélike Warm Sourdough Chocolate Cake because its sharp flavor intensifies the bitterness of the chocolate—it also contains the perfect scant amount of flour necessary to bind the ingredients together. Since the almost liquid center of this dessert makes transferring to another plate nearly impossible, the cake must be baked in metal rings, placed directly on ovenproof serving plates in individual-size portions. I remove the rings once the cake is baked, set the hot plate on top of a cool, larger plate, dust the top of the cake with powdered sugar, and garnish it with a scoop of vanilla ice cream or whipped cream. This recipe can be baked in soufflé cups, but the presentation won't be quite as beautiful because the cake never rises high above the rim of the mold, as a soufflé does.

Once the cake is baked, it must be eaten immediately. However, the batter can be made ahead, piped or spooned into the metal rings set on the ovenproof plates (or soufflé cups), and refrigerated for up to 3 days.

HAVE READY:
Pastry brush
Eight 3½-by-1-inch metal rings or eight tuna fish cans with both ends removed and well rinsed or eight 4-ounce soufflé cups
Eight 6-inch ovenproof plates
2 large mixing bowls
Mixer fitted with whisk attachment
Rubber spatula
Piping bag with plain wide nozzle or large metal spoon
Six 8- to 10-inch underliner plates, optional
Powdered sugar dredger or fine-mesh strainer

2 tablespoons unsalted butter, melted
4 tablespoons heavy cream
1 large egg

2 large egg yolks

3 tablespoons granulated sugar, in all

14 ounces imported bittersweet chocolate—such as Valrhona, Lindt, Tobler, Suchard—in all, melted and kept warm

2 ounces (about ¼ cup) strained (strain to remove the undissolved flour bits) White Starter

3 egg whites

Confectioners' sugar for dusting

Vanilla ice cream or whipped cream

Preheat the oven to 500 degrees F. Be sure the oven racks are placed well apart to allow plenty of air circulation. Brush the insides of metal rings with butter and place them directly on ovenproof plates. (If you're using soufflé cups, you don't need to butter them.) Whip the heavy cream to soft peaks and refrigerate.

Place whole egg, yolks, and 2 tablespoons of sugar in the bowl of a mixer fitted with a whisk attachment. Beat on high speed until the mixture reaches a mousselike consistency, about 5 minutes. Remove the bowl from the mixer. Stir in half the melted chocolate, all the whipped cream, and the White Starter with a rubber spatula. Set aside.

In a clean bowl, beat the egg whites with the remaining tablespoon of sugar until stiff. Using a rubber spatula, fold together the egg-white mixture and chocolate mixture until combined. Stir in the remaining melted chocolate.

Pipe or spoon the mixture into the rings or soufflé cups, filling them about ¾ inch full. (*Note:* At this point, the cakes can be covered with plastic wrap and refrigerated until ready to use. Add 1 minute of cooking time if they are baked chilled.)

Place four plates on each oven rack. Bake for 5 to 6 minutes. When finished baking, the cakes should be just firm enough around the outside to hold their shape but very soft in the center. Because home ovens tend to heat unevenly, all the cakes may not be done at the same time.

Dust the cakes with an even layer of confectioners' sugar. With a towel or potholder, carefully remove the rings. (If you are using soufflé cups, serve directly from the cups.) Top the cakes with ice cream or whipped cream, and serve immediately on the underliner plates if desired.

SOURDOUGH ONION RINGS

MAKES ONE TO SIX SERVINGS (EAT AS MANY AS YOU LIKE!)

There are two kinds of onion rings—aside from the kind that are just plain bad. They should be either bready, the sort you might find at a great fast-food joint, or lacy and crisp, the batter light as tempura. For years I tried to get the chefs in the kitchen at the restaurant to come up with a perfect onion ring. And they got pretty darn close with one lacy/crisp version made with soda water, beer, flour, and baking soda. I was proud of the experimental batches and had one of our regular customers, writer Jonathan Gold, sample a few. He liked them, but he didn't look satisfied. It turned out he'd just read a description of yeasted onion rings in an old southern cookbook and was wondering if we could get an even better onion ring if we added the one thing that had made our reputation at the bakery: sourdough starter. Of course, I thought. Immediately, I headed to the kitchen and had a new batch made. They were spectacularly good: shatteringly crisp, the caramel-like sweetness of the onion set off by the mellow sour of the starter. Hold the ketchup. There is one drawback, however; the batter must be used right away—it becomes too thin if left to sit.

ONE-DAY RECIPE

HAVE READY:
Large bowl
Medium-size bowl
Shallow bowl
Wooden spoon or whisk
Heavy-bottom skillet
Candy or frying thermometer
Mesh strainer or slotted spoon
Baking sheet
Paper towels

Ice cubes
1 pound 2 ounces (about 2 cups) White Starter

4 ounces ($^{1}/_{2}$ cup) cold sparkling water
$^{1}/_{2}$ teaspoon sea salt, plus extra for seasoning
3 large onions, peeled and cut into $^{1}/_{2}$-inch slices
4 ounces (about 1 cup) all-purpose or unbleached white bread flour
Peanut or canola oil

Fill a large bowl with ice cubes, then place the medium-size bowl on top of the ice. Place White Starter, sparkling water, and salt in the medium-size bowl and stir to combine.

Separate the onion slices into rings, leaving the centers intact.

Place flour in a shallow bowl and add the onion slices. Toss the onions in the flour to coat.

Heat 1 inch of oil in a heavy-bottom skillet to 375 degrees F. Dip the flour-coated rings, one at a time, into the starter mixture, then drop them in the hot oil. Fry only what the pan can hold in one layer. Fry the rings until they are golden brown, 2 to 3 minutes, turning if necessary. Remove the rings with a mesh strainer or slotted spoon to a baking sheet lined with paper towels. Sprinkle with salt to taste. Keep the rings warm in a 225-degree F oven until all are fried. Be sure the oil returns to 375 degrees F before adding the next batch of onions. It's vital that the onion rings be fried at the right temperature—if the oil is too cool, they'll be greasy.

SOURDOUGH PANCAKES

MAKES ABOUT FOURTEEN 4- TO 5-INCH PANCAKES.

More tangy than buttermilk, lower in fat than sour cream, sourdough starter might be exactly what you need to make your Saturday morning pancakes more delicious than ever. Maple syrup is already in this Sourdough Pancake batter; you may want to sprinkle these pancakes with fresh raspberries and powdered sugar, or sautéed apple slices and cinnamon.

ONE-DAY RECIPE

HAVE READY:
Large mixing bowl
Whisk
Fine-mesh strainer
Griddle or nonstick skillet
Spatula
Pastry brush

1 pound 2 ounces (about 2 cups) White Starter
2 tablespoons maple syrup
3 tablespoons safflower or corn oil, plus extra for oiling griddle
2 large eggs
½ teaspoon sea salt
½ teaspoon baking soda
1 teaspoon baking powder

Place White Starter, maple syrup, oil, and eggs in a large mixing bowl and whisk to combine.

Push salt, baking soda, and baking powder through a fine-mesh strainer directly into the bowl and whisk to incorporate. The batter should be thicker than heavy cream and feel very elastic.

Preheat a griddle or nonstick skillet and lightly brush it with oil. Pour ¼ cup of batter for each pancake onto the hot griddle. Cook the batter over medium-high heat until bubbles cover the surface. Flip the pancake with a spatula and continue cooking until the underside is brown, about 1 more minute.

Remove the pancakes from the griddle and keep them warm in a 250-degree F oven until all the batter is used. Serve warm.

Sourdough Waffles

MAKES ABOUT EIGHT 8-INCH WAFFLES.

You'll never go out for Sunday breakfast if you take the time to stir together this easy batter on Saturday night. These Sourdough Waffles always seem to turn out with a perfectly crisp exterior and a light, sourdough-flavored interior. Serve them with warm honey or maple syrup.

Two-Day Recipe—First Day

HAVE READY:
Small saucepan
Large mixing bowl
Whisk
Plastic wrap

4 ounces ($^1\!/_2$ cup) unsalted butter
8 ounces (1 cup) whole or low-fat milk
9 ounces (about 1 cup) White Starter
1 teaspoon salt
1 tablespoon brown sugar, packed
6 ounces (about 1$^1\!/_2$ cups) all-purpose flour

Place butter and milk in a small saucepan and warm over low heat until the butter melts. Set the mixture aside at room temperature to cool.

Place White Starter, cooled milk-butter mixture, salt, brown sugar, and flour in a large mixing bowl and whisk together. Cover the bowl tightly with plastic wrap and let the batter stand at room temperature for 8 to 14 hours.

SECOND DAY

HAVE READY:
Waffle iron
Pastry brush

2 large eggs
¼ teaspoon baking soda
Vegetable oil

Preheat the waffle iron 10 to 15 minutes before you will be ready to use it.

Uncover the batter and whisk in eggs and baking soda until well combined. The batter should be thick and elastic. Lightly brush the hot waffle iron with vegetable oil. The oil should sizzle on the iron, signaling that it is hot enough. Pour ½ to ¾ cup of batter onto the hot waffle iron. Close the lid and let the waffle cook until it is golden and crisp, 3 to 5 minutes. Repeat with the remaining batter.

Rye Blini

MAKES APPROXIMATELY 8 DOZEN SMALL OR 2½ DOZEN LARGE BLINI.

Blini are yeasted pancakes traditionally served with caviar, gravlax, or smoked salmon. These Rye Blini are made with a sourdough Rye Starter, whose flavor perfectly matches the taste of cured fish.

The batter can be prepared ahead and left at room temperature for 1 hour. Just before serving, you can fold in the beaten egg whites. The blini are best served warm.

ONE-DAY RECIPE

HAVE READY:
Small saucepan
Candy or long-stemmed, instant-read cooking thermometer, optional
Wooden spoon
3 large mixing bowls
Plastic wrap
Wooden spoon
Fine-mesh strainer
Whisk
Rubber spatula
Cast-iron skillet or heavy-bottom sauté pan or griddle
Metal spatula
Paper towels

1 pound (2 cups) whole or low-fat milk
2¼ cakes (1¼ ounces) or 1 tablespoon plus 1 teaspoon packed fresh yeast
13 ounces (about 1½ cups) Rye Starter
4 tablespoons sugar in all
6 ounces (about 1½ cups) unbleached all-purpose flour
2 tablespoons buckwheat flour
2 teaspoons baking powder
2 teaspoons baking soda
¾ teaspoon sea salt

4 eggs, separated
4 ounces unsalted butter

Warm milk in a small saucepan to about 85 degrees F or until a drop or two tested on the back of your hand feels warm. Stir in yeast with a wooden spoon until it is dissolved.

Transfer the mixture to a large mixing bowl and stir in Rye Starter and 2 tablespoons of sugar until well combined. Cover the bowl tightly with plastic wrap and allow the mixture to sit at room temperature for 30 minutes.

Set strainer over a large mixing bowl. Rub flours, baking powder, baking soda, and salt through the strainer and into the bowl. Add 3 egg yolks and stir with a whisk until well mixed.

Add the yeast-starter mixture to the egg mixture and stir until well mixed. Set aside.

Whisk 4 egg whites with the remaining 2 tablespoons of sugar in a large mixing bowl until soft peaks form.

Fold the egg whites into the flour mixture with a rubber spatula until thoroughly blended.

Melt about ½ tablespoon butter over medium heat in skillet, sauté pan, or preheated griddle. As soon as the butter begins to bubble, drop as many tablespoons of batter as will fit into the pan. Be sure to keep the pancakes spaced well apart—they spread as they cook. You may have to adjust the flame to ensure that the pan never gets so hot that the butter burns or so cool that the blini don't sizzle as they hit the pan.

Cook the blini for 2 to 3 minutes on one side, until they are nicely browned. Flip the blini and cook the opposite side. Remove the blini to a serving platter. Wipe the pan with a paper towel, add butter, and cook the second batch in the same manner. Repeat the process until all the batter is used.

CRISP SAVORY TOASTS

MAKES 10–20 TOASTS, ACCORDING TO SIZE OF LOAF.

Sometimes all a dish needs is something crisp on the side to make it special. Salads, soups, and pastas, for instance, often could use a piece of crisp, garlicky toast, something to make them more than everyday eating. These Crisp Savory Toasts are like a spectacular version of garlic bread, sprinkled with Parmesan cheese and heated up with a few dried red pepper flakes. They are a good example of a food that you can make far better in your own kitchen than you could ever purchase.

ONE-DAY RECIPE

HAVE READY:
Mortar and pestle or mixing bowl and spoon
Sharp bread knife or electric meat slicer
Baking sheet

4 ounces (2 tablespoons) unsalted butter, softened
1/2 teaspoon dried red pepper flakes
1 large clove garlic, minced
1 shallot, minced
One 1-pound to 2-pound boule, such as Rosemary–Olive Oil, Olive, Normandy Rye, or Multigrain bread
Imported Parmesan cheese, freshly grated

If you are slicing the bread by hand, freeze it just until it is firm enough to slice thinly. If you own or have access to an electric meat slicer, freeze the bread for several hours, until almost frozen.

Preheat the oven to 300 degrees F.

Place the butter, red pepper flakes, garlic, and shallot in mortar and mash with the pestle into a smooth paste.

Slice the bread as thinly as possible, between 1/4 inch and 1/8 inch thick. Place the slices on a baking sheet. Thinly spread the garlic-butter mixture on one side of each slice and sprinkle lightly with Parmesan cheese.

Bake the toasts until the tops are lightly browned, 30 to 40 minutes. The toasts should be dry but still a bit moist in the center.

CRISP SWEET TOASTS

MAKES 10–20 TOASTS, ACCORDING TO SIZE OF LOAF.

4 ounces (8 tablespoons) unsalted butter
½ cup sugar
1 teaspoon cinnamon

The same method can be used with butter, sugar, and cinnamon to make Crisp Sweet Toasts, which would be ideal for afternoon tea, for breakfast, or as a simple dessert. Start by using a sweeter bread, such as the Fig-Anise, Fruit-Nut, or Rye-Currant breads. Follow the chilling and slicing directions for Crisp Savory Toasts.

For the topping, melt butter. Then combine sugar and cinnamon in a small bowl.

Brush the slices with the melted butter and sprinkle the tops with the sugar-cinnamon mixture.

Bake according to the directions for Crisp Savory Toasts.

PULLED CROUTONS

MAKES 8 CUPS.

S tart with a wonderfully flavored bread and you'll get wonderful croutons. Pulled Croutons are more interesting to me than the perfectly square sort. Pulling instead of cutting the strands gives the croutons a nice rustic, uneven look. Don't save them for just salads; they're terrific in soups and on top of pasta too.

ONE-DAY RECIPE

HAVE READY:
Mixing bowl
2 baking sheets

One 2-pound boule, such as Country White, Walnut, Rosemary–Olive Oil, or Olive Bread, one to three days old
6 tablespoons extra-virgin olive oil
1 teaspoon coarse salt
¼ teaspoon coarsely ground pepper
Chopped fresh herbs, such as parsley, celery leaves, thyme, oregano, or basil, or chile flakes, optional

Cut the boule in half. Pull one-half-inch pieces from the inside of the bread, avoiding the crust. This size is ideal for salads. Pull smaller pieces if the croutons will be used on pasta.

Preheat the oven to 325 degrees F. If both baking sheets won't fit on the center oven rack, separate the racks to allow plenty of air circulation.

Toss the croutons in a bowl with olive oil, salt, and pepper. Spread the croutons in a single layer on the baking sheets and bake until golden brown and crisp, about 12 to 18 minutes, depending on size. Check periodically; it may be necessary to toss the croutons several times and to rotate the baking sheets to ensure even baking.

The croutons should be lightly colored and crisp throughout. After baking, allow the croutons to cool; then they can be tossed with chopped herbs and dried chile flakes. Good croutons have no shelf life; they need to be eaten a few hours after they have been baked.

GARLIC PULLED CROUTONS

2 cloves garlic, crushed

Follow the directions for Pulled Croutons, but make a garlic-flavored oil by placing the olive oil in a small saucepan and adding crushed cloves of garlic. Gently simmer for 5 minutes. Strain the oil, then toss the croutons in it, then bake.

APPENDIX: SOURCES

KING ARTHUR FLOUR

Not only sells organic and nonorganic flours of all types but has an excellent catalog of baking equipment, including proofing baskets, baguette pans, *lames*, thermometers, scales, baking stones, baker's peels, and more. P.O. Box 876, Norwich, VT 05055-0876. Phone: (800) 827-6836.

BOB'S RED MILL

Mail order for all flours—unbleached bread flour, unbleached high-gluten flour, coarse-ground whole-wheat flour, durum and semolina, also pumpernickel meal (rye chops), various seeds and organic grains, wheat germ, and bran. Most important, Bob's sells Guisto's nine-grain cereal mix, which I use in my multigrain bread. 5209 S.E. International Way, Milwaukie, OR 97222. Phone: (503) 654-3215. Fax: (503) 653-1339.

WALNUT ACRES

A general foods catalog that carries everything from organic meat and vitamins to dried fruits, whole-wheat bread flour, unbleached bread flour, and grains. Penns Creek, PA 17862. Phone: (800) 433-3998.

ARROWHEAD MILLS

Sells organic flours that are also available in most health food stores. P.O. Box 2059, Hereford, TX 79045. Phone: (806) 364-0730.

CAPITOL MILLING CO.

Manufactures all types of wheat flours and miscellaneous wheat products. Distributor of other grain flours. Custom miller to fit any bakery's needs.

Wholesale only. P.O. Box 2796 G.M.F., Los Angeles, CA 90051. Phone: (213) 628-8235. Fax: (213) 617-1937.

MORGAN & COMPANY

Suppliers of the freshest walnuts, the moistest figs, and the plumpest raisins, plus a variety of other dried fruits. Unfortunately, at this time, these choice ingredients are available only wholesale. 5132 N. Palm, No. 79, Fresno, CA 93705. Phone: (209) 261-0378.

WILLIAMS-SONOMA

Catalog and store locations throughout the country. Has basic baking equipment for the home kitchen, including baguette pans, baking stones or tiles, baker's peels, and thermometers. P.O. Box 7456, San Francisco, CA 94120-7456. Phone: (800) 541-2233.

VON SNEDAKER'S MAGIC BAKING SHEET

This is great in any recipe that calls for parchment paper—such as *Fougasse*, Olive-Onion Bread Sticks, Pretzels, and English Muffins. 12021 Wilshire Blvd., Suite 231, Los Angeles, CA 90025. Phone: (310) 395-6365.

CONSULTING MARKETING SERVICES

Supplies proofing baskets, linen, *lames*, proofing boards, wooden baker's peels, and so on. Provides bakery layouts, training, equipment, and formulas for bakeries of all sizes. Phone: (415) 359-0557.

ALLIED BAKING EQUIPMENT

Commercial bakery equipment. 12015 E. Slauson Ave, Unit K, Sante Fe Springs, CA 90670. Phone: (310) 945-6506.

FBM (FRENCH BAKING MACHINES)

Sells commercial ovens, also mail orders for proofing baskets, *lames, couche,* and thermometers. 2666 Rt. 130, Cranbury, NJ 08512. Phone: (609) 860-0577.

BREAD BAKER'S GUILD OF AMERICA

A nonprofit organization created to provide education in artisan baking and production of high-quality bread products. P.O. Box 22254, Pittsburgh, PA 15222. Phone: (412) 765-3638.

MARGIE BEYERS CERAMICS

They produce ceramic baking pans, including French baguette pans, pizza stones, and other types of bread pans. 7159 Beach Drive S.W., Seattle WA 98136. Phone: (216) 935-6282.

INDEX

About the Author

Nancy Silverton is the pastry chef/owner of Campanile restaurant and the baker/owner of La Brea Bakery, both in Los Angeles.

Born and raised in Los Angeles, Nancy was eighteen, a liberal arts student at California State University, Sonoma, when she began working as a vegetarian cook in her dormitory kitchen. After apprenticing at a small northern California restaurant, she attended the Cordon Bleu in London. Returning to Los Angeles, she was employed as an assistant pastry chef at Michael's restaurant in Santa Monica.

Soon after completing a series of pastry courses at the Ecole le Notre in Plaiser, France, Silverton was appointed head pastry chef at Wolfgang Puck's Spago restaurant.

In 1985, she and her husband, Mark Peel, moved to Manhattan and spent six months revamping the restaurant Maxwell's Plum.

La Brea Bakery was opened in January 1989; Campanile was opened in June 1989.

Silverton's many honors include the Southern California Restaurant Writers 1995 Restaurateur of the Year award and the James Beard Best Pastry Chef of the Year award (1990). In 1995, *Chocolatier* magazine named her one of their ten best pastry chefs of the year.

Nancy Silverton is the author of two successful cookbooks: *Desserts* and *Mark Peel and Nancy Silverton at Home: Two Chefs Cook for Family and Friends.* She and Mark Peel are currently working on another cookbook. They have three children: Vanessa, Benjamin, and Oliver.

PUMPKIN BREAD

BAGUETTE

WHOLE-WHEAT BOULE

MULTIGRAIN BREAD

GEORGE'S SEEDED SOUR

RED PEPPER–SCALLION BREAD

HAMBURGER BUNS

RUSTIC OLIVE-HERB BREAD,
RUSTIC BREAD,
ITALIAN BREAD STICKS

PAIN DE MIE